DEVELOPMENTAL READING IN HIGH SCHOOL

GUY L. BOND

ASSOCIATE PROFESSOR OF EDUCATION
COLLEGE OF EDUCATION
UNIVERSITY OF MINNESOTA

EVA BOND

PROFESSOR OF PSYCHOLOGY
RICHMOND PROFESSIONAL INSTITUTE
COLLEGE OF WILLIAM AND MARY

NEW YORK
THE MACMILLAN COMPANY

To Arthur I. Gates

PREFACE

This is a book for high school teachers. It is written for the teacher who is perplexed by the realization that her pupils cannot read the materials of her course. The need for the high school teacher of today to assume the new and difficult responsibility of teaching reading is becoming ever more apparent. It is evident also that she must have help in undertaking this task. It has been the sincere desire of the authors, from their experience and study, to add to the help that is available. With this desire uppermost we have made an attempt to keep this book as readable and practical as is consistent with accuracy. Many controversial topics have been either purposely omitted or generalized so that the teacher would not be confronted with a body of research which might prove confusing.

Written primarily for teachers and teachers-in-training, this book has grown out of a study of questions asked by high school teachers in various parts of the United States, concerning problems that they have faced in teaching reading. The more useful reading skills and techniques have been discussed; and specific, practical procedures have been given by which these skills and techniques may be developed.

The authors are indebted to many people without whose aid this book would never have reached completion. First among these is Dr. Arthur I. Gates, from whom much friendly counsel and stimulation have been received over a number of years. Dr. Gates read the manuscript and offered many helpful suggestions.

We are grateful to Dr. Dora V. Smith and to Dr. Margaret McKim for reading the manuscript and for various suggestions.

We wish to thank the many research workers who have had a most important part in clarifying the problems and methods of reading at the high school level. It is not feasible to acknowledge individually all the valuable studies in the field of reading that make a book such as this possible. Nonetheless, we wish to make it known that the findings of these indefatigable research workers have influenced these pages. We wish also to thank the many students and teachers who have helped us through the problems they have raised and the suggestions they have offered. Among those especially deserving mention are Miss Hazel Olsen, Dr. J. H. Shores, Mr. Harold J. McNally, and Miss Bertha Handlan.

We are deeply grateful to Dr. E. A. Bond and Fredricka Hoffa Bond for their many hours of untiring work, their valuable suggestions, and their unwavering interest. Parts of the manuscript were read and critically appraised by Dr. Austin D. Bond and Dr. Elden A. Bond.

GUY L. BOND

EVA BOND

April, 1941

CONTENTS

SECTION I

INTRODUCTION

CHAPTER
PAGE

I. NEED FOR TEACHING READING IN HIGH SCHOOL . . 3

Good Reading Important for Effective Living . . 3

Teachers Appreciate the Importance of Good Reading 5

The Development of Reading Is Part of the Teaching of Every Subject 7

Reading in the Daily Life of High School Students 11

Reading Ability of High School Students . . . 19

Selected Bibliography 26

II. BASIC CONSIDERATIONS DETERMINING THE NATURE OF THE READING PROGRAM 28

The Theory of Simplicity of Reading 28

The Theory That Reading Is a Complex Process 29

Reading Purposes 32

Major Tasks of the Reading Program 40

The Twofold Aspect of a High School Reading Program 46

Summary 46

Selected Bibliography 47

SECTION II

THE ALL-SCHOOL READING PROGRAM

III. THE DEVELOPMENTAL READING PROGRAM . . . 51

The Meaning of the Developmental Reading Program 52

vii

CHAPTER   PAGE

Factors Contributing to the Absence of Reading
Programs 57
The Scope of the Developmental Program . . . 60
Administrative Considerations in Setting up a De-
velopmental Reading Program 62
Summary 65
Selected Bibliography 66

IV. THE DEVELOPMENT OF READING TECHNIQUES AND SKILLS   68
Silent Reading Skills and Techniques 70
Oral Reading 94
Summary 99
Selected Bibliography 102

V. DEVELOPMENT OF VOCABULARY 104
Three Phases of Meaning 104
Importance of Meaning 107
The Development of Meaning 114
An Illustration of the Building of Meanings . . 125
Summary 129
Selected Bibliography 130

VI. DEVELOPMENT OF READING INTERESTS 131
Reading Interests of High School Students . . 132
Factors Affecting Reading Interests 136
Suggestions for Guiding Interests 139
The Interrelationship between Interests and Reading
Abilities 148
Summary 149
Selected Bibliography 150

VII. DEVELOPMENT OF A DIFFERENTIATED ATTACK . . . 152
An Experiment in Speed of Reading Various Types
of Materials 152
Adjusting Reading Rate to Suit the Purpose and the
Material 160

CHAPTER   PAGE

Selecting the Reading Techniques to Suit the Purpose
and the Material 162
Refining a Technique to Meet the Purpose or Material 166
Summary 168

VIII. DEVELOPMENT OF ABILITY IN READING THE MATERIALS
OF THE CONTENT SUBJECTS 169
General Procedures Helpful in all Content Fields 170
Reading in the Social Studies 175
Reading in Literature 181
Reading in Mathematics 185
Reading in Science 189
Summary 194
Selected Bibliography 195

IX. DEVELOPMENT OF INDEPENDENCE IN READING . . . 197
A Trip to the Library 197
The Meaning of Independence in Reading . . 200
The Need for Independence in Reading . . . 202
The Encouragement of Independence in Reading . 205
An Illustration of Developing Independence in
Reading Graphs 212
Summary 215
Selected Bibliography 215

X. APPRAISALS OF READING ABILITIES 217
Purposes of Measurement of Reading Abilities . . 219
The Use of Appraisals in Improving Instruction in
Reading 220
The Use of Reading Appraisals in Improving Instruction in the Content Subjects 224
The Use of Appraisals in Reading to Aid in the Selection of Materials 229
The Use of Appraisals in Reading to Aid in the
Guidance of Students 230

CHAPTER   PAGE
        The Use of Appraisals in Reading to Contribute to
           Research in Education   231
        Reading Outcomes That Should Be Appraised .   . 232
        Testing Procedures   234
        Administration of Tests   238
        Summary   241
        Selected Bibliography   242

                            SECTION III

        THE PROGRAM FOR THE RETARDED READER

XI.   READING DISABILITY   247
        Selection of Remedial Cases   247
        Causes of Reading Disability   253
        Summary   273
        Selected Bibliography   274

XII. DIAGNOSING READING DISABILITY   276
        Purpose of Diagnosis   277
        The Program of Diagnosis   278
        Outcome of Diagnosis   294
        Summary   294
        Selected Bibliography   296

XIII. REMEDIAL PROGRAM   298
        Organization   298
        Principles of Remedial Teaching   302
        Remedial Instruction for Specific Difficulties .   . 310
        Summary   320
        Selected Bibliography   320

                            SECTION IV

                        CO-ORDINATION

XIV. CO-ORDINATING THE READING PROGRAM   325
        Co-ordination between Elementary and Secondary
           School Reading Programs   326

PAGE

Considerations in Co-ordinating a Reading Program   327
The Co-ordinator of the Reading Program   .   . 330
Duties of the Co-ordinator 332
Duties of the Teachers 340
Duties of the Administrator   342
Summary   343
Selected Bibliography 345

APPENDIX 347
INDEX 355

SECTION I

INTRODUCTION

CHAPTER I

NEED FOR TEACHING READING IN HIGH SCHOOL

GOOD READING IMPORTANT FOR EFFECTIVE LIVING

A democratic society requires a public that can read. This is not a new point of view. Victor Hugo, in the year 1834, saw the necessity for a well-educated and reading public for France and advocated teaching the peasants to read. He saw the relationship between poor reading and social maladjustment when he said:

> You are bent on economy; do not be so lavish in taking off the heads of so many during the year. Suppress the executioner; you could defray the expense of six hundred schoolmasters with the wages you give your eighty executioners. Think of the multitude; then there would be schools for the children, workshops for the men.
>
> Do you know that in France there are fewer people who know how to read than in any other country in Europe? Fancy, Switzerland can read, Belgium can read, Denmark can read, Greece can read, Ireland can read—and France cannot read! It is a crying evil.[1]

The demand is not only for the present high percentage of literacy (for the status of which we are so justly proud) but also for a greater degree of literacy than is now usual. The schools—elementary, secondary, and college—must assume increased responsibility to society in the training of a public that is able to read effectively, is independent in reading, has the desire to read, and can select materials for reading that

[1] Hugo, Victor. *Claude Gueux,* 1834.

contribute to the continued development of wholesome, challenging members of that society. Too many Americans are not only ineffectual in reading for relatively simple purposes, but they also show immaturity in the selection of what they read. Too often the reading of adults is narrow in scope; it is questionable whether such reading results in the social outcomes that are desirable.

Educators realize that reading contributes to the effectiveness of the adult. In his economic and business life the individual's ability to read well is of real value. It enables him to keep abreast of business and occupational trends and conditions. There are few craftsmen who do not find it both profitable and interesting to read their trade journals and other material related to their trade. The amount of printed matter prepared for meeting the problems of the housewife gives evidence of her wide use of reading. Reading permeates the occupational life of the American public, as the following statement of the Educational Policies Commission suggests:

> Most economic enterprises of importance today presuppose that the rank and file worker can read and write. The factory employer must be able to read safety signs in workrooms. The truck driver who could not read traffic signs would indeed be a menace. The retail salesman must be able to record orders and addresses accurately. It is impossible to operate modern mass production industry, fabricating products with interchangeable parts, unless the average person can read instructions. The typical large business requires ready alphabetic and arithmetic literacy at a thousand crucial points. Market reports, agricultural research findings, and the ability to write for and to install machine parts lose most of their significance where farmers cannot read and write. Arithmetical training permits exact measurement to be woven into the very warp and woof of our industrial economy.

We take this contribution of the school for granted, since it has been supplied for several generations. It is important, however, that this economic essential be maintained and improved. Illiteracy and near-illiteracy should be removed wherever they exist. Reading and arithmetic should be more often focused upon economic problems and issues, and should increasingly involve a background of reality in the economic sphere. The advance of technological economy implies corresponding progress in alphabetic and arithmetic literacy. This is a prerequisite to efficiency both as a producer and a consumer.[2]

Reading also plays an important role in civic life. It produces a well-informed citizenry. Through reading the individual keeps informed on the political, social, and economic problems of his national and local governments. He is also made aware of his responsibilities as a citizen. The educator realizes that in a like manner reading permeates other phases of adult life. As one educator has aptly stated:

> Reading is a basic tool in the living of a good life. . . . Those who can use it to learn from books, as well as be amused by them, have access to the stores of knowledge. They can furnish their minds so that the prospect of hours spent alone is less bleak. Nor, in the hours they spend with others, need they fear that hollow sound of empty conversation.[3]

TEACHERS APPRECIATE THE IMPORTANCE OF GOOD READING

Elementary school teachers are meeting their responsibility to society and to the children by giving an increasing emphasis to instruction in reading. On the other hand, the teaching of reading in high schools has been left almost entirely to chance. Many teachers in high schools, however, are beginning to see the need for the continued development of the

[2] Educational Policies Commission. *Education and Economic Well-Being in American Democracy,* 1940, p. 43.

[3] Adler, Mortimer J. *How to Read a Book,* 1940, p. vii.

reading abilities of their students. It is becoming more and more evident that the elementary school cannot assume the full responsibility for teaching reading. The realization that the secondary school must undertake its part in reading development and that the teaching of reading cannot be left to chance is creating an earnest desire on the part of the secondary school teacher to contribute to reading growth.[4] This concern over the student's reading abilities is both directly and indirectly the result of the complex social and economic times in which we are living. It is apparent that if a child is to become an effective member of a democratic society in this highly interrelated world, he must be an able and critical reader.

The schools have changed and are changing their curricula to meet the needs of the pupils in a changing world. When the task of the secondary pupil was that of accumulating isolated facts, the ability to do intensive reading of a single textbook was all that a given subject demanded of him. But the high school of today is endeavoring to develop, in addition to the accumulation of integrated factual experiences, broad concepts, generalizations, and appreciations. Hence the student must be a more extensive and proficient reader than formerly was the case.

Educators of youth are now beginning to sense that good reading ability is central to the schoolwork of a student. They realize that a student must be an able reader to do good work in any subject. This is so since the study of reading will not only improve the ability to do effective reading, but will also

[4] Center, S. S., and Persons, G. L. *Teaching High School Students How to Read,* D. Appleton-Century Company, 1937.

Davis, H. C. "Improving Reading Ability of High School Seniors," *California Journal of Secondary Education,* Vol. XII, November, 1937, pp. 424-29.

La Brant, L. L. "An Evaluation of the Free Reading in Grades Ten, Eleven, and Twelve, for the Class of 1935," *Contributions to Education,* Vol. I, No. 2, The Ohio State University Press, 1936.

contribute to the learning of the other subjects of the curriculum. Educators appreciate that through the means of reading each student can do his own work at his own pace and that many of the most efficient teaching practices depend for their successful operations upon the student's ability to read well. They know further that a student will be a more effective participating member of his group if he has adequate reading ability than he will be without this power.

Coupled with the changing demands on reading in the high school is an increasing tendency for all students to remain in school for longer periods of time. Pupils who formerly left school because of inadequate reading ability are no longer being taken up in gainful employment and are therefore continuing in school. The tendency to remain in school, added to the changes in the curricula and the social demands upon reading, makes the problem even more apparent.

Just as educators are sensing the importance of good reading ability for successful school adjustment so others concerned with the social and personal advancement of youth are aware of the importance of reading in enabling each youth to live a rich and complete life. For reading is a worth-while and highly stimulating recreational experience; it adds many and vivid meanings to the individual's other experiences; it stimulates and fosters interests; and, since through it one can get away from the humdrum of his existence, reading contributes to his mental health. Thus, reading adds to the development of a wholesome personality.

THE DEVELOPMENT OF READING IS PART OF THE TEACHING OF EVERY SUBJECT

One of the authors [5] conducted an investigation on the ninth-grade level for the purpose of finding the relationships be-

[5] Bond, Eva. "Reading and Ninth Grade Achievement," *Contributions to Education*, No. 756, Bureau of Publications, Teachers College, Columbia University, 1938.

tween the various reading abilities and the scholastic achievements in the different subject-matter areas. The effect of
differences in age and in intelligence was eliminated by the
statistical procedure. The data indicate that:

1. Reading ability is an important factor in scholastic success.

2. Different subjects require special reading abilities.

Swenson[6] and Shores,[7] working with eighth-grade pupils
in companion studies, investigated the relationships among
various reading abilities—reading vocabulary, rate, and comprehension of materials similar to textbook materials of history
and science—and achievement in history and science. With the
exception of rate of reading, they found that:

1. All the reading abilities measured were significantly interrelated.

2. The reading abilities were significantly related to achievement.

3. There were constant trends indicating that for each of
the two fields (science and history) certain reading abilities
were more closely related to reading in that field than were
other reading abilities. But the reading abilities closely related to reading science materials were not necessarily the
same as those closely related to reading history. The studies
show that while there is much in common among the different reading abilities, there is much that is different. The
differences seem to be uniquely related to reading specific
subject-matter materials. For example, the various measures
of vocabulary were highly interrelated. But vocabulary ability
in science was more highly related to the ability to compre-

[6] Swenson, Esther J. "The Relation of Ability to Read Material of the Type Used
in Studying Science to Eighth-Grade Achievement," unpublished master's thesis,
Graduate School, University of Minnesota, 1938.

[7] Shores, J. H. "The Ability to Read Historical Materials as Related to Eighth-
Grade Achievement and General Reading Abilities," unpublished master's thesis,
Graduate School, University of Minnesota, 1938.

hend materials from the field of science than was either general vocabulary ability or vocabulary ability in other subject-matter areas.

In another study, working with ninth-grade students, Shores investigated the relationships between certain reading skills and reading comprehension of scientific materials, and between the reading skills and reading comprehension of historical materials. Then he compared these two groups of relationships. He concluded:

> By the time the students have reached the ninth grade their reading proficiency is to a considerable extent specific to the content field in which the reading is done.[8]

Certain types of reading were more highly associated with reading the materials of history than with those of science, and other skills were more highly related to reading the materials of science than the materials of history. He stated also:

> The fact that ninth-grade teachers should be concerned with the teaching of reading in the content materials of science and history is plainly indicated.[9]

Shores feels that the teaching of the reading abilities should be done by the teacher of that subject.

Bond[10] investigated interrelationships among tenth-grade abilities and achievements. His data imply that the developmental process of learning to read must take into account the building up of a proficiency in reading for each of various

[8] Shores, J. H. "Reading and Study Skills as Related to Comprehension of Science and History in the Ninth Grade," unpublished doctor's dissertation, Graduate School, University of Minnesota, 1940, p. 144.

[9] Ibid., p. 146.

[10] Bond, Elden. "Tenth-Grade Abilities and Achievements," *Contributions to Education*, No. 813, Bureau of Publications, Teachers College, Columbia University, 1940.

purposes in many subject-matter fields. It appears that each field of human experience, such as science, social science, and literature, places a unique burden upon the student's vocabulary and background of meaning. In addition, the student reading in a given field must approach that reading with the purposes requisite for reading in that field. It is likely that there is a degree of overlapping between the reading purposes in various fields. Nevertheless, it is probable that each field stresses certain of these purposes more than it does others. An hypothesis that seems tenable is that the reading techniques and various balances between techniques are determined in no small measure by the specific purpose for which the reading is being done. It might, then, be implied that the developmental process of learning to read should enable the student to build an ability to adjust the various techniques to the purposes and materials of a specific subject-matter area.

The five investigations just discussed were conducted in three widely separated cities. We may assume that the materials and methods of instruction were undoubtedly different since it would be unreasonable to believe that the materials and methods would be the same in Mansfield, Ohio; in Minneapolis, Minnesota; and in Kansas City, Missouri. The methods of appraisal and of statistical analysis were different. Yet, in all cases, the findings point to two fundamental conclusions:

1. Reading abilities are highly related to achievement in junior and senior high school subjects; the degree to which a reading ability is related depends upon the subject-matter area in question.

2. The various reading abilities (with the exception of reading speed) are highly related to each other and to the ability to read the materials of various high school subjects; the degree of relationship between the reading abilities and the reading of the material of any given subject depends upon

the subject in question. This degree of consistency between the findings of these researches strengthens their conclusions.

Thus, in order to read effectively the materials of a subject, a student must have the reading abilities required for reading the materials of that subject. The requisite reading abilities for any one subject-matter area are not necessarily the ones required for another. Since the necessary reading abilities must be developed for each subject, and should be developed where they are needed, it follows logically that reading instruction should be an integral part of the teaching of each content subject and should be the responsibility of the teacher of that subject. That specific instruction is helpful is indicated by Jacobson, who says that his data—

> warrant the conclusion that giving reading instruction in the field in which the content is to be mastered is superior to giving it in another subject-matter field and expecting the ability to transfer to a content field.[11]

Reading in the Daily Life of High School Students

When students become aware of the importance of reading to living and achieving, they are strongly motivated to improve their reading techniques and abilities. The following discussion by a group of high school boys and girls known to the authors illustrates this point.

One day just as the history class was about to begin, Jean asked, "Arnold, what are you doing?"

"I'm studying my history lesson," was Arnold's reply.

"Oh, I thought you were reading something," Jean commented.

"As a matter of fact, that's what I am doing. I'm reading my history lesson," he remarked.

[11] Jacobson, Paul B. "Two Experiments with Work-Type Reading Exercises in Ninth Grade," *University of Iowa Studies in Education*, Vol. VIII, No. 5, University of Iowa, 1933, pp. 77-78.

The teacher, overhearing the conversation, said, "Arnold, your last statement is better than your first. This is true because it implies that you understand the way by which you are adding to your knowledge of history. Reading is so much a part of what we do in this class that we hardly realize how much use we make of it."

"How much use do we actually make of reading in our schoolwork and in things we do outside of school?" became the question that challenged that group of students. The more thought and attention they gave to reading as a tool to serve them, the greater was their realization of how incomplete their lives would be if for some reason they were unable to read. One boy compared the inability to read with the loss of one of the senses. He said that the loss of the ability to read and the consequent inability to understand the printed page would be similar to the loss of the ability to hear and the consequent inability to understand the spoken word. The students decided to discuss the question again during the class hour of the next day.

In order to be ready for the discussion, the class decided that each pupil keep a record of the activities in which he engaged before the next meeting and of the way reading contributed to his activities. Then during the next class period they would be able to formulate an opinion of the extent to which reading was serving them. In addition, they would gain an understanding of the extent to which reading might serve them more fully if they made more complete use of it. The well-defined purpose aroused a new interest in these pupils. This interest proved to be a strong incentive for studying the question thoroughly.

When the time came for sharing the results of their independent activities, a group of eager, enthusiastic and well-prepared students assembled. It was apparent that they had spent much time and thought preparing for the discussion.

Charles, one of the students in the group, began the class discussion by giving a résumé of his record of the ways in which reading had served him since the previous class hour. He included in his résumé a list of the different reading techniques he had used to meet the purposes of his day's reading activities. Some little time and thought were given to the query of another student; namely, "Do you think that Charles could have made a better use of reading?" The students considered each of Charles's activities in the light of his reading purposes and the way in which these purposes could be met most effectively. Many of the group had engaged in somewhat similar reading activities. The students found that they had made a variety of approaches to the same activity. The merits of the various approaches were considered. One such activity had been the preparation of the history lesson. The history homework was composed of ten pages of textbook reading. One student, who found it difficult to understand much of the material of the lesson, had read and reread it. Another student had outlined the content of the passage. She could not remember much about the passage, but she had it all down in her notebook.

A third student, who had devoted a relatively short time to the preparation of the history lesson, had glanced through the ten pages of material, noting the headings and the first sentence or so of each paragraph. He said that by that method he had been able to get a general idea of what the lesson was about. It was clear that his purpose in reading the material was quite different from that of the student who had outlined the passage paragraph by paragraph.

A fourth student had first skimmed the material in order to get a general impression of it. Then he had read it through, pausing from time to time to draw inferences of what he had read and to predict what the discussion in the next section would include. Still another student had devoted the first few minutes of his study time to reviewing the things he already knew about the topic which the passage discussed. Then he read the passage and, upon finishing it, jotted down in his notebook certain generalizations he had formulated as a result of the reading.

One other student said that he had been so intrigued by a map included in the passage that he had spent an entire study period reading it. Consequently, he felt that he had not studied the lesson at all. Charles thought that perhaps a careful reading of the map might have been as productive of learning as a careful reading of the verbal content of the passage.

As a result of sharing their experiences, the students worked out an effective plan of reading for the purpose of increasing general information on an historical topic. This plan proved to be a combination of some of the approaches the students had used. They analyzed other reading activities in order to work out efficient approaches.

At this point in the class discussion, one pupil asked if reading might not have been used to advantage in other activities in which Charles had engaged, but in which reading had played no part. Charles had played baseball all afternoon. During the game an argument had ensued over a question of a baseball rule. It had been somewhat grudgingly settled by abiding by the opinion of the umpire, but if the umpire had had recourse to an official rule book, a more amicable solution of the altercation might have resulted.

Another student asked if anyone had used reading for any purpose on the previous day when some other activity would have been a wiser one. Mary felt that she had used a great deal of time and energy in going to the library, locating and reading material about a forthcoming political meeting. She said that a better plan would have been to telephone the political party's headquarters to ascertain the fact in which she was interested. In other words, she believed that an individual should be able to decide when to use and when not to use the activity of reading.

Edward, who was leading the class discussion that day, stopped it at this point so that the class might summarize what had been said, before the period ended. Among the concepts and generalizations the students formulated were these:

1. Reading makes up a large part of our school life. It appears that almost three fourths of the time we devote to schoolwork is spent in reading.

2. This estimate of time used in reading is enlightening to us. The understanding of the important part that reading plays in achievement in various subjects is equally interesting. As compared with the good reader, the poor reader seems to be at a disadvantage in learning his school subjects.

3. A conscious effort to improve our reading abilities would very likely increase our efficiency in most, if not all, of the subjects that we study.

4. Some of us are using very much more effective ways of reading than are others. It is worth while to analyze the way we read from time to time to see if we can improve our way of reading.

5. Reading enters into a very large percentage of the activities in which we engage. When there is a problem to be solved, it is important to see how reading may help in its solution. It is also important before beginning a new activity to consider how reading can contribute to it.

One boy proposed a topic that the other students wanted to discuss at the next class meeting. He said, "I am glad to learn more about how I may use reading in my school life. But I should like to know if reading will be as useful a tool to me when I leave school as it now is. To what extent do our fathers and mothers use reading in their daily lives?"

They decided to gather information on the topic before the next meeting so that they would be able to discuss it more intelligently.

To introduce the topic the next day the teacher told the group the uses he had made of reading that day. He said: "It is my custom to glance through the morning newspaper while I breakfast. This glance must necessarily be a cursory one since my time is limited. However, this morning—

"1. I looked at the front-page headlines. I read the first paragraph of each news item contained thereon and read in the entirety two of the news items in which I was especially interested.

"2. I carefully noted the statement of the weather forecast for today.

"3. I paged through the paper and read the comic strips.

"4. I located the sports pages and read the headlines and many of the columns pertaining to sports events.

"5. I consulted the index to locate radio and movie items. I turned to the table of outstanding radio broadcasts and carefully noted those to which I shall listen this evening.

"6. I located and read the editorial page.

"During the progress of the school day thus far, I have read for a great variety of purposes many different kinds of materials. I have used many different reading abilities and techniques.

"1. I read the bulletin board to note administrative announcements.

"2. I glanced through my class notes in order to organize today's class discussions. In addition, I searched through several books to locate facts that I was unable to recall and read materials dealing with the topics to refresh and enlarge my knowledge of them.

"3. I read the morning mail. Some of it I glanced at and discarded; the rest I sorted for filing and answering.

"4. I read critically and analytically several of your class papers. The purpose of reading these papers is to find out how adequately you present the topics and to make comments about the papers whenever I think such suggestions will prove helpful to you. I like to find out the insight you have into the significant concepts and generalizations of the topic you consider. Also in the reading of these papers, I search carefully for evidence of original thinking.

"As · you can see from this enumeration, I, as a typical teacher, read frequently, use many different techniques and abilities, and am motivated by a variety of purposes in my reading activities."

The following reports of several of the pupils are illustrative of all the reports:

John: My sister works in a brokerage office. Most of her working day is spent in reading. A part of her job is to read the financial news in all the daily papers and in several weekly magazines. This includes reading financial statements of various kinds. She reads news as it comes out on the teletype news ticker and on the tape that records the stock market transactions. She also reads and answers a large number of letters each week.

Mary: My dad is a lawyer. Men in his profession spend a fairly large proportion of their working day reading. Sometimes it is necessary for a lawyer to spend several hours reading, studying, rereading, and restudy-

ing a single passage. My father says that the material he reads requires an analytical type of reading.
This type he learned in law school.

Joan: My mother is a public health nurse. She uses reading to learn about case studies of her patients. She
also reads mortality and disease statistics, government
publications, and lots of other materials. She says
that reading is an indispensable tool to her and that
she wishes she could read more efficiently.

Edward: My father is a carpenter. He has to read blueprints,
graphs, color cards, materials about price and quality
of supplies, about heating, and all sorts of things.
He says, too, that when he gets home at night, he is
too tired to do anything but read. He reads a great
deal on rainy days. He reads the newspaper, *The
Saturday Evening Post,* and *Building Trades.*

The outcome of the class discussion was a realization that
adults, other than teachers and students, in all walks of life
read many kinds of materials and for many purposes, using
various reading techniques and skills.

However, the pupils were well aware of the fact that many
adults of their acquaintance confine their reading to picture
newspapers and magazines, baseball score-cards, and the like.
Reading such materials is profitable in itself, but it is a meager
diet indeed. These boys and girls regretted the fact that
many adults who have finished high school can do little more
than decipher the printed page; and that other adults cannot
read sufficiently well to enable them to be contributing members to, or even intelligent followers in, a democratic society.

The conclusion reached by the pupils is all too true. Many
adults have little understanding of the uses to which they
could put reading in making their lives happier, more abun-

dant, and independent. They have never taken a step in the fresh, rich air of the world of literature. All their lives they have been circumscribed by walls of illiteracy because of their inability to use reading efficiently. Forced to echo the opinions of others by their inability to read for the purpose of forming their own, many adults become uninteresting and prosaic individuals.

Reading Ability of High School Students

It is generally agreed that the teaching of reading both from the developmental and from the remedial aspects should be extended into the high school.[12] Such an extension is needed to prepare students to meet the new and increasing demands that the curriculum and living in our society make upon them. The reading that is expected of the high school student is in general more difficult than that of the elementary school student. The student must acquire new and refined reading techniques in order to do the more difficult reading.

Whenever students are observed, whether they be reading in a high school classroom, study hall, or library, it is very evident that some of them are in difficulty and that the majority are not reading as effectively as might be hoped. The measurement of reading ability indicates to some extent the magnitude of the problem with which the high school is confronted. When the reading abilities of a group are appraised, wide variations in abilities are found.

The results of the measurement of the reading abilities of all the students just finishing the tenth grade in a Midwestern city are shown in Table I. An inspection of this table shows a wide range in reading ability of these 225 students. They range in comprehension ability from a grade equivalent to

[12] Gray, W. S. "The Nature and Extent of the Reading Problem in American Education," *Educational Record,* Vol. XIX, January, 1938, pp. 87-104.

TABLE I

Distribution of the Mental and Reading Grade Scores of Tenth-Grade Pupils on the Stanford-Binet Test of Intelligence and the Gates Reading Survey Test

Number = 225

GRADE LEVEL	MENTAL GRADE [13]	CHRONO-LOGICAL GRADE [14]	LEVEL OF COMPRE-HENSION [15]	VOCABU-LARY [15]	SPEED [15]
13.0+	16		2	8	10
12.5—12.9	12		13	11	5
12.0—12.4	16		33	18	9
11.5—11.9	15	2	37	26	21
11.0—11.4	8	4	31	27	16
10.5—10.9	22	26	27	25	8
10.0—10.4	32	81	29	14	11
9.5—9.9	25	100	25	36	13
9.0—9.4	26	12	17	19	23
8.5—8.9	19		4	11	24
8.0—8.4	17		2	6	18
7.5—7.9	10		0	3	24
7.0—7.4	2		1	5	18
6.5—6.9	3		2	7	16
6.0—6.4	1		1	7	2
5.5—5.9	1		1	2	2
5.0—5.4					3
4.5—4.9					1
4.0—4.4					0
3.5—3.9					1
High Score	13.0+	11.8	13.0+	13.0+	13.0+
Median	10.1	10.0	10.8	10.6	9.1
Low Score	5.9	9.0	5.7	5.6	3.6

[13] Mental Age measured by Stanford-Binet Test of Intelligence, and translated into Mental Grade according to Table I, Appendix 2, p. 604, Arthur I. Gates, *The Improvement of Reading,* Revised, The Macmillan Company, 1935.

[14] Gates, Arthur I., ibid.

[15] Gates, Arthur I. *Gates Reading Survey,* Bureau of Publications, Teachers College, Columbia University.

TABLE II

Distribution of the Mental and Reading Grade Scores of a Tenth-Grade History Class on the Stanford-Binet Test of Intelligence and the Gates Reading Survey

Number = 41

GRADE LEVEL	MENTAL GRADE [16]	LEVEL OF COMPRE-HENSION [17]	VOCABULARY [17]	SPEED [17]
13.0+	3		2	1
12.5—12.9	3	1	2	0
12.0—12.4	4	2	4	2
11.5—11.9	2	7	6	4
11.0—11.4	2	9	4	5
10.5—10.9	7	8	6	3
10.0—10.4	4	3	3	2
9.5—9.9	5	4	7	4
9.0—9.4	3	4	2	4
8.5—8.9	4	2	1	5
8.0—8.4	2	0	1	3
7.5—7.9	1	0	0	4
7.0—7.4	0	1	1	2
6.5—6.9	1	1	2	1
6.0—6.4				1
High Score	13.0+	12.7	13.0+	13.0+
Median	10.5	10.9	10.8	9.6
Low Score	6.7	6.6	6.7	6.2

that of an "average" pupil who has been in the fifth grade seven months (5.7) to at least that of an "average" person entering college (13.0). This range of more than seven years in reading ability within one grade level in a given school

[16] Mental Age measured by Stanford-Binet Test of Intelligence, and translated into Mental Grade according to Table I, Appendix 2, p. 604, Arthur I. Gates, *The Improvement of Reading*, Revised, The Macmillan Company, 1935.

[17] Gates, Arthur I. *Gates Reading Survey*, Bureau of Publications, Teachers College, Columbia University.

is typical of the range that might be found in almost any high school class of equal size. It should be noted that the comprehension ability of the majority of these students clusters within three grades scores of each other. However, that does not alter the problems with which this high school is confronted.

It is obvious that the adjustment of instruction to such a wide range of reading ability presents many major problems. Among the problems that a wide distribution makes are these: adjustment of instruction, purchase of suitable materials, curriculum reorganization, remedial programs.

A further inspection of Table I shows as great a range in vocabulary as in level of comprehension. This fact indicates that these students are very differently prepared to understand the concepts and verbal aspects of class discussions, lectures, and reading materials.

The students also vary greatly in the speed with which they read. Their range in speed of reading is from the speed of a child who has been six months in the third grade (3.6) to more than that of the "average" college freshman (13.0+). While speed of reading is not as important as comprehension and vocabulary, nevertheless this range indicates that there are wide variations in the amount of time that it would take the students to read the class assignments. One of the faster readers in the group would be able to read in an hour what it would take one of the slower readers several hours to read. Obviously some of these students are totally unprepared to do eleventh-grade reading. Others are prepared for materials that are considerably more exacting than those usually assigned to them. In fact they probably do not find the materials of the high school challenging. The spread in reading ability constitutes one of the more serious problems with which the high school is confronted.

Reading Abilities of a History Class

The distribution of reading abilities within a history class of forty-one students is given in Table II. An inspection of this table shows that the range within the class section is almost as much as the range for the grade group as a whole. It may be seen that there was one student in this history class whose reading comprehension grade score was 12.7 and there was at the opposite extreme a student with a comprehension grade score of 6.6. The median comprehension score for the class was 10.9. The spread from the highest to the lowest in reading comprehension was over six years. It is evident that the history teacher had great difficulty in selecting material upon the topics of the course for the extreme cases of this distribution. Obviously a student whose level of comprehension was equivalent to that of an "average" sixth-grade child could not be expected to read tenth-grade materials with understanding.

Table II on page 21 shows that there are likewise wide differences in vocabulary and in speed of reading. It is evident that instruction in this class should be adjusted to the varying reading abilities of its members.

Reading Abilities of Individuals

To complicate the problem further, there are differences in the development of the reading abilities for any given individual. It is sometimes true that these differences are rather great. Figures I and II show profiles of such individuals. The reading abilities of the individual pictured in Figure I are somewhat varied. This student ranks high in reading comprehension and vocabulary, but relatively low in speed of reading. His comprehension score is equal to a grade score of 12.4. His vocabulary score of 11.9, though somewhat lower than the comprehension score, nevertheless is actually a grade above the one in which he is. His reading rate is 9.5. Thus he is over a year retarded in speed of reading. There is a difference of almost three years between his level of comprehension and his speed of reading. Though somewhat slow, this student is a very accurate, careful reader.

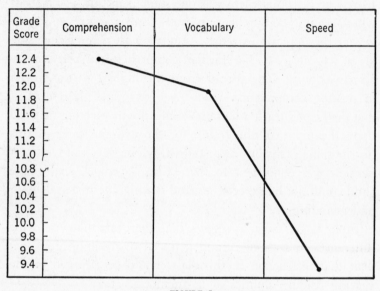

Grade Score	Comprehension	Vocabulary	Speed
12.4			
12.2			
12.0			
11.8			
11.6			
11.4			
11.2			
11.0			
10.8			
10.6			
10.4			
10.2			
10.0			
9.8			
9.6			
9.4			

FIGURE I

Profile of a Slow, Accurate Reader

The reading abilities of the individual pictured in Figure II are also varied. In both level of comprehension and in vocabulary the grade score is 8.6. The rate grade score is 12.3. Again, there is a wide range, but of a different sort. In the case of this student it is questionable whether his high rate of speed is helping him. Inasmuch as the fundamental purpose of reading is to get meaning from the printed page, this student cannot be considered an effective reader of high school materials.

The wide variation noted in this high school class is typical of tenth grades throughout the United States. Every teacher in high school is faced by the reading problem. "I have to teach my students how to read the materials of my course before I can begin teaching the course itself," is a comment frequently made by high school teachers. Thus teachers in

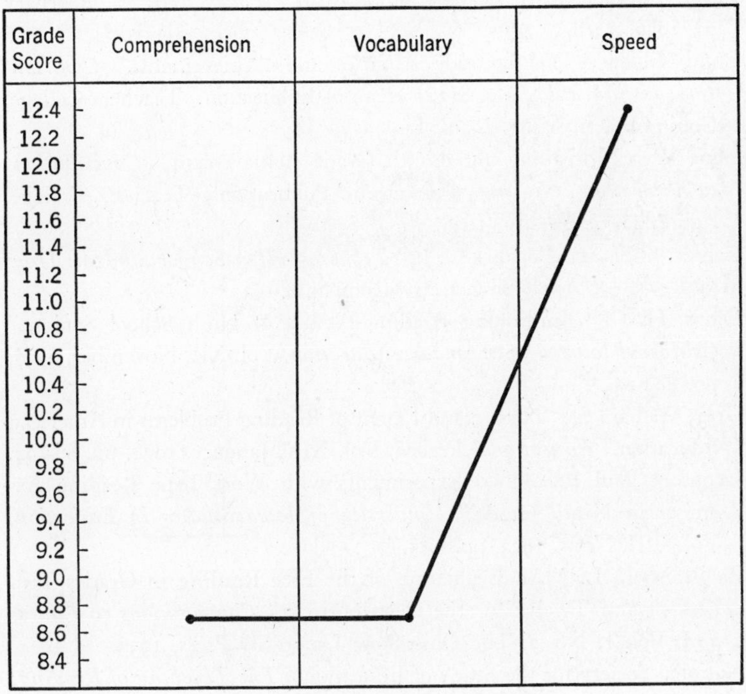

Grade Score	Comprehension	Vocabulary	Speed
12.4			
12.2			
12.0			
11.8			
11.6			
11.4			
11.2			
11.0			
10.8			
10.6			
10.4			
10.2			
10.0			
9.8			
9.6			
9.4			
9.2			
9.0			
8.8			
8.6			
8.4			

FIGURE II

Profile of a Fast, Inaccurate Reader

the various academic fields are obliged to make provision for reading instruction as an integral part of their course work. The fact of the matter is that to a considerable extent they have been concerned with the reading problem. However, there has been no well-rounded, co-ordinated reading program which includes all students and which enlists the services of all teachers. It is the purpose of this book to discuss the formation of such a program.

SELECTED BIBLIOGRAPHY

Adler, Mortimer J. *How to Read a Book,* Simon and Schuster, 1940.

Barry, Jerome. "Americans Cannot Read," *Today,* Vol. V, February 22, 1936, p. 18.

Bond, Elden. "Tenth-Grade Abilities and Achievements," *Contributions to Education,* No. 813, Bureau of Publications, Teachers College, Columbia University, 1940.

Bond, Eva. "Reading and Ninth Grade Achievement," *Contributions to Education,* No. 756, Bureau of Publications, Teachers College, Columbia University, 1938.

Center, S. S., and Persons, G. L. *Teaching High School Students How to Read,* D. Appleton-Century Company, 1937.

Davis, H. C. "Improving Reading Ability of High School Seniors," *California Journal of Secondary Education,* Vol. XII, November, 1937, pp. 424-29.

Gray, William S. "Nature and Extent of Reading Problems in American Education," *Educational Record,* Vol. XIX, January, 1938, pp. 87-104.

Jacobson, Paul B. "Two Experiments with Work-Type Reading Exercises in Ninth Grade," *University of Iowa Studies in Education,* Vol. VIII, No. 5, 1933, pp. 1-85.

La Brant, L. L. "An Evaluation of the Free Reading in Grades Ten, Eleven, and Twelve for the Class of 1935," *Contributions to Education,* Vol. 1, No. 2, The Ohio State University Press, 1936.

National Society for the Study of Education. *The Teaching of Reading: A Second Report, The Thirty-Sixth Yearbook,* Part I, Public School Publishing Company, 1937.

Schuster, M. Lincoln. "Can College Graduates Read?" *Publishers Weekly,* Vol. CXXV, February 24, 1934, pp. 837-39.

Shores, J. H. "The Ability to Read Historical Materials as Related to Eighth-Grade Achievement and General Reading Abilities," unpublished master's thesis, Graduate School, University of Minnesota, 1938.

Shores, J. H. "Reading and Study Skills as Related to Comprehension of Science and History in the Ninth Grade," unpublished doctor's dissertation, Graduate School, University of Minnesota, 1940.

Strang, Ruth, and Rose, F. C. *Problems in the Improvement of Reading in High School and College,* Revised, The Science Press Printing Company, 1940, Chapter I.

Swenson, Esther. "The Relation of Ability to Read Material of the Type Used in Studying Science to Eighth-Grade Achievement," unpublished master's thesis, Graduate School, University of Minnesota, 1938.

CHAPTER II

BASIC CONSIDERATIONS DETERMINING THE NATURE OF THE READING PROGRAM

Reading is a psychological process. Just as there are many theories of psychology, so also there are conflicting theories concerning the nature of the reading process. Proponents of the various schools of psychology have contributed to the body of psychological knowledge. Proponents of the various theories concerning the nature of reading likewise have contributed to the knowledge of reading. Among the approaches to reading that may be recognized in the literature are the two following:

1. The theory of simplicity of reading
2. The theory that reading is a complex process

The Theory of Simplicity of Reading

Reading is regarded by some as a relatively simple process, which can be learned in the elementary school. The basic factors in the process include speed of perception, suppression of vocalization, adequacy of eye movements, span of recognition, and others. This point of view is that psychologically reading is not a complicated situation but rather that efficient reading depends on the mastery of certain factors basic to reading, which are probably few in number.

When instruction is based upon this theory, the mechanical aspects of reading tend to be given a role of undue importance. Much of the time and effort of the teacher is spent upon drill designed to increase the length of line of printed matter that the student can see at one glance. Eye-movement habits of the student are carefully studied and improved. Not much effort is expended in an attempt to give the student experience in reading material of many sorts. Theoretically, at least, it is assumed that practice in the reading of one kind of material enables the student to read materials of all sorts.

A program of reading, based upon the simplicity theory of the nature of reading, would not concern itself with the development of various types of reading, but it would be concerned merely with giving the child a general skill of reading. It considers that once a child learns to read he is adequately equipped with the reading tool and should be given opportunities to use and practice this ability. It assumes that the critical evaluation the child makes of what is read is quite distinct from the reading skill involved and should not be considered a part of reading development. Thus, it is assumed that only the simplest skills are to be considered as reading activities. There are, however, other problems of interpretation of the printed page which are very real. They are, according to the simplicity theory, better thought of as problems of mental activity or thinking than as problems of reading. While the theory of simplicity is very attractive, many educators believe that it is too limited in scope.

The Theory That Reading Is a Complex Process

The second theory is that reading is made up of numerous skills and techniques, the kind and quality of which vary with the purpose of the reader and with the reading situation. Lists, such as Horn and McBroom's,[1] of specific reading skills illus-

[1] Horn, Ernest, and McBroom, Maude. "A Survey of a Course of Study in Reading," Extension Bulletin No. 93, *College of Education Series,* No. 3, University of Iowa, 1924.

trate the complexity of the reading situation. Other lists[2] indicate some of the life situations in which reading abilities are used; they give insight into the variety of purposes for which people read.

From the point of view of this approach, reading is a continuous and a tremendously important process as well as a very complex one. While the major emphasis upon the learning of reading skills remains in the elementary school, there is a recognized need for the acquisition of new reading skills and for the improvement of existing skills at higher levels of school life. There is an ever-growing body of research that seems to support this view.

Because children encounter new reading activities in each new subject at every level,[3] it becomes desirable to provide specific instruction in the reading techniques and skills that are needed for that subject. Furthermore, provision should be made for diagnosis of the reading difficulties of each child and for remedial instruction. Since extreme individual differences exist in reading ability, considered as a whole as well as in various aspects of that ability, it is imperative that diagnostic and remedial measures be instituted when there is an indication of need.

The analysis of the reading of fifty ninth-grade children, who were examined in the Educational Clinic at Northwestern University, showed that a wide variety of specific deficiencies existed.[4] Failure to acquire one or more of the many techniques or skills involved in reading is believed to be a fre-

[2] McKee, Paul. *Reading and Literature in the Elementary School*, Houghton Mifflin Company, 1934, pp. 48-55.

Hathaway, Gladys. "Purposes for Which People Read," *University of Pittsburgh, School of Education Journal*, Vol. 4, March, 1929, p. 83.

[3] McCallister, James M. *Remedial and Corrective Instruction in Reading*, D. Appleton-Century Company, 1936.

[4] Witty, Paul A. "Diagnosis and Remedial Treatment of Reading Difficulties in the Secondary School," *Educational Trends*, Vol. 3, April, 1934, pp. 7-13.

quent source of difficulty in reading.[5] Anderson[6] states that there is not a general reading ability that is acquired once and for all time to a sufficient degree to meet all needs of the reader. A good reader in one type of reading is likely to be a good reader in other types, but there are many exceptions.

A program of reading based upon the theory that reading is a complex process would concern itself with whether or not the child has adequate purposes for reading, whether or not he has a sufficient meaning background for interpreting what he is reading, whether or not he is adjusting his reading to the task at hand. It would assume that such mechanical habits as good eye movements, wide span of perception, etc., are the result and not the cause of ability sufficient to read the material. The emphasis would be placed on an endeavor to obtain a balance between the reading techniques employed and the thought-getting processes which are involved in an adequate interpretation of the passage.

The following generalizations from investigations seem to support the second view:

1. Such mechanical aspects of reading as eye movements, length of perception, and others vary markedly with changes of material difficulty and with the purposes for which that material is being read. This view lends some evidence to the conclusion that rhythmic eye movements are the result of and not the cause of effective reading.

2. A too limited informational background inhibits the development of reading efficiency.

3. When the purpose for which the individual is reading is altered, his effectiveness as a reader frequently changes. This would not be true if reading were a simple process.

[5] Gates, Arthur I. *The Improvement of Reading*, Revised, The Macmillan Company, 1935, p. 12.

[6] Anderson, E. M. "Individual Differences in the Reading Ability of College Students," *University of Missouri Bulletin*, Vol. XXIX, No. 39, 1928, p. 53.

4. Measurements of a pupil's abilities in various types of reading often show wide discrepancies among these abilities.

5. When corrective measures are employed upon one specific type of reading, the gain in the effectiveness of reading is usually most pronounced in that type.

6. Material difficulty cannot be determined by a single factor, but is determined by many factors, such as difficulty of vocabulary, complexity of phraseology, length of sentence, complexity of concepts, and so forth.

7. The theory of complexity is more nearly allied than the other theories with the principles of learning in other fields.

READING PURPOSES

The Role of Purpose

The student approaches reading with a goal in mind. In other words, he has a reason for reading. His reason might be to find out how his favorite baseball player hit in the last game. It might be reading purely for enjoyment. He might be reading to organize his biology lesson. His reading might be for the purpose of enabling him to work an algebra problem. Or, for that matter, his purpose in reading might be simply to pass the time away until the bell rings. Irrespective of the type of reading or of who is doing the reading, there is a reading purpose.

Preferably, reading should take place only when the reader has a well-defined goal. He should be aware of the purpose for which he is reading. In reading for any one given purpose, one or more types of reading, usually various types, are useful to realize the goal. If the purpose for reading is clear to the student, he will be more likely to employ suitable reading techniques. The individual, thus, should know how to set up clearly defined reading goals for himself.

The teacher's task is to set up situations that enable the

student to establish goals, toward a realization of which the student will read. The nature of these situations will be determined by the limitations and needs of each student. For example, a student might rank high in many reading abilities, but be somewhat limited in his proficiency in reading to follow directions. During the course in science, the teacher may set up a situation into which the student is so guided that he desires to make a barometer. The student locates a descriptive account of the making of a barometer. The purpose for which this student is reading is to draw out from the passage the detailed step-by-step description of how to proceed in constructing a barometer. While it is true that during the reading of the passage he will use other reading techniques, such as locating the information in the article, remembering factual detail, etc., the major emphasis will be upon the organized type of reading that is required in understanding directions.

It can be seen that if the situations are well chosen, they will aid fundamentally in establishing the desired types of ability. Situations such as the one cited above enable the student to gain experience in selecting the types of reading which are essential to the realization of his goal. This is probably true, however, only if the student is aware of and desirous of reaching the goal that is set.

Reading Purposes Listed by Teachers

As a means of determining how fully teachers realize the purposes for which they read, a group of them was asked to list their reading purposes. One hundred sixteen students in a summer session class in a college of education (the majority of whom were elementary school teachers) listed the purposes for which they read. A tabulation of the lists of purposes is shown in Table III.

TABLE III

*Reading Purposes Listed by Students in a College of Education
Summer Session Class*

SILENT READING	NUMBER	PER CENT OF TOTAL
Information		
To increase general information	73	19
To gather information	63	17
To obtain and act upon directions	24	6
To verify facts and opinions	15	4
To form an opinion	11	3
To evaluate material	7	2
To form a basis of judgment	5	1
To understand a situation	3	1
To judge appropriateness	2	1
Recreation		
For sheer enjoyment	113	30
To enlarge interests	24	6
To idle time away	14	4
To satisfy curiosity	1	0
ORAL READING		
To provide recreation	6	2
To alter public opinion	3	1
To give factual data	2	1
To give directions	1	0
MISCELLANEOUS		
To improve reading abilities	8	2
Unclassified	3	1
To develop ego	1	0

The most frequent answer was: "For enjoyment and to gain information."

It is interesting to note that, although the majority of the students were classroom teachers who had been engaged for a part of each day in the teaching of reading, a large proportion of them were unable to list more than two purposes for reading.

Less than ten per cent of the students listed oral reading of any kind. Yet it is probably true that everyone in the group reads orally many times a month for the purposes of giving directions, giving factual details, altering public opinion, or providing recreation.

Reading for enjoyment and reading for the purpose of gathering general information or for increasing the amount of his general information were listed by practically every student. But the students, for the most part, were unable to go further than the listing of two of these purposes. An individual who wishes to do a good and a thorough piece of work of any kind should be able to formulate for himself what he is doing, how it should be done, and what it should accomplish. Just as truly when reading, the individual should know why the reading is being done, how it should be done, and what it will accomplish for him. Teaching students to formulate reading purposes and reading procedures is an integral part of teaching reading. It is very likely that the college and the graduate students whose reading purposes are listed above had had little or no training in setting up their own reading purposes. It is likely that they would have benefited from such training and experience.

Purposes and Types of Reading

An organized statement of the purposes for which one reads, adapted from the list prepared by McKee,[7] together with a listing of some of the types of reading employed to realize these purposes, follows: [8]

[7] McKee, Paul. *Reading and Literature in Elementary School*, Houghton Mifflin Company, 1934, pp. 48-55.

[8] While it is realized that the types of reading employed will vary somewhat due to the specific purpose involved, the types listed for each general purpose are probably indicative of the nature of the reading abilities that might be used.

I. Silent Reading

   A. For the purpose of securing information

Purpose 1. Gathering information

Types of reading
   a. Locating information
   b. Scanning information
   c. Reading to remember details

Purpose 2. Understanding a situation

Types of reading
   a. Reading to get the central thought
   b. Reading to discover related facts

Purpose 3. Forming an opinion

Types of reading
   a. Skimming to get the general impression
   b. Reading to draw inferences
   c. Reading to predict outcome

Purpose 4. Verifying facts and opinions

Types of reading
   a. Using index and reference materials to locate material in which the facts are presented
   b. Scanning to find exact or related data
   c. Reading for exact comprehension

Purpose 5. Obtaining and acting upon directions

Types of reading
   a. Use of meaning background to iso-

late reference materials where the directions may be found

b. Locating the reference material, through use of card catalog, index, etc.

c. Reading to follow directions

Purpose 6.   Forming a basis of judgment

Types of reading

a. Locating pertinent information

b. Reading to draw inferences

(1) Using illustrative materials, such as graphs, maps, tables, etc.

(2) Using verbal materials

c. Reading to predict outcome

Purpose 7.   Evaluating material

Types of reading

a. Skimming material for general impression

b. Reading for appreciation

c. Reading to note details of organization, quality, interest value, and factual content to draw inferences

Purpose 8.   Judging appropriateness of material

Types of reading

a. Reading to get central meanings

b. Reading to note details of organization, quality, interest value, and factual content to draw inferences

Purpose 9. Increasing general information

Types of reading
a. Skimming
b. Scanning
c. Noting details
d. Making inferences

B. For the purpose of recreation

Purpose 1. Idling time away

Type of reading
Reading to get the general significance

Purpose 2. Enlarging interests

Types of reading
a. Skimming materials
b. Locating interesting materials
c. Reading to get the central meaning

Purpose 3. Satisfying moods

Type of reading
The type is so determined by the mood to be satisfied that it is impossible to list types.

Purpose 4. Satisfying curiosity

Types of reading
a. Skimming
b. Scanning
c. Reading to note details
d. Reading to make inferences

Purpose 5.   For sheer enjoyment

Type of reading

Reading to get the general significance

II. Oral Reading

A. Purpose of providing others with information

Purpose 1.   Giving directions

Type of reading

Oral reading in which the stress is put
upon organization and sequence

Purpose 2.   Giving factual data related to a group
problem

Type of reading

Oral reading which stresses details

Purpose 3.   Altering public opinion

Type of reading

a. Oral reading which stresses the prediction of outcome of events
b. Oral reading which stresses general
concepts or significance

B. Reading aloud for the purpose of providing recreation

The purposes are the same as listed in the outline
under "Silent Reading—For the purpose of recreation." The types of reading are similar, too, with
added emphasis on an oral interpretation of meanings.

As can be seen from this listing, which makes no pretense of being complete, there is a great deal of overlapping of types. The purpose probably determines in a general way the abilities that will be used. It also determines the emphasis that will be placed on any one ability. Setting up various types of situations, then, is an important factor in a well-rounded reading program. Such a diversified program of reading will help the student gain a fuller appreciation of the uses of reading. It will also enable him to establish awareness of and practice in using the reading abilities that will prove most beneficial in meeting any of the various reading purposes.

Major Tasks of the Reading Program

In order to obtain a clear understanding of the role of purpose in the development of reading abilities, it is pertinent at this point to consider the more important tasks of the complete developmental reading program. It must be realized that the entire program of reading instruction is designed to develop effectiveness in each of five areas. It will be seen from the discussion that follows that each of these areas is developed from the initial lesson continuously and contemporaneously throughout the program. It also will be seen that fundamentally the instruction at any one educational level varies in degree as well as in kind.

These five areas are:

1. Development and refinement of reading techniques and skills
2. Development of vocabulary and background concepts
3. Development of reading interests and tastes
4. Development of independence in reading
5. Development of a differentiated attack

Development and Refinement of Reading
Techniques and Skills

Reading techniques and skills are continuously being developed. The beginning learnings introduce relatively simple reading skills. As the student progresses in reading development, these simple reading skills are added to and refined. The high school student has not only refined the skills and techniques he used in the early elementary school, but he has also added new ones. The college student and the adult continue to refine as well as add to the reading techniques and skills.

For example, one such skill is the proper handling of reading material. The developmental nature of this skill can be seen in the contrast between the child's opening of his first book and the adult's adept manipulation of his morning paper during a rush hour on the subway. While this latter situation may not be the ultimate, it approaches the ultimate in respect to the manipulation of materials when it is refined to the point of avoiding entanglements.

This refining and additive process is equally true, though less observable perhaps, of each of the many types of techniques involved in reading. It includes the development of an ability to eliminate the laborious and time-consuming techniques. The elimination of laborious and time-consuming techniques is being developed from the onset of instruction throughout the reading lifetime of the individual. This ability takes two forms. In the first place, the actual elimination of faulty techniques, such as lip reading, head movements, vocalization, etc., is continually being accomplished. In the second place, the student is learning to eliminate temporarily time-consuming though valuable techniques, such as word analysis, in order to get a better balance between the extent to which he employs such techniques and the purpose at hand. An example of this growth may be found in comparing the reading of the child who points to and studies intently each individual word, to his later reading as the editor of a large newspaper who skims articles to determine news value. The number of laborious techniques this individual has eliminated for the rapid and successful accomplishment of this specific task is legion. However, if this same editor were reading a description of some fishing tackle he was expecting to buy, his reading would be more laborious and time-consuming in character. The techniques employed are determined by the purpose and difficulty of the reading situation as well as by the importance of the task.

Development of Vocabulary and Background Concepts

While the growth in meanings and concepts is the concern of the entire educational program, reading makes a real contribution to this growth. In addition to aiding in the development of general meanings and concepts, reading contributes markedly toward increasing the scope and refinement of word meanings.

Inasmuch as reading should be the understanding of the printed page, the meaning backgrounds the individual brings to the reading are of paramount importance. The more able the individual is to attach meanings to the symbols of the passage and the more able he is to select the precise meaning for each symbol or phrase of symbols, the more fluent will be his reading of the passage. The more complete the background of meaning the individual brings to the reading of a passage, the more complete will be the understanding of it. The deeper and finer the background for appreciation is, the deeper and finer will be the appreciation. The broader and more accurate the background of concepts is, the broader and more accurate will be the concepts. The freer from prejudice the individual's attitudes with regard to the subject of a passage are, the less prejudiced will be his interpretation of it. The greater the number and the accuracy of the generalizations the individual has formulated before the reading of a passage, the more accurate will be the resulting generalizations. In other words, meaning backgrounds are basic to good reading—it matters not whether it be the reading of literary materials, scientific materials, social-scientific materials, or materials from any other field of human endeavor.

Development of Reading Interests and Tastes

Reading interests and tastes are not achieved suddenly. They grow from the time the child reads his first well-written and artistically illustrated story until in old age he lays aside his last book. The progress in reading interests and tastes, which contribute toward making the individual a wholesome and challenging personality, is as truly developmental as are the other areas of the reading program.

One evening at sunset a child, who was walking with an artist in a park, said, "See that beautiful rock."

"What do you see?" queried the artist.

"I see a large gray and black rock. It is beautiful against the green grass and trees," the child answered.

"In that rock formation," remarked the artist, "I see many hues and degrees of intensity of color, gloriously contrasting one with another. I see purples and reds, yellows, greens and blues, blue-greens and purple-reds. The shadows and lights form a myriad of color. Look closely, my child, for you have only begun to use your eyes to appreciate the beauties of nature. Let me help you."

It was not long before the young child, too, saw the soft, delicate colors hidden in the irregularities of the rock formations. Vast new avenues of color had been forever opened to her.

So it is with reading. Each new interest, value, and appreciation opens broad avenues to new worlds of pleasure. It is the teacher's privilege to guide the student toward more complete appreciations, just as it was the artist's privilege to help the child make fuller use of her eyes as a tool to see colors that had always been within her vision, but not within her power to enjoy.

Development of Independence in Reading

As the child progresses through the program, he should be developing a growing degree of independence. Independence in reading is the ability of the individual to rely upon his own resources to locate and use printed materials in meeting a goal. An illustration of the growth in independence is the comparison of the degree of independence achieved by the child who no longer depends upon the teacher to give him the meaning of a word but looks it up in his picture dictionary, to that of the adult who traces the meaning of an obscure word to its historical origin; or the independence of the child who finds a sentence in his reading selection to prove a point, as contrasted with that of the adult who surveys the literature of a field to obtain evidence bearing on an hypothesis. These illustrations show different degrees of independence. The problem of finding the word in the picture dictionary is perhaps fundamentally as difficult for the child at his stage of development as is that of determining the historical origin of a word for the person who purposes to read with that degree of precision.

Development of a Differentiated Attack

By a differentiated attack is meant the ability to adjust

reading skills and techniques and the higher intellectual processes to the purposes for which the reading is being done and to the materials that are being used. This is illustrated by the continuous growth in differentiation that is necessary from the child who reads a simple story for appreciation on the one hand, and bulletin board directions on the other; to the adult who reads a novel on the one hand, and an income tax blank on the other. It can readily be seen that while the nature of the differentiation is similar in this illustration, the degree of refinement is rather marked. The child has to make relatively few such adjustments in reading; the adult has to make a vast number of such differentiations. As the child's reading ability develops, there is a greater demand for the ability to apply reading skills and techniques and the higher intellectual processes because of the increasing specificity of experiences which he encounters. The child can meet this demand only to the extent that the reading program develops his expertness in differentiating his reading attack.

In the Arabian times Aladdin had his lamp. The modern Aladdin has his book to transport him through time and space, give him adventure, aid him in solving his problems, and bring to him interesting companions and the gifts of literature.

This realization of the value of the ability to read may well make its first exciting appearance when the young child forms his initial association of the printed word with the idea it symbolizes. In order to appreciate the importance of reading, however, the individual must be taught the many applications reading may have to his daily living. It is unreasonable to suppose that the student can incidentally gain an understanding of the many uses, both recreational and informational, to which reading may be put. A conscious effort must be made in the reading instruction to insure the continuous development of this realization throughout the school life of the individual.

THE TWOFOLD ASPECT OF A HIGH SCHOOL READING PROGRAM

The reading program in the high school may be divided into two rather distinct divisions. The first of these embraces the students who have the ability to continue their growth in each of the five areas through the developmental program; the second, those relatively few students who have markedly failed to make adequate progress in any or all of the five areas of the reading program. The latter group of students, in addition to continuing the developmental program, should be given remedial instruction designed to meet their individual needs.

SUMMARY

Two theories of reading were briefly discussed. The theory upon which this book is based is that reading is a continuous process. Reading is a very important and complex process. It is made up of numerous skills and techniques, of which the kind and quality vary with the purposes of the reader and with the type of reading situations.

Silent and oral reading purposes and the various types of reading that might be useful in realizing the goals were listed. It was shown that there is always a reading purpose, irrespective of the type of reading done or of who is doing it. The purpose may be an unconscious one or it may be consciously defined. Students should have instruction and experience in setting up reading purposes to enable them to set up their own purposes in out-of-school reading during their school and adult life.

Reading instruction in both oral and silent reading should include the following areas:

1. Development and refinement of reading techniques and skills
2. Development of vocabulary and background concepts
3. Development of reading interests and tastes
4. Development of independence in reading
5. Development of a differentiated attack

SELECTED BIBLIOGRAPHY

Anderson, E. M. "Individual Differences in the Reading Ability of College Students," *University of Missouri Bulletin,* Vol. XXIX, No. 39, 1928.

Buswell, Guy T. "How Adults Read," *Supplementary Educational Monographs,* No. 45, University of Chicago, 1937.

Gates, Arthur I. *The Improvement of Reading,* Revised, The Macmillan Company, 1935.

Hathaway, Gladys. "Purposes for Which People Read: A Technique for Their Discovery," *University of Pittsburgh School of Education Journal,* Vol. IV, March, 1929, pp. 83-99.

Horn, Ernest, and McBroom, Maude. "A Survey of a Course of Study in Reading," Extension Bulletin No. 93, *College of Education Series,* No. 3, University of Iowa, 1924.

McCallister, James M. *Remedial and Corrective Instruction in Reading,* D. Appleton-Century Company, 1936.

McKee, Paul. *Reading and Literature in the Elementary School,* Houghton Mifflin Company, 1934, pp. 48-55.

Paul, Vera A. "The Improvement of Oral Reading," *The Teaching of Reading: A Second Report, The Thirty-Sixth Yearbook of the National Society for the Study of Education,* Part I, Public School Publishing Company, 1937.

Smith, Nila B. *American Reading Instruction,* Silver, Burdett and Company, 1934, Chapter 8.

Thorndike, E. L. "Improving the Ability to Read," *Teachers College Record,* Vol. XXXVI, October, November, December, 1934, pp. 1-19, 123-44, 229-41.

Thorndike, E. L. "Reading Is Reasoning: A Study of Mistakes in Paragraph Reading," *Journal of Educational Psychology,* Vol. VIII, June, 1917, pp. 323-32.

Witty, Paul A. "Diagnosis and Remedial Treatment of Reading Difficulties in the Secondary School," *Educational Trends,* Vol. III, April, 1934, pp. 7-13.

Witty, Paul, and Kopel, David. *Reading and the Educative Process,* Ginn and Company, 1939.

SECTION II

THE ALL-SCHOOL READING PROGRAM

CHAPTER III

THE DEVELOPMENTAL READING PROGRAM

Growth in the ability to use and understand speech is a developmental process. That is, each new speech ability which an individual learns grows out of his previously learned abilities.

An infant one month of age neither knows how to speak nor comprehends the words he hears. But it is not long before he gives evidence of understanding, to some extent, words which are spoken to him. Although his progress in the developmental process of using and understanding speech appears to be slow at first, it is actually very rapid. By the time he is twelve months of age, the average child can say three words and understand many more that are spoken to him. During the short span of the next twelve months, the average child has increased his spoken vocabulary to nearly three hundred words. By the time he enters school he knows between two thousand and three thousand words.[1]

At first a single word suffices for a sentence. The young child conveys the meaning of his wish to have the ball handed to him by pointing to it and saying, "Ball." It is not long, however, before he is using sentences containing words other than nouns. At about twenty-two months of age, he may be heard to say, "Me, ball." Later, as the young child develops in the use of language, the sentence becomes, "Hand me the

---

[1] Smith, M. E. "An Investigation of the Development of the Sentence and the Extent of Vocabulary in Young Children," *University of Iowa Studies, Studies in Child Welfare,* Vol. 3, No. 5, 1926, p. 92.

ball" or "Please throw the ball to me." By the time the child enters school, he knows how to use sentences containing several words. In these sentences he is able to use all the basic speech forms that adults use.[2]

As the child progresses through elementary school, high school, and college, and into adult life, the adding of new words and new meanings of words is a continuous process. This sequence in the growth of ability in the oral use of words is a "developmental" process. Each new learning depends upon previous learnings. Likewise growth in reading is "developmental."

THE MEANING OF THE DEVELOPMENTAL READING PROGRAM

Reading Growth in the Elementary School

The majority of elementary school students have been progressing in the development of reading in a continuous and satisfactory fashion. These students enter the seventh grade with a good background of meanings, good reading skills and techniques, wholesome interests and tastes, and a fair degree of independence. In a rather general way they are able to adjust their reading to the purpose at hand. Their developmental progress reflects the fact that the reading program has been one of major concern to the elementary teachers. While it is true that a few children have failed to establish the necessary reading abilities and therefore constitute remedial problems, still, the guidance of the children by the elementary classroom teacher has, for the most part, been successful. The purpose of the developmental program in reading in the secondary school is to continue this growth.

As materials and methods continue to become more effective on the elementary school level, and as the teachers become

[2] Goodenough, Florence L. *Developmental Psychology,* D. Appleton-Century Company, 1934.

more able to adjust these materials and methods to the differ-ences of individual children, the remedial program will be needed for fewer and fewer children. For an ever-increasing percentage of the children, the developmental program will become the complete reading program from the very first year of school life through the completion of formal education and into adult life.

This optimism seems justified when we realize that leaders in educational thinking have been and are continuing to be sincerely concerned and interested in the elementary school reading program. Their interest and concern have led them to devote no small measure of their time and effort to studying and analyzing the learning process as it is related to reading. Probably in few other fields has the work of educational leaders been so gratifying and the result so practical as in the field of reading. The co-operative endeavor of many elemen-tary school teachers and research workers has aided immeas-urably in making the outlook for reading appear very hopeful. As the methods, materials, and other results of research that are now available have a wider use in the schoolroom, increas-ingly more effective reading on the part of the children may be expected.

Reading Growth in Secondary School

The fact that in the secondary school the continued im-provement in reading has been left to chance is a dark cloud on the reading horizon.

No better results should be expected from this procedure than from leaving a vegetable garden to grow by itself with-out any outside care after it is once started.

Suppose a man wants to grow a fine vegetable garden. He analyzes the soil and prepares it well for planting. He deter-mines the nature of the various seeds. He plants each in the kind of soil best suited to its development. He carefully feeds and waters the plants. They respond to all this care by growing into strong, hardy plants.

But suppose that during the warm growing season, when the greatest degree of growth should be expected, the growing plants are no longer systematically watered or cultivated. The yield will be disappointingly small in spite of the fine early care. True, some areas may receive water and cultivation, but the ones that do are determined by a chance process. Some of the sturdier plants will continue to grow and bear fruit, but even these sturdy plants would have increased their yield with more care. Some of the more neglected plants will wither and die from the very warmth that with proper care would have fostered their growth. Only continued care of the plants throughout their whole period of growth would allow them to develop to the fullest extent.

The secondary school developmental reading program is concerned fundamentally with the continued refinement and development of the more mature aspects of the self-same types of abilities that were being refined and developed in the elementary school. This refinement and development likewise continue as long as the individual continues to learn. The newer demands made on reading by the secondary school curriculum make it unreasonable to expect the elementary school to complete the developmental process.

The time to develop and refine an ability in reading is the time when that degree of development and refinement will be useful to the student in his reading. For this reason it is apparent that the elementary school cannot develop in the child refinements of reading abilities which will be essential to the successful pursuance of high school work. Nor can the high school develop all those essential for later educational achievement. For that matter, teachers in one subject-matter field cannot be expected to develop in the student the refinements of reading abilities that are required in the study of other fields.   The English teacher, for example, should not be expected to develop the ability to read an algebraic formula; nor should the mathematics teacher be expected to teach the ability to appreciate poetry.   Moreover, no one teacher can build up the word and meaning backgrounds that are necessary for effective reading in other content fields.

Developmental Reading in the Content Subjects

The reading abilities essential to achievement in the various content subjects differ considerably.   The extent to which reading skill is a factor in achievement depends upon the scholastic achievement in question.   In other words, we cannot hope that the ability to read simple literary materials rapidly and with a relatively high power of comprehension will take care of all the needs of the several academic subjects.   Each subject demands specialized and rather highly complicated groupings of reading skills which must be developed in the study of the particular subject itself.   The teacher of general science, for example, might conceivably find it expedient to devote a portion of the first few weeks of the course to improving the reading ability of the students in the reading of scientific materials, so that they may be better able to comprehend adequately those materials.   He should, in addition, be constantly alert throughout the entire course in general science to the reading problems the children are meeting and should develop the reading abilities necessary to enable the children to meet adequately those more difficult situations.

Have you ever heard a child say, "I spent last period in the study hall reading my lesson for general science.   I read it over and over, but I couldn't seem to understand what it meant"?   In such cases the child's mental ability is usually adequate, but what he needs is help with his reading. He needs simple, interesting materials about the particular subject which is being considered in that day's general science lesson. This is just one of many such instances which are constantly occurring in connection with classwork and homework assignments throughout the country.

The teacher of each subject should teach the children how to read that particular subject. Efficiency in work-study reading habits, for example, seems to be a greater factor in achievement in mathematics than does high ability in some of the other aspects of reading comprehension. Furthermore, scientific and mathematical reading requires careful, slow reading of comparatively small amounts of material, whereas a fast rate of reading simple materials is a definite help in enlarging vocabulary and broadening literary acquaintance. There is a need, therefore, on the secondary school level for a concerted attack by all teachers upon the problems of reading in the five areas with which reading instruction concerns itself.

Consider the change in degree of independence involved in the use of reference materials at different stages of school life. This will illustrate the growth of an individual in the refinement and development of independence. In the first grade the child might be expected to secure the answer to the question independently by reading a passage in a carefully chosen, graded selection handed and designated to him by the teacher. At the sixth-grade level the child might find the answer to a question by going to the library, locating books on the shelf to which the teacher had referred him, and then locating the information in these books by the use of the index or table of contents.

The sophomore in high school, in answering a specific question, might be expected to go to the library, locate books of a type recommended to him by the teacher, and use the index to ascertain whether or not pertinent material was contained in these presentations. He might also be expected to consult the indexes of the several periodicals in the library for additional pertinent facts.

The college student confronted by a problem would be expected to locate independently information pertinent to the specific problem in mind. By using the card catalogue, readers' indexes of various kinds, etc., he would be expected to find the needed information from a wide range of materials. He might be expected to more nearly exhaust the materials on a specific topic than would a high school sophomore. The graduate student, on the other hand, in dealing with a specific problem, would be expected to exhaust all the available pertinent and related materials.

From the above illustration it is evident that the sixth-grade child is neither in need of nor ready for the degree of refinement in independent use of reference materials that is necessary at the more advanced educational levels. This phase, as well as other phases of the developmental program, is, therefore, simply a conscious, systematic continuation of the reading program of the elementary school.

Factors Contributing to the Absence of Reading Programs

As indicated in the foregoing discussion, if the continued development of reading is to be achieved, the high school must inaugurate thoroughgoing reading programs. A casual survey of the practices on the high school level clearly indicates an absence of such programs.

There are several factors which have contributed to the absence of a systematic endeavor to improve the reading efficiency of the students. In the first place, the population of the high school has increased greatly in the past few years. This change in population has come about because of com-

pulsory school attendance laws and because of lack of occupational opportunity. The relatively recent influx of students
into the high school has brought many poor readers who,
previous to that time, would not have continued their education. For the most part, those interested in the reading problem in the high school have been unduly concerned with
diagnostic and remedial work with these poor readers. Consequently, there has been a failure to realize the need of the
entire high school population for continued instruction in
reading.

Another factor contributing to the lack of a systematic endeavor to improve the reading efficiency of the students is that
not until recently has the developmental nature of reading
been recognized. This lack of awareness of the developmental
nature of reading has also resulted in an undue emphasis upon
remedial procedures. Those schools that have been aware of
the problem of reading have directed their attention toward
remedial instruction for the students in need of it rather than
reading instruction for the entire student body.

Again, there has been little, if any, knowledge of the degree
to which the learnings in the high school depend upon reading
abilities. Recent research, experimentation, and thinking in
the field of reading have given some indication of the degree
to which abilities in reading permeate the entire educational
process.[3]

[3] Bond, Elden. "Tenth-Grade Abilities and Achievements," *Contributions to Education*, No. 813, Bureau of Publications, Teachers College, Columbia University, 1940.

Bond, Eva. "Reading and Ninth Grade Achievement," *Contributions to Education*, No. 756, Bureau of Publications, Teachers College, Columbia University, 1938.

McCallister, James M. *Remedial and Corrective Instruction in Reading*, D. Appleton-Century Company, 1936.

National Society for the Study of Education, *The Teaching of Reading: A Second Report, The Thirty-Sixth Yearbook*, Public School Publishing Company, 1937.

Shores, J. H. "Reading and Study Skills as Related to Comprehension of Science and History in the Ninth Grade," unpublished doctor's dissertation, Graduate School, University of Minnesota, 1940.

Furthermore, we are only just becoming aware in some slight degree of the significance of reading achievement in the personal and social adjustment of the individual and of its contribution to his economic efficiency.[4]

And finally, there has been no clear formulation of how or in what way the high school can contribute to reading development. The lack of such formulation may be accounted for by the relative recency and incompleteness of experimentation in this field. Nevertheless, the demand for continued development in reading made upon the high school must be met.

Many forward-looking teachers have recognized in its larger significance the problem cited above and have been making real contributions to the reading development of the children who have been fortunate enough to have been under their tutelage. One such teacher, for example, upon finding that the students were having difficulty in reading the textbook, appraised the students' reading as they read for a variety of purposes. He found, as a result of his appraisal, that some students were having trouble in organizing the ideas in a sequential fashion, while others were experiencing difficulty in getting the significant generalizations from a passage. A third group was reading too hurriedly to note details.

The teacher wished to give instruction in the types of reading abilities necessary for the reading of historical literature, which the students were finding troublesome. He decided that the reading entailed in preparing for the forthcoming

---

[4] Blanchard, Phyllis. "Reading Disabilities in Relation to Maladjustment," *Mental Hygiene*, Vol. 12, October, 1928, pp. 772-88.

Gates, Arthur I. "Failure in Reading and Social Maladjustment," *The Journal of the National Education Association*, Vol. XXV, No. 7, 1936, pp. 205-6.

Monroe, Marion. *Children Who Cannot Read*, University of Chicago Press, 1932, p. 105.

Educational Policies Commission. *Education and Economic Well-Being in American Democracy*, 1940, p. 43.

pageant, "The Settlement of Jamestown," would offer an opportunity to provide instruction in the reading techniques in which the students were deficient.

Appropriate reading experiences were set up for the various groups. The task assigned to the first group, which was having trouble with organization, was that of formulating the outline around which the pageant would be written. The task of the second group, which was having trouble in reading to get the significant generalizations, was that of reading to find the significant features of the settlement of Jamestown to make up the final scene. The task of the third group was reading to find the details of the dress and customs of that time. The teacher did not, however, let his instruction end at that point; but he showed the students of each group how they should read for their purpose. He also discussed with the members of the class the various types of reading abilities that had been used in the preparation of the material for the historical pageant, and the fact that they had to adjust their reading to the nature of the problem at hand.

While such isolated efforts to improve reading instruction have no doubt had beneficial effects, the problem can be met adequately only by a unified developmental reading program encompassing all teachers and all students.

THE SCOPE OF THE DEVELOPMENTAL PROGRAM

The scope of the developmental program on the high school level is very broad. It should utilize all of the reading experiences, both oral and silent, that lend themselves to the continued growth of the student in the major areas with which the program of reading instruction concerns itself; namely:

1. Development and refinement of reading techniques and skills

2. Development of vocabulary and background concepts
3. Development of reading interests and tastes
4. Development of independence in reading
5. Development of a differentiated attack

From the preceding discussion, it is evident that the developmental program permeates each of the subject-matter fields in which reading is used. In addition, it permeates the recreational and other reading of the individual.

Instruction in reading the materials of each subject-matter field includes problems that are unique to that field. For example, in the area of the development and refinement of reading techniques and skills, the development of the ability in reading chemical formulas is quite unique to the field of chemistry. Getting the meaning from a printed page, even though that printed page consists of chemical abbreviations, is as truly a task of reading as is the reading of any abbreviations or, for that matter, any kind of material.

Or, again, when one is reading in the field of biological sciences, he is confronted by many new words. His initial approach to the recognition of these words is sounding out or analyzing them. Later he handles them as sight words, although in both cases he may know the meaning background behind each word. For example, the term for one type of flying reptile is *pterodactyl*. Although the meaning was known to the reader, if he had had no experience with biological vocabulary, it would have been necessary for him to use the laborious technique of analysis rather than the more rapid one of sight recognition in order to recognize the word *pterodactyl*. No amount of analyzing words in other fields would give him the sight recognition of all such words found in the biological sciences. The biology teacher is well aware of the need for systematically building up a biological vocabulary. Most high school teachers find it necessary to teach their students how to read the materials of their course. It is unquestionably true, however, that a co-ordination of their efforts would result in more effective teaching and learning.

There are problems of reading instruction in each of the subject-matter fields that are unique to that field. The illustrations cited above show such problems in the first of the five areas of reading instruction. Illustrations could be drawn from any of the areas and any content field. The fact that it takes many types of situations to foster growth in all these areas and the fact that there are problems unique to a specific subject-matter field make the broad scope of the developmental program mandatory.

Administrative Considerations in Setting up a Developmental Reading Program

The organization of a developmental reading program in the high school will depend upon local conditions, such as size, internal organization, personnel, and financial condition. Irrespective of these conditions, a developmental reading program should include all students and all teachers. While this is true, it is recommended that a beginning be made the first year with an all-inclusive program for the freshman class only. Then the program should be introduced on the higher levels as rapidly as is feasible. It is probably wise to make the reorganization of the total school a gradual one. It should be pointed out, however, that for those students who are included it is necessary to have a well-integrated, complete developmental program, encompassing all their school subjects and including active participation on the part of all their teachers.

Time must be allotted for basic instruction in reading. This instruction should be supplemented by active participation in the teaching of reading by the subject-matter teachers as a part of their regular classroom instruction. Provision for the instruction in reading abilities that are common to many fields could be made, for example, by setting aside two periods a week for such instruction. The general reading instruction might fit most easily into the home-room period, in which case the instruction in the basic reading techniques and abilities would be done by the home-room teachers.

The fact that all home-room teachers are to undertake this teaching makes necessary considerable in-service training for the teachers. In order that they may adequately perform their twofold task, it is necessary for them to know both how to teach the general aspects of reading and how to include, in the teaching of their content subject, the reading instruction necessary to develop those reading abilities needed in that subject.

Whatever organization is undertaken, it should be relatively simple in nature and should be easily operated. A cumbersome, complicated program of co-ordination is neither necessary nor desirable. (The co-ordination of the reading program will be discussed at greater length in Chapter XIV.) Whatever the organization, it should be understandable to the teachers. This implies that their part should be clearly defined and explained.

The following are some of the responsibilities that must be assumed by each member of the faculty:

1. The teacher must know how to interpret the results of the initial standardized tests.

2. He must, in addition, be able to make the appraisals of one kind or another that will enable him to understand the various reading abilities and limitations of the students.

3. He must be able to make use of the appraisals so that he can better individualize reading instruction.

4. He must have an awareness of the reading difficulties encountered in his subject-matter field and the contributions his

subject can make to the reading development of the students.

5. He must know how to organize and carry out the reading activities that make up a part of the instruction in the content subject.

6. He must have some conception of the place of reading in the other content subjects so that he may work co-operatively with the other teachers in this school-wide endeavor.

7. He must know the varying levels of reading difficulty of the materials in his subject-matter field, including a knowledge of the library facilities, so that he may better adjust reading assignments to the needs and abilities of his students.

The introduction of a reading program, like the introduction of instruction in any other subject into the high school curriculum, presents a personnel problem. It necessitates finding the person or persons who can teach it satisfactorily. It involves the in-service training of the present teaching staff, the requiring of a background in reading methods as a part of the educational equipment of all new teachers, and the placing of the responsibility for co-ordinating the reading program on a member of the staff or a teacher-committee.

It is imperative, however, that the responsibility for co-ordinating the program be put in the hands of someone who has been thoroughly trained in the psychology of reading. The proportion of the co-ordinator's time that should be devoted to the reading program will depend upon the specific school situation. The co-ordinator, regardless of the size and needs of the school, should not be expected to carry a full teaching load and at the same time act as the co-ordinator of the program. Ideally, the medium-sized and larger high schools should have on their teaching staff a person who devotes his entire time to the reading program and who is endowed with supervisory or administrative ranking.

A minimum budget should include an item sufficient to

cover the cost of the testing program, including special examinations needed for remedial cases, mimeographed instructional directions to the teachers, and an item covering the salary of the co-ordinator. There is probably no place in the high school curriculum where a use of the school resources would be so productive in furthering the educational effectiveness of the high school as in installing a reading program.

SUMMARY

Growth in reading is developmental. Each new learning is prepared for by previous learnings. The developmental program in reading is for the purpose of providing for the continued growth of the reading abilities of high school students. It is concerned fundamentally with the continued refinement and development of the more mature aspects of the same types of abilities that were being refined and developed in the elementary school.

It is not possible for the teachers in one subject-matter field to develop in the student the refinements of reading abilities that are required in the study of other fields. The reading abilities essential to achievement in the various content subjects differ considerably. Each subject demands specialized and rather highly complicated groupings of reading skills which must be developed in the study of the particular subject itself.

Factors that have contributed to the absence of a systematic endeavor to improve the reading efficiency of high school students are:

1. The high school has had a greatly increased population during the past few years.

2. Only recently has the developmental nature of reading been recognized.

3. There has been a dearth of knowledge as to the degree

to which the learnings in high school depend upon reading abilities.

4. Educational leaders are only now becoming aware of the significance of reading achievement in the personal and social adjustment of the individual and of its contribution to his economic efficiency.

5. There has been no clear formulation of how the high school can contribute to reading development.

The developmental program permeates each of the subject-matter fields in which reading is used. In addition, it permeates the recreational and other reading of the individual. It includes all students and all teachers. In addition to basic instruction in reading, there is an active participation in the teaching of reading on the part of the subject-matter teachers within their regular classroom instruction.

SELECTED BIBLIOGRAPHY

Bond, Elden. "Tenth-Grade Abilities and Achievements," *Contributions to Education,* No. 813, Bureau of Publications, Teachers College, Columbia University, 1940.

Bond, Eva. "Reading and Ninth Grade Achievement," *Contributions to Education,* No. 756, Bureau of Publications, Teachers College, Columbia University, 1938.

Gray, William S. "The Nature and Organization of Basic Instruction in Reading," *The Teaching of Reading: A Second Report, The Thirty-Sixth Yearbook of the National Society for the Study of Education,* Part I, Public School Publishing Company, 1937.

Hovious, Carol. "What Should Be Done about Reading in Secondary Schools?" *California Journal of Secondary Education,* Vol. XI, January, 1936, pp. 17-21.

McCallister, J. M. *Remedial and Corrective Instruction in Reading,* D. Appleton-Century Company, 1936, Chapter 2.

Shores, J. H. "The Ability to Read Historical Materials as Related to Eighth-Grade Achievement and General Reading Abilities," unpublished master's thesis, Graduate School, University of Minnesota, 1938.

Shores, J. H. "Reading and Study Skills as Related to Comprehension of Science and History in the Ninth Grade," unpublished doctor's thesis, Graduate School, University of Minnesota, 1940.

Strang, Ruth, and Rose, F. C. *Problems in the Improvement of Reading in High School and College,* Revised, The Science Press Printing Company, 1940, Chapter IV.

CHAPTER IV

THE DEVELOPMENT OF READING TECHNIQUES AND SKILLS

There are many teachers who know little about their own methods of reading. To determine how aware teachers are of reading techniques and skills, a group of teachers were asked to list the ones they use in daily life. The group consisted of one hundred sixteen students in a summer session class in a college of education. The majority of these students were elementary school teachers. A tabulation of the lists they made is given in Table IV.

These students were unable to compile a suitable list of the reading techniques which they should have been teaching. It is rather difficult to find a plausible reason to account for the results. It might have been that they were not acquainted with the fact that the reading skills and techniques they teach to elementary or to secondary school children are among the reading skills and techniques they themselves use in their own daily reading. It might be argued that if the task had been the listing of reading skills and techniques taught in the elementary school, this group of teachers and teachers-in-training would have been able to prepare more adequate and accurate lists. But such an explanation does not seem a very plausible one. When one realizes that the students under discussion represent a sampling of elementary school teachers who are actually engaged in teaching children to read, he can easily see that definite steps should be taken to improve teachers' conception of how to teach reading.

The responses included under "unclassified" in Table IV were such statements as: "just reading," "educational," "interesting materials," "short stories," "fiction," "reading for skills," etc.

TABLE IV

Reading Skills and Techniques Listed by Students in a Class of the Summer Session in a College of Education

Number = 116

READING SKILLS AND TECHNIQUES	NUMBER	PER CENT OF TOTAL
Reading to get the general significance	101	21
Oral reading	54	11
Skimming	39	8
Work type	37	8
Sentence, paragraph, and story comprehension	27	6
Noting details	29	6
Organizing	24	5
Scanning	16	3
Locating information	15	3
Reading critically	10	2
Following directions	9	2
Speed	9	2
Word recognition techniques	8	2
Reading to predict outcomes	4	1
Reading graphs, maps, tables, etc.	1	0
Unclassified	100	21

These data and those in Chapter II show that teachers are, on the whole, unaware of their reading purposes, techniques, and skills. This indicates either that these teachers disagreed concerning their particular objectives, or that they were not sufficiently conversant with the teaching of reading and would profit by including, in their professional training, courses in the teaching of reading.

Silent Reading Skills and Techniques

In the development of reading ability the learning of adequate skills and techniques is essential. This chapter will be concerned with a discussion of some of the more important of these skills and techniques.

Word Recognition Techniques

The development of word recognition techniques is not so much a problem in the high school as in the elementary school. It does, nevertheless, constitute a phase of reading instruction in the high school that should not be neglected. The development of ability in word recognition techniques on the high school level tends to involve adjustments of the old techniques more than it does the establishment of additional ones. The average student entering high school has already established a fairly competent diversified attack upon words. If he is an effective reader, he adjusts his attack to the word being analyzed. In the high school the student's improvement is the result of cue reduction; that is, he learns to depend more and more upon the content and less and less upon laborious techniques. In any subject-matter field that has a technical vocabulary, the student will find himself analyzing these technical words more intently than is necessary to analyze words with which he is more familiar.

For example, in order to foster development in word recognition, some biology teachers try to teach some of the more common Greek and Latin derivatives which are frequently used in the technical vocabulary. They do this so that the size of the units of analysis may be increased and the meanings may be immediately evident. Learning the root *saurus* will aid in the analysis of words such as *Dinosauria, Pterosauria,* and *Ichthyosaurus.* It also has the advantage of giving the meaning of such words. This approach tends to keep at a high level the running content. The content, thus, may aid the student in recognizing other technical words. For some students this approach may be wasteful because it tends to cause them to break into units words that might otherwise be recognized as wholes.

Other instructors, instead of teaching the Greek and Latin roots, list the technical words included in the passages and give their pronunciation and meanings. Then, when the student encounters these words, he can usually handle them as sight words. Since it involves taking words out of context, this approach is time-consuming. Consequently, it is subject to the same limitations as word drill in the elementary school.

Still other instructors in the biological sciences attempt to select materials which will give the student the opportunity to read relatively nontechnical matter with the vocabulary burden of technical words kept at a minimum. Unfortunately, such materials are relatively scarce. Seldom are nontechnical materials sufficiently precise to meet the demands of the biological sciences on the high school level. In order to select materials most effectively, it is necessary for the teacher to have a wide knowledge of the literature of biology and a reasonably accurate knowledge of the needs and reading abilities of the members of the class.

Probably the most effective way of developing adequate techniques of word recognition is a composite of the three methods discussed above with the greatest emphasis upon the third. This procedure implies that the students will be reading materials selected to accord with their reading abilities. It further implies that the teacher will take out of the content certain words for class or individual discussion when he deems it necessary to add these words to the vocabulary of the students. When this is done, it will usually be expedient to point out the derivation of words of similar origin or roots. The sequence should be: (1) selecting material at the appropriate level of difficulty, (2) inspecting words taken from the content, (3) grouping words that have derivations which are the same as or similar to those previously encountered. It is wasteful to reverse the procedure—studying roots as such, listing examples, and then depending upon the memory to transfer to contextual reading.

Eye Movements

The eyes move along the line in a series of pauses and forward jumps from left to right. Then follows a *return sweep* from the end of one line to the beginning of the next. During a pause, or *fixation,* the actual recognition takes place. At times the reader, for one reason or another, loses the meaning or gets into some other difficulty. Then he finds it necessary to jump back along the line for the purpose of picking up the meaning. Such return jumps are called *regressions*. The amount of a line of print the eyes see at any one fixation is termed the *eye span*.

The role of these eye movements in reading has been studied probably as much as any other factor associated with skill in reading. It is the unquestioned fact that good readers of any given material have effective eye movements for reading that material. Among the points of view of those who have studied the problem are two contradictory ones. Some investigators believe that poor eye movements are the *cause* of reading disability. And others believe that faulty eye movements are the *result* of inability to read the material.

The writers hold the latter point of view. The major problem does not seem to be that of training eye movements. It is rather the improvement of reading. This point of view is aptly stated by Witty and Kopel in the following quotation:

Research has demonstrated that improvement in eye movement occurs when reading gains are produced by remedial programs which make no direct attack upon faulty eye movement. In fact, eye-movement training *per se* has been shown to yield no appreciable gain in reading ability. Indeed the poor reader's difficulty is rarely a mechanical problem; it is usually an inadequacy in perceiving or associating meaning with words and other language symbols.[1]

As Horn has stated:

The classroom teacher needs to be concerned with movement of the eyes little more than with the movements of the bones of the inner ear.[2]

Even a good reader who encounters a passage such as the following will immediately notice that he makes many more fixations and regressive eye movements than he does in reading material in which the vocabulary is more familiar to him.[3]

Connected with the anterior end of the basal plate is the large bilobed *posterior dorsal cartilage* (*p. d. c.*); it appears to be formed from the united anterior ends of the trabeculae. Below and projecting in front of it is the *anterior dorsal cartilage* (*a. d. c.*), which is probably homologous with the upper labial cartilage of some Fishes and Amphibians. Also belonging to the series of labial cartilages are the paired *anterior lateral cartilages* (*a. l. c.*) and the great ring-shaped *annular cartilage* (*an. c.*) which supports the edge of the buccal funnel.[4]

For the majority of students in high school, exercises designed to develop effective eye movements would not, in themselves, result in more effective reading. On the other hand,

[1] Witty, Paul, and Kopel, David. *Reading and the Educative Process,* Ginn and Company, 1939, pp. 17-18.

[2] Horn, Ernest. *Methods of Instruction in the Social Studies,* Charles Scribner's Sons, 1937, pp. 201-2.

[3] Those students suffering from defects in orientation will be discussed in the chapter on remedial reading.

[4] From a college zoology textbook: Parker, T. Jeffery, and Haswell, A. William. *A Textbook in Zoology,* Vol. II, The Macmillan Company, 1921, p. 123.

such exercises might make the student so conscious of the mechanical aspects of reading that his effective reading would be inhibited.

The remedy for the student who has faulty eye movements is to give him material that will not place so great a burden on his reading abilities as the material on which he showed faulty eye movements. Probably the most effective way, for the person inexperienced in reading such materials, to read the passage on page 73 is by the use of so-called "faulty" eye movements. As the student gains in the ability to read materials similar to the passage taken from the college text, the number of fixations and regressions will automatically become fewer.

Rate of Reading

The concept of "rate of reading" should include not only the number of words per minute at which the student can read relatively simple materials, but also the speed with which he can accomplish the purpose for which he is reading and the speed at which he can read materials of different degrees of difficulty. Bond[5] found that reading speed is not a general attribute. Students differentiate their rate of reading when the purpose for reading, the subject-matter content of the material, or the comprehension difficulty of the material changes.

While it is important that the student be able to read as rapidly as is compatible with his purpose, exercises to develop speed *per se* might be open to question. It is probable that the rate of reading of the majority of students[6] increases auto-

[5] Bond, Elden. "Tenth-Grade Abilities and Achievements," *Contributions to Education,* No. 813, Bureau of Publications, Teachers College, Columbia University, 1940, p. 63.

[6] Certain students who have faulty habits, such as head movements, excessive articulation, lip movements, word-by-word reading, overanalysis, etc., will need special remedial training to increase their speed of reading. But this phase of the problem cannot be considered an aspect of the developmental program at the high school level and is discussed, therefore, in Chapter XIII as a phase of remedial instruction.

matically for any one type of reading as the students gain in ability to comprehend sentences, paragraphs, and stories, to get the central meanings of passages, to predict outcomes, to increase their vocabularies, and to develop facility in using various study skills and techniques. In other words, the way to make the majority of students *rapid* readers is to make them *effective* readers.

However, it is important for the student to improve in the technique of adjusting his speed of reading to the purpose at hand and to the difficulty of the material. The increasing of speed, then, becomes a matter of temporarily eliminating thought processes and techniques of word and phrase recognition which are not essential to the purpose at hand. For example, it would be foolish indeed to approach the reading of a mathematical problem at the same rate as the skimming of an article to gain an impression of it. Instruction in the various content subjects can aid materially by pointing out those purposes for which the student should read at a relatively slow rate and those for which he should read faster.

Let us suppose that a high school student looks through his new text in Occupations for the purpose of getting an idea of the scope of the course. For this purpose his speed of reading is very rapid. In less than a half hour he can become well aware of the material covered. This same student, on the other hand, may spend as much as two or three hours in reading to find the facts about and weigh the values of a single occupation discussed in the book.

Skimming

Skimming is a rapid sort of reading which has many uses. First, it may be used to get a single fact from a passage. For example, an individual may glance through a newspaper item about a forthcoming event just to find out when it begins.

The effective reader with such a purpose temporarily eliminates his more laborious and time-consuming reading techniques by simply gleaning enough of the meaning so that he can locate the part of the article that contains the fact he wishes to know.

Skimming may also be used to gain a general impression of a passage, chapter, or book. A person selecting a book from a library or bookstore would probably skim through several before deciding on one. He would glance at the style and organization of each book and perhaps read a few passages carefully. Then, if it did not challenge him, he would put it aside and try another until he found one that promised to be interesting and valuable.

The value of skimming lies in the fact that it is the most rapid sort of reading. From the above examples it may be seen that skimming is a useful technique for the adult. It saves him considerable time in locating information. Besides aiding him immeasurably in selecting materials that he wishes to read intently, skimming enables him to gain a general impression of a passage that he does not care to read with a greater degree of thoroughness. Because of the great abundance of material available on practically any topic, ability to skim has become an essential reading technique.

The student, as well as the adult, finds the ability to skim a useful technique on many occasions. In the curriculum organized around topical units, one of the major tasks of the student is that of locating pertinent or related materials. The ability to skim is obviously time-saving to the student and for this reason makes possible a more adequate grasp of literature in accordance with his purpose.

Students can learn to acquire this technique by practice in locating single facts from passages and in getting general impressions of books and short selections. (Those students who are handicapped by excessive articulation, overanalysis, etc., will need special remedial work. A discussion of these diffi- culties will be found in Chapter XIII.) Practice should be di- rected toward increasing the speed with which the various materials may be skimmed. Students, for example, may be asked to skim a passage to find a quotation which supports a statement. Instruction in this ability should be given in each of the content subjects. The materials of each subject are some- what different in style and content. Therefore, the student may be able to skim effectively in one field and yet be unable to skim in another unless instruction and practice are pro- vided for the materials in both fields.

A student may wish to know the exact date of an event. From his background of knowledge he knows that the event occurred during the Napoleonic Wars. From the index in a history book he locates the section that deals with this period. Then he skims the material, noticing primarily the dates given until he finds the one for which he is searching.

Or the student may wish to know whether a certain element is a radioactive element. He decides, through his background of experience and knowledge of the subject, the appropriate key words to use in locating through the index the material to read. Then he skims the material until he finds the infor- mation desired. The skimming he does in this instance has to be somewhat more thorough and time-consuming than was the skimming to locate the historical date.

Locating Information

The ability to locate information is made up of a hierarchy of reading skills, including the use of such helps as card cata- logues, encyclopedias, various indexes, and tables of contents.

The ability to locate information in the various reference books and materials is a reading technique which is practically indispensable in the life of a high school student. It is important for the student to be able not only to locate material quickly and accurately from one source, but also to exhaust the sources of information. Consequently, he must gain facility in the use of all available reference books, indexes, and card catalogues.

Most high school students and many college students and adults have little conception of the many functions of the dictionary. The time required for the teacher and a group of high school students to page through a dictionary carefully enough to take note of the many kinds of information it contains will be repaid manyfold in the resultant saving of time for those students during their school and adult life. The different reference books, indexes, and digests will be useful to students only as the students learn their functions, become familiar with them, and have experience in using them.

Instruction in the use of these reference materials should be given in the general reading period and should be followed by the use of special reference materials pertaining to the various subject-matter fields. Students should have experience in using these materials in more than one library if that is possible. It should be pointed out that skimming, which is also a technique in this hierarchy, is used after the general location of information has been made. First, the passage dealing with the topic is located through the use of the various reference aids, and then skimming is used to find the material wanted.

Reading Graphs, Tables, Maps, Charts

Another reading technique is the ability to read charts, graphs, tables, pictographs, and other pictorial and tabular material. There seems to be in the reading matter of adults an increasing use of such materials. But teachers frequently assume that the development of the ability to read such materials is not a part of the reading program. However, since many high school students are unable to interpret graphs and charts accurately, there is a real need for instruction in how to use them. The student who is able to comprehend such material becomes a much more effective interpreter of the printed page.

Wrightstone [7] investigated in grades seven to twelve the children's growth in reading maps and graphs. He concluded that even comparatively simple exercises in map-reading and graph-reading may be used through the twelfth grade with the expectation of increased pupil growth and comprehension. He made the plea for more systematic instruction in these reading skills than is now being given.

Students should be taught that graphic materials are as much a part of a selection as is the verbal material and that they should be read as carefully. Adequate instruction should be given in the interpretation of many different kinds of graphs and a wide variety of charts, tables, and maps. Horn has pointed out:

> As in the case of reading maps, the reading of graphs requires specialized ability, and the development of these abilities cannot be left either to chance or to incidental teaching. When students are taught to read graphs, as they should be, there is reason to believe that these aids will add materially to the effectiveness of instruction.[8]

One social science teacher, for example, prepared large reproductions of various graphic illustrative materials which were used in class discussions whenever they added significantly to the understanding of a problem. Before the end of

[7] Report of unpublished study by Wrightstone in "Child Development and the Curriculum," *The Thirty-Eighth Yearbook of the National Society for the Study of Education,* Public School Publishing Company, 1939, pp. 343-48.

[8] Horn, Ernest. *Methods of Instruction in the Social Studies,* Charles Scribner's Sons, 1937, p. 388.

the year, the students not only knew how to read graphic illustrations, but they also included graphic materials in their own writings and in their classroom discussions frequently referred to various types of them.

Sentence, Paragraph, and Story Comprehension

Comprehension is the ability to understand the meaning which a series of printed symbols is intended to impart. In other words, it implies the ability to obtain from a passage what the author had to say. This definition holds for a word, a phrase, a sentence, a paragraph, as well as for a longer passage. The ability to comprehend these units in general becomes increasingly more difficult from the word, through the sentence, to the understanding of the entire passage. For example, understanding a sentence requires understanding a sufficient number of words so that the reader can accurately arrive at the meaning of all.

The paragraph in turn is usually more difficult to comprehend than any sentence it contains. Since the meaning of a paragraph is more than a simple summation of the meanings of the sentences, understanding a paragraph involves more than simply understanding each sentence. It entails, for example, giving proper weight to each of its sentences and ascertaining the relationships among them. For the same reason understanding an entire passage is, in turn, more difficult than interpreting the paragraphs of which the passage is composed.

From the standpoint of the teacher, the considerations discussed above are important because they point inevitably to the fact that, while it is necessary to be able to understand the words in order to arrive at the meaning of a sentence, the mere understanding of its words will not of itself guarantee the comprehension of the sentence. Likewise, the understanding of a sentence is basic to the understanding of a paragraph. The relation is reciprocal. Before a sentence can be understood, all the key words must be understood. This understanding, however, may depend on the specific meaning of the key words in that sentence. While the content gives the meanings of many words, the content is understood only where the meanings of the words and the interrelationships between those words are known or implied. It follows that in developing comprehension ability, it is necessary for the student to be effectual in his ability to read and understand the meanings of the words. Then, he must see the relationship between the words. It should be noted that the bases of adequate comprehension are a large background of meanings and understandings plus the ability to determine relationships between the meanings and understandings.

Since the most necessary elements in comprehension are meaning backgrounds and vocabulary understandings, the suggestions for improving them given in Chapter V will apply to increasing comprehension. In developing comprehension, the student should use materials for the interpretation of which he has adequate meaning backgrounds. As he reads, however, he should make a conscious effort to increase his meaning backgrounds.

The student should read with a definite problem in mind and should continually relate to his problem the various concepts contained in the material he is reading. He should likewise make an effort to see the relationships between the various concepts within a paragraph and between the paragraphs in a passage. So an effective way of developing comprehension is to encourage the student consciously to try to reach a goal for which the reading is being done. The material must, of course, be suited to his developmental level of meaning background and understanding.

Power of Comprehension

Power of comprehension is the ability to comprehend materials of varying levels of difficulty. The student with a high level of comprehension will be able to understand passages which call for wide backgrounds of experiences, meanings, concepts, and the ability to see complex relationships. The student with a low power of comprehension will be able to understand only passages containing the more obvious relationships between less difficult word meanings, concepts, and understandings. The results of testing power of comprehension, then, tell how difficult a passage the student may be expected to read with understanding if he is given unlimited time. Power of comprehension is probably more highly correlated with intelligence than any of the other reading techniques and skills.

Reading to Get the General Significance of a Passage

Reading for general significance is the specialized type of reading comprehension which places emphasis upon getting the central thought of a passage. This rapid sort of reading stresses the relationship between the units which make up the passage and requires a high degree of skill in generalizing.

One of the most commonly used types of reading ability is that of reading to get the general significance of a passage. One frequently uses this ability for recreational and other daily reading activities. Newspapers, magazines, and many other materials are read in this way when it is not necessary to employ a more exacting kind of reading. Since many details are passed over, such reading is relatively rapid.

In order to improve a student's ability to get the general significance of a passage, the teacher should use highly interesting materials. He should take advantage of materials related to any especially interesting phase of schoolwork. He should also use the student's own choice of recreational reading.

Extensive reading of interesting material, the difficulty of which is at the student's level of development, will, in and of itself, prove helpful in increasing his ability to get the general significance. The student should not be required to review or give a detailed account of the material. The task set for the student must be in the nature of responding to a single item, such as, "What is this paragraph about?" or "State, in a single sentence, the central theme of the passage." However, the task should call for a generalized, though accurate, interpretation of the material.

Various potential opportunities for developing the ability to read to get the general significance of a passage are present in the day-by-day activities of the high school student. For example, the writing of headlines for news items provides excellent practice in this ability. Items submitted by the class for the school newspaper may carry a headline chosen as the best of those written by the members of the class. An exercise in writing headlines may be constructed by clipping items out of the newspaper and having the students read the news items for the purpose of composing a headline for each. Or, again, the students may read the paper for the purpose of preparing a short summary statement of news events for presentation as a class news broadcast.

Reading to Note Details

It is unfortunate that many teachers stress a type of reading which is among the most infrequently used by adults. The ability to note details is a specialized type of comprehension which emphasizes observing and remembering important and significant facts. This exacting process requires a careful, detailed reading of a passage. In reading a selection describing the way in which a person was dressed, for example, one would note the exact colors and style of the garments rather than the general impression of the wearer's taste in dress. This is the type of reading which students must do frequently in order to pass examinations which require the memory of details.

The practice of asking questions demanding memory of details encourages students to use this reading technique at the expense of others. Although this skill is important for such purposes as collecting data, verifying facts, etc., there are other reading techniques which are of greater value to adults. It is unfortunate that teachers find it so easy to ask detailed questions that this process has become one of the most practiced reading techniques.

Even though this type of reading is one of those most practiced by students, there are some who cannot use it effectively. This failure to establish the ability to read for details may be a result of the fact that the student does not realize that he can note several details in one reading. In the second place, the student may not have clearly set noting details as his reading goal and may have become so engrossed in the general meaning of the passage that he fails to note the details contained in it.

In order to develop the skill of noting details, the student should be encouraged to get as many of them in one reading as is possible. One way of doing this is to have him read a passage, turn over the page, and then see how many detailed questions he can answer without recourse to rereading. He should then reread the passage to determine the accuracy of the responses and to fill in the omitted items.

In order that the student may not lose sight of his goal of collecting factual detail, the purpose for which he is collecting those details should be of intrinsic value to him. Then, the student will have a real reason for collecting the factual details for which some use is going to be made.

A reading situation that proved to be intrinsically interesting to one high school boy follows:

John was going to a summer camp on a mountain lake. A letter from the camp officials, stating the clothes and equipment needed for the summer's outing, had been received. John read the letter carefully, noting details. Then he located advertisements in newspapers, read them to note such details as where the various articles could be procured, their prices, sizes, etc. John also read historical and geographical descriptions of the country round about the camp, noting factual details, the knowledge of which would make his summer's experience an interesting one. Such a reading situation, intrinsically interesting to the reader as it was, aptly illustrates the need of the ability to read to note details.

Reading to Organize

Ability to organize is that type of reading comprehension which places special emphasis upon understanding the arrangement of the thought in the passage. It makes possible the establishment of the sequence or of the interrelationship between the ideas presented.

The better understanding of the relationship between the various ideas which are used in the presentation of a topic gives a more complete grasp of the subject under discussion and enables the reader to retain for a longer period of time its salient points. This is among the more important and usable of the reading techniques and will probably aid the student in achieving a higher power of comprehension. It is, therefore, an important aid to effective study.

Reading to appreciate the general significance of a passsage should usually precede any attempt of the student to organize it. When the general significance of the material is understood, the student may reread it for the purpose of establishing for himself some sort of sequence which the thought of the passage presents.

Many high school students are unable to outline relatively simple material. This fact is shown by their scores on such standardized tests as Sub-test 3 in the Iowa Silent Reading Comprehension battery of tests. These scores indicate, likewise, that there are many students in the high schools for whom more instruction in reading for the purpose of organizing the material read should be given than the elementary school has been able to provide.

Experience in the use of this reading technique may be gained by the students through providing them with passages to read and outline. In selecting the material to be organized, the teacher should be sure that the thought has been arranged in a sequential way. The students may gain experience in this reading technique by outlining selections from their science or social science texts and from reference books. Students should be encouraged to include in their outlines the main thoughts of the passage, arranged in logical sequence, and expressed in their own words. They should, of course, omit unnecessary facts and minutiae.

When a class activity has been completed and a report has been written, the writing of center and subheadings provides experience in formulating and stating in an organized and concise way what the material is about.

Rereading a book, passage, or chapter for the purpose of reviewing it is another effective way of gaining experience in ability to organize. Since such rereading is a part of most courses of the high school, practice in organizing may quite naturally be directed by the teacher as a part of his regular classwork. As we have already seen, much of the instruction in reading on the high school level can be done most effectively in the classroom as an integral part of the instruction in the content subject itself.

Another useful way to gain experience in organizing the materials read is to practice writing a brief summary of a passage after it has been read. The student who purposes to read so that he may write a summary of the article, passage, or book will necessarily read to understand the relationship between the various ideas which are used in the presentation. Reading which enables the individual to gain a more complete grasp of the subject and to retain the salient points for a longer period of time is a type that is very useful to the student both as a student and later as an adult.

The inexperienced student may find it useful to pause in his reading from time to time so that he may think through the material and enumerate to himself the sequential order of the presentation. Pauses to think through the relation of one item to another and to understand the arrangement of thought will enable the student to organize the material in his mind as he continues his reading. It should be reiterated, however, that a prereading of the material for the purpose of understanding its general significance is desirable before reading for the purpose of organizing it.

Reading to Follow Directions

Ability to follow directions is that type of reading comprehension which enables an individual to understand precisely what a passage tells him to do. This exacting sort of reading is a relatively slow process which calls for understanding the step-by-step sequence.

For example, this is the technique used by the examiner in reading the directions of a standardized test preparatory to giving it. It is necessary for him to read slowly, carefully, and for the purpose of understanding each step in the process. While it is true that a person who has read many such directions will be able to read them fairly rapidly, still he should not read directions with the same rate of speed that he uses to get the general significance of a passage.

Any teacher who has worked with high school students knows that a large proportion of students do not know how to do the slow, careful, precise type of reading that is required for following directions. A reading problem of one high school girl illustrated to her the need for an ability to read to follow directions. Barbara wished to use the yarn she received on her birthday to knit a sweater. The reading tasks included those of locating patterns; reading to note significant details, such as amount of yarn required and kinds of knitting stitches to use; and reading and following the directions as the sweater took shape. Inability to read accurately to follow directions certainly could have had unhappy results for Barbara.

Instruction in reading to follow directions should first make clear to the students that material of this sort should be read slowly and carefully. It is all too true that readers establish one general rate of reading and tend to use that speed at all times, irrespective of the difficulty or kind of material they are reading.

Instruction should also convince the reader that he must understand each step in the process. Since this type of reading is necessary for any laboratory course, there is ample opportunity for the student to gain experience in it. In all probability he will show improvement in this ability if he gains an insight into the two basic facts just presented; namely, that this exacting sort of reading should never be done in a hurry, and second, the step-by-step sequence of the directions must be understood.

Reading to Predict Outcomes

The ability to predict outcomes is a type of comprehension which enables the reader to postulate from a series of events what is most likely to be the result. This kind of reading requires a marked degree of ability both in seeing the relationships in a series of happenings and in weighing and judging which of several results is the most likely. Such reading, then, requires logically evaluating a series of factors from the point of view of the significance each might have in determining an outcome.

This type of reading is frequently used in reading political or economic topics. The reader tries to arrange the thoughts in their proper order so that he may formulate an idea of what will happen next. For example, an individual during a political campaign reads articles dealing with the various candidates for office. He estimates what will happen if one candidate is elected. He then predicts what will happen if some other is elected. Then he weighs each outcome to see which he would prefer and registers his vote in the light of his decision.

Teachers frequently include in their procedure instruction in ability to predict outcomes. The teacher of a group of first-grade pupils, after reading the first part of a story, may ask, "And what do you think happens next?" After several of the children have expressed an opinion and told why it is their opinion, the teacher will finish reading the story.

Variations of this teaching technique may be used in the elementary school, the high school, the college, and the graduate school. The teller of the tale may be a fellow student, a teacher, a writer, a research worker, etc. The series of happenings may be real or postulated, simple or intricate, few or many, depending upon the capabilities of the readers. But whatever the variation, the technique will be found useful in giving the student experience in seeing relationships between a series of happenings, in weighing and judging several possible outcomes, and in predicting the most likely one.

Teachers of mathematics seek to instill this ability in their students. They expect the student to acquire the habit of reading a mathematical problem, noting the relationships between the various relevant factors, and then predicting results of the calculations. The use of this technique keeps students from going too far astray in their mathematical calculations. No student who could logically evaluate the series of factors in a problem about the cost of the Erie Canal would have the canal cost more than the total estimated wealth of the United States! If the result he obtained after working the problem was not in line with his estimate, he would set himself the task of finding his error.

Students will find this reading technique useful in school and adult life. In order that the student may achieve an increasingly high level of reading development, he should have experience in reading many different types of materials for the purpose of predicting outcomes. The number and difficulty of relationships should be gradually increased.

Reading to Form Sensory Impressions

The ability to form sensory impressions of what is read is an impressionistic sort of reading comprehension. It requires the ability to feel, taste, smell, hear, and see the sensory images aroused by the printed words.

This ability enables the individual to appreciate the various types of pictures the author is trying to create with his words. It entails recalling experiences and associating them with those the author is setting forth. The larger the background of experiences the individual has, the more likely he is to receive the sensory impressions portrayed. Of all the sorts of reading experiences, this one probably gives the most vivid and real enjoyment. It is also important to one who is reading for the purpose of following directions to make something, because it enables the reader to visualize the steps in the process as he reads about them.

It is a truism that the individual increases his background of experience as he grows older. It is likewise a truism that this very increase in meaning background results in greater chance for the reader to respond to the sensory stimuli the printed word is expected to arouse. Nevertheless, students continue to read without apparent enjoyment materials which they have the meaning backgrounds to appreciate. By reading and sharing experiences, it is possible for students to learn that words, phrases, and passages can elicit visual and other forms of imagery.

Striking comparisons can be made between words which stimulate one sense and those which stimulate more than one. The following examples [9] are indicative:

WORDS	SENSES APPEALED TO
soft	touch
cottony	touch and sight
white	sight
snowy	sight and temperature
closed	sight
slammed	sight and sound
weep	sight
sob	sight, hearing, and movement
gray	sight
leaden	sight and pressure
cut	sight
chop	sight, hearing, and movement

[9] White, Wendell. *The Psychology of Making Life Interesting*, The Macmillan Company, 1939, p. 32.

It might be found helpful to encourage the students to look for such words in their reading in order to lengthen the list given above. Students should be encouraged to use words, phrases, and descriptions that arouse more than one sensory response.

Students should also be directed toward reading passages containing impressionistic materials so that their reading experiences may be made more vivid and real.

The following exercise develops the ability to see the pictures contained in printed words:

ILLUSTRATING HERO STORIES

Most of us like to read books or magazines that are illustrated. The pictures arouse our interest and help us to understand the stories.

You have already looked at the illustrations for "The Golden Cup of Kasimir." Turn back to page 321 once more and study the picture carefully. Notice how the picture helps you to see the ancient Polish castle and the strange way men dressed in those times. Recall the high spot of the story that the illustration pictures, and notice how the artist has shown the cruelty of Batu as he leans over the parapet and the bravery of Stefan as he hurtles toward the river below. . . .

The members of the class would no doubt find it interesting to plan illustrations for other hero stories which they read. Here is one way to get started:

Divide the class into committees. Each member of each committee will volunteer to read at least one hero story. . . .

In planning the illustrations for your hero story, make notes as you read the story. Your illustrations should be planned in such a way as to make the most important high spots of the story clear and to increase the enjoyment of anyone who reads the illustrated story. Plan at least two pictures for your story. . . .

Make your plan for each illustration brief and clear so

that an artist could draw the kind of picture you have in mind.[10]

Reading Critically

Ability to read critically enables the individual to determine the validity and reliability of statements read. One uses this reading technique when he purposes to determine the accuracy of the material presented.

This is an exacting sort of reading which calls for careful comparison of the statements made with the experience background that the individual has. It involves, among other things, comparing the expressed opinions of various authorities and weighing their statements in relation to the reader's own understanding. It is easy to see that the effectiveness of critical reading depends in no small measure upon the extent of the reader's background.

High school students, quite without specific instruction, read the presentation of a topic in several textbooks and reference books for the purpose of formulating an opinion as to the authoritativeness of each. The ability to evaluate critically various presentations upon the same topic is a useful reading technique. Students may well be given experience in determining the accuracy of statements in many different kinds of materials. It seems logical that the greater part of this training and experience will be a result of the evaluation of materials read as a part of the course work in the various content subjects. Book reviews, if required, should be in the form of critical evaluations, rather than in the form of outlines. The former type of review usually necessitates a greater degree of comprehension of the material than does the mere outlining of it.

The larger the background of knowledge the student has in any one subject, the better able he will be to evaluate any new

[10] Pooley, Robert C., and Walcott, Fred G. *Growth in Reading,* Scott, Foresman and Company, 1939, pp. 326-27.

material dealing with it. The students will grow in ability to read critically in any subject-matter field as they increase their knowledge of word and meaning backgrounds in that field and as they learn to analyze the material critically.

ORAL READING

Effective interpretive oral reading depends upon the same techniques and skills that are used in effective silent reading. Anything that is done to perfect the abilities that are needed for proficient silent reading aids in establishing a good foundation for interpretive•oral reading. While there is a close relationship between oral and silent reading abilities, there are certain fundamental differences between the two. Oral reading is usually a slower process than is silent reading. The reason it is slower is that oral reading involves a greater use of the speech mechanism. Oral reading is usually done in a situation consisting of more than one individual, in which case the reader is concerned not only about getting the meaning from the printed page, but also about imparting that meaning to others. He is desirous of enabling them to interpret adequately and to enjoy his presentation of the thought of the passage. For that reason he puts special emphasis upon interpreting the meaning he wishes to convey to the listeners. The oral reader is attentive to such other things as appearance, posture, gesture, facial expression, enunciation, pronunciation.

The Social Worth of Oral Reading

Oral reading is the oral presentation of printed or written material. It usually implies a manuscript, a reader, and an audience. Although a very small part of the reading of an individual is oral, it is important that he develop the abilities to do effective oral reading. There are occasions both in school and out when it is necessary for an individual to read aloud. The social worth of oral reading is dependent upon the excellency of that reading. For that reason one who does oral reading—and practically everyone does—wants to do it well. A poor presentation wastes the time not only of the reader, but also of the group for whom he reads. If a person reads to a large group but once in his entire life, the time spent in school learning to do oral reading well will not have been wasted.

Most individuals who are obliged to read to an audience find themselves wishing they had developed their oral reading ability more fully. The business man reading to his service club, the woman to her women's club, the student to his classmates, the high school teacher to her associates at faculty meetings, and the mother reading to her children—all would be happier if the school had prepared them better for their tasks. It is needless to say that in the majority of cases the audience also would have been glad to have heard the results of better oral reading instruction.

Studies showing the frequency of use of oral reading in comparison with that of silent reading tend to deny the value of oral reading instruction since oral reading is used so infrequently. This situation may be compared with the supplying of a community with water. About one per cent of the total water is used for drinking. Yet surely this fact does not mean that little or no attention should be given to the quality of the drinking water. The fact that oral reading is used infrequently does not mean that it merits no attention.

Oral Sight Reading

Many factors make oral sight reading very difficult. Among these factors is the inability to anticipate what comes next. The ability to foretell the thought of a passage is a prerequisite of interpretive oral sight reading. Only the mature reader has this ability. Good oral readers frequently focus their attention upon words seven or eight ahead of the ones they are speaking. This enables them to give an adequate interpretation and to work out troublesome words before it is necessary to express them. They need to interpret immediately by the voice the meaning of the passage. The oral sight reader cannot pause too long or reread the passage in order to reacquaint himself with the content. He may frequently become so concerned with vocal expression that he forgets what he has read and has difficulty in giving it an adequate interpretation.

The materials for oral sight reading should be relatively easy, containing few or no reading difficulties. If the student reads with a high, strained voice or with a staccato expression or shows other signs of emotional tension, the task set for him is probably too difficult and should be at a lower level.

Emotional Factors in Oral Reading

When, as is usual, oral reading is done in the audience situation where the reader has a direct responsibility to his listeners, it should be prepared reading. The audience situation is highly charged with emotional concomitants. There are probably few educational experiences so filled with the possibility of detrimental emotional reactions as that wherein a student who has little oral reading ability is forced to stumble through an oral presentation for which he has had little opportunity to prepare. Such an experience tends to cause feelings of confusion and frustration. These feelings cause inadequate reading and inadequate personal adjustment. They also lay the foundation for insecurity in future performances of oral reading.

The adolescent student is inclined to be self-conscious and is very desirous of gaining favorable personal recognition. These considerations and the fact that the adolescent is undergoing certain physiological changes which may add to his sense of insecurity make it necessary to be very considerate of his feelings in oral reading situations. Easy, familiar materials supplemented by an opportunity for adequate preparation should be provided so that the oral presentation of the high school student may be successful and satisfying.

The possibility of emotional reactions in the audience situation can be lessened somewhat by developing a co-operative attitude on the part of the audience. Just as truly as the reader has a responsibility to the listeners, so does the audience have a responsibility to the reader. The responsibility of the audience is that of courteously attending the reader so that there is as little distraction as possible. It is relatively easy to build a co-operative attitude in a high school class because each student wants attentive listeners when he reads. This co-operation between the students and the speaker may be facilitated by taking care that there are at hand no books or other distracting materials. Such situations should be approached by the students with the attitude of expected pleasure. The passages to be read should be sufficiently worth while to make the occasion one of enjoyment. There is little justification for using the time of the entire class unless both the reader and listeners derive pleasure and benefit from their experience. In order to profit from listening to oral reading, the student must learn how to listen.

Oral reading should be approached by the group with a definite purpose in mind. This purpose may be to acquaint the group with factual knowledge so that the students may have the information necessary to carry on their group enterprise. Or it may be to give the class directions for carrying forward their enterprise. Or the purpose may be that of providing recreation. Whatever the purpose, if it is real to the students, an audience situation will be set up that fosters not only attentive listening, but also a conscientious and appropriate presentation.

Instruction in Oral Reading

During the course of instruction in a content subject, students are frequently called upon to read orally. For example, the students read such writings as reports, essays, poems, stories, problems, communications addressed to the class, the minutes of the class or club, directions, or authoritative material to substantiate a point of view. Whatever the material, it is important for the teacher to be sensitive to the emotional condition of the reader and to know how to put him at his ease. If it is seen that the student is in difficulty, the interjection of a question or a comment may be sufficient to give the student time to regain his poise. At other times it may be well for the student to tell in his own words the content of the rest of the passage rather than to continue with the oral reading of it.

It is very unwise indeed in the majority of instances for either the teacher or a member of the class to criticize the oral reading presentation. The teacher should offer only constructive suggestions. The student will profit more from the constructive suggestions relative to the improvement of his oral reading when given to him in a private conference, where he will be under no embarrassment and where it is possible for him to discuss the suggestions with the teacher. In fact, even constructive suggestions may prove to be detrimental to the developmental growth in oral reading if the criticisms are given to the student in the presence of others.

If it is evident that a specific student has difficulty in keeping his poise when he is reading orally to the group, opportunities should be provided for him to develop good oral reading ability. At first the student who is ill at ease and whose oral reading is halting or unusually rapid should be encouraged to talk informally to groups of three or four people. Later the number may be increased. Then opportunities should be provided for him to read aloud relatively easy material which he has prepared for oral reading. When he is able to read such material easily and well, he may then read material of greater difficulty. When he becomes proficient in reading prepared material orally, he may then read orally at sight.

In one school, students read orally before a microphone which was in a vacant room. The auditors were in an adjoining room. Later, after the student had had several experiences in reading before the microphone, he read in the presence of two or three students. It was not long before even the poorest oral readers were able to read before the entire group. When the reading situation is freed from inhibiting emotional concomitants, the students are able to progress rapidly in the development of their oral reading ability.

A person can improve the quality of his oral reading by listening to the reading of good radio announcers and trying to emulate their reading techniques and also noticing their rate of reading, enunciation, pronunciation, etc.

Instruction designed to improve oral reading entails such considerations as a careful selection of materials, a reading situation free from emotional tension, a real purpose for oral reading, constructive suggestions by the teacher, and a use of good radio announcers as models. While the chapters that follow for the most part will be concerned with silent reading, much of the discussion is quite as applicable to oral reading.

Summary

The reading techniques and skills that should be taught on the high school level include:

1. *Word recognition techniques.* The student needs to have a well-rounded attack upon new words, including (a) the use

of context clues, (b) the use of the general shape of the word, (c) the use of large known parts of words, (d) phonetic analysis. It is important for the student to have a differentiated attack upon new words so that he will be able to work out quickly and accurately the meaning of a word that is unfamiliar to him.

2. *Reading speed.* The student should learn to adjust the speed of reading to the purpose for which he is reading and to the difficulty of the material that is being used to accomplish that purpose.

3. *Skimming.* The technique of skimming is a reading technique that may be used for the purpose of learning a single fact from a passage, of acquiring a general impression of the topics discussed in a passage or book, and of gathering a general impression of a passage or book. Skimming is a rapid sort of reading that is of great use to both the student and the adult.

4. *Locating information.* This ability is made up of a hierarchy of reading skills, including the use of card catalogues, encyclopedias, various indexes, tables of contents. It is a reading technique that is practically indispensable to an independent reader.

5. *Ability to read graphs, maps, tables, and charts.* This reading technique is the ability to get the meaning that pictorial and tabular materials contain or display. Since students by and large are somewhat ineffective in reading such materials, definite instruction in the reading of a wide variety of them should be provided.

6. *Sentence, paragraph, and story comprehension.* Comprehension is the ability to understand the meaning that the series of printed symbols contains. The ability to read understandingly many and different types of materials for many and different purposes is the ultimate goal of reading instruction.

All the reading techniques and skills contribute to comprehensive reading.

7. *Reading to get the general significance of a passage.* This ability is the specialized type of reading comprehension that places emphasis upon getting the central thought of a passage. It requires a high degree of skill in generalizing.

8. *Reading to note details.* This ability is the specialized type of reading comprehension that places emphasis upon observing and remembering the important and significant facts presented in a passage.

9. *Reading to organize.* This ability is that type of reading comprehension which places special emphasis upon understanding the arrangement of the thought in a passage. It entails the understanding of the interrelationships among the ideas presented in a passage.

10. *Reading to follow directions.* This ability is that type of reading comprehension which enables an individual to read a passage and understand precisely what it tells him to do. It calls for the understanding of the step-by-step sequence of the directions.

11. *Reading to predict outcomes.* This ability is a type of comprehension that enables the reader to postulate from a series of events what is the most probable result. The ability to see and weigh relationships between a series of happenings and to predict a possible outcome is one that should be continuously developed.

12. *Reading to form sensory impressions.* This type of reading requires the ability to feel, taste, smell, hear, and see the sensory stimulations that the printed words arouse. The larger the background of experiences the individual has, the more apt he is to receive the sensory impressions portrayed. This ability makes reading pleasurable.

13. *Ability to read critically.* This ability is a type of reading

comprehension that enables the individual to determine the accuracy of the material presented. In order to read critically in any given field, it is necessary that the reader have a word and meaning background in that field. This exacting sort of reading requires a careful comparison of the statements in the passage with the experience background of the reader.

14. *Oral reading.* Although a very small part of the reading of an individual is oral, it is important for him to develop the ability to do effective oral reading. The social worth of oral reading depends upon its excellency. Because oral reading is infrequently used does not mean that it merits no attention. Effective interpretive oral reading depends upon the same techniques and skills that are used in silent reading. Anything that is done to perfect the abilities that are needed for proficient silent reading will aid in establishing a good foundation for interpretive oral reading.

SELECTED BIBLIOGRAPHY

Bond, Elden. "Tenth-Grade Abilities and Achievements," *Contributions to Education,* No. 813, Bureau of Publications, Teachers College, Columbia University, 1940.

Gates, Arthur I. *The Improvement of Reading,* Revised, The Macmillan Company, 1935, Chapter 4.

Harris, Albert J. *How to Increase Reading Ability,* Longmans, Green and Company, 1940, Chapters 4, 9, 10.

Horn, Ernest. *Methods of Instruction in the Social Studies,* Charles Scribner's Sons, 1937, pp. 201-2.

McKee, Paul. *Reading and Literature in the Elementary School,* Houghton Mifflin Company, 1934, Chapters 9 and 11.

Seashore, R. H., Stockford, L. B. O., and Swartz, B. K. "A Correlational Analysis of Factors in Speed of Reading Tests," *School and Society,* Vol. XLVI, August 7, 1937, pp. 187-92.

Strang, Ruth, and Rose, F. C. *Problems in the Improvement of Reading in High School and College,* Revised, The Science Press Printing Company, 1940, Chapter II.

Tinker, Miles A. "The Influence of Form of Type on the Perception of Words," *Journal of Applied Psychology*, Vol. XVI, April, 1932, pp. 167-74.

Tinker, Miles A. "The Role of Eye Movements in Diagnostic and Remedial Reading," *School and Society*, Vol. XXXIX, February 3, 1934, pp. 147-48.

Traxler, Arthur E. "Relation Between Rate of Reading and Speed of Association," *Journal of Educational Psychology*, Vol. XXV, May, 1934, pp. 357-65.

Witty, Paul, and Kopel, David. *Reading and the Educative Process*, Ginn and Company, 1939.

CHAPTER V

DEVELOPMENT OF VOCABULARY

One phase of vocabulary development necessary to reading, that of recognizing a word from its printed symbol, has been discussed as a reading technique. You will recall that improvement in recognizing words and building up a sight vocabulary usually results from cue reductions[1] through which the student learns to depend more upon the content than upon close inspection of each part of a word. Cue reduction also takes place in learning to recognize a larger unit by focusing attention on fewer of its components.

THREE PHASES OF MEANING

When children first come in contact with a word, it is probably not necessary for them to associate it with more than one object. Mere recognition of a word constitutes one phase of meaning.

It might be helpful to pause at this point and observe the efforts of three first graders learning to read the word *cat*. A meaning must be attached to this word if the reading is to be more than mere verbalization. It is interesting to note that on hearing the word *cat* each child will get a different picture. One child's cat might be a gray house cat; another's might be yellow; while the third might be a black and white gingham cat with a red bow, tinkling bell, and button eyes.

---

[1] Hollingworth, H. L. *Psychology*, D. Appleton-Century Company, 1928, p. 7.

Any of these various backgrounds would probably suffice for the mere recognition of the printed word.

A second phase of meaning for an individual is the number of connotations a word has for him. In order to get a more generalized concept of the word *cat,* the child will have to establish many meaning backgrounds. This process of learning the word *cat* continues throughout the life of the individual. *Cat* has many meanings. To the hunter or naturalist, it means a family of animals including the domesticated cat, tiger, lion, leopard, puma, cheetah, lynx, to say nothing of the lowly bobcat. To the sailor, *cat* might give the added meanings of a type of sailboard and a strong tackle used to hoist an anchor to the cathead of a ship. To the sportsman, *cat* may in addition imply a type of baseball and other games and equipment used in playing them. To the historian, *cat* has an added meaning—a whip made of rope or leather.

It can be seen from this incomplete list that even the simplest words have many distinct meanings. Part of the development of word meanings is, therefore, an extension of the various meanings that different words have.

Meaning background has a third phase of development: the depth or vividness of understanding and appreciation. While two individuals may both recognize that the word *cat* may mean lion, the hunter who has bearded a lion in his den will be likely to bring to this meaning of *cat* a more vivid impression than will the individual who has had no such experience. It is possible that the hunter who has actually been confronted by a lion will think *lion* when he reads *cat* because of the vividness of experience.

The young child who has had many experiences with house cats will bring a deeper and different understanding to the learning of *cat* than will the child whose experience has been limited to a toy cat. Of course, the child whose only experience with *cat* has been that of playing with a toy cat will be better prepared for the reading than will a child whose experience background is even more barren.

Furthermore, there are different types of appreciation. The child who has had and loved a toy cat may have a different sort of appreciation of *cat* from that of the child who has had the experience of pulling a live cat by the tail and has suffered the consequences. It is difficult to say which would have the deeper and more lasting impression. These two children are apt to bring to the reading of the word *cat* quite different generalized backgrounds. One child might infer that all cats are objects that he can play with in any fashion without any reaction on the part of the cat; the other might bring the generalized inference that it is hazardous to play with any cat.

These illustrations show that there are three phases of meaning which have an influence upon an individual's effectiveness as a reader and upon the interpretations and inferences he makes while reading. These are:

1. *Simple recognition.* The individual is able to attach a meaning to a symbol.

2. *Extensiveness of meanings.* The individual is able to associate two or more distinct meanings with a symbol.

3. *Depth or vividness of meanings.* The individual is able to make use of deeper and finer appreciations and broader concepts and generalizations in interpreting a symbol.

It must be recognized that these phases are not discrete but overlap in both their importance and development. In reality it could be said that the growth of all three phases of meaning is probably continuous and contemporaneous. The teacher should recognize that for any one word one of the three phases might be lacking and that attention might be focused upon it. For example, if the child was interpreting

the word *realize* in the sentence—*He realized large profits*—
as *understand* rather than *gain,* the correct meaning for this
situation should be brought to his attention. The teaching of
vocabulary entails more than merely teaching the child to
recognize words. It encompasses both the enriching and the
extending of word meaning.

IMPORTANCE OF MEANING

Inasmuch as reading should be the understanding of the
printed page, the meaning backgrounds the individual brings
to the readings are of paramount importance. The more able
the individual is to attach meanings to the symbols of the
passage and the more able he is to select the precise meaning
for each symbol or phrase of symbols in the passage, the more
fluently he will read it. The deeper and finer the reader's
background for appreciations, the deeper and finer will be
his appreciation. The broader and more accurate the background of generalizations and concepts, the broader and more
accurate will be the resulting generalizations and concepts.
The freer from prejudice the individual's attitudes with regard
to the subject of the passage, the less prejudiced will be his
interpretation of it.

In other words, meaning backgrounds are basic to reading,
whether it be the reading of literary, scientific, or social scientific materials, or those from any other field of human endeavor. Two ways in which meanings contribute to reading
are: first, meanings increase the effectiveness of the individual
as a reader; and second, meanings color the interpretation and
appreciation of what the individual reads.

Illustrations of the role played by meaning background in
various reading skills and techniques will show its importance
to the effectiveness of the reader.

Word Recognition

As we have learned, contextual clues are of great importance to adequate ability in word recognition. Contextual clues depend for their effectiveness upon the individual's having a rather keen background of meanings. For example, one would not expect the individual who did not know the appropriate meaning of the word *board* to derive the recognition of it in the phrase, *room and board*.

Of course, not even a complete knowledge of the meaning of the word *wiring* would enable the reader to know what was meant by the sentence—*The man is wiring*—unless the reading just preceding delimited the meaning of it. However, the person knowing the content of the passage could not derive its meaning unless he knew the appropriate meaning of the word.

Again, a boy reared in a rural area might have the experience background that would enable him to understand the phrase *grain elevator* as used in the sentence—*The grain elevator was built near the railroad track*. The experience background of a boy reared in an urban area might prepare him to understand this phrase—*Ten tons of wheat were loaded on the grain elevator to be taken to the top floor of the building*. Very likely a confused meaning would result if the boy with the rural experience background undertook to recognize the words *grain elevator* in the sentence dealing with an urban concept, while the boy with the urban experiences would be confused in reading the sentence dealing with the rural concept because of an inappropriate understanding. Thus, in order for a student to use the context to derive the meaning of an unfamiliar word, it is often necessary for him to have a background that will enable him to select the specific meaning appropriate to that context.

Rate of Reading

The speed at which an individual reads a passage depends in no small measure upon his familiarity with the subject and upon the terminology used in the discussion. His familiarity with the subject may speed up the reading, since it enables him to derive the meaning without hesitation. But on the other hand, it may slow him up considerably, since it forces him, because of his broad background of experiences, to inspect the reading matter intently in the light of his many generalizations.

Another reader, without the necessary subject-matter or content background, may be slowed up by the very nature of the concepts. He will find it necessary to think them through carefully as he proceeds. A third reader, familiar with the concepts, might find his rate lessened because of an inadequate vocabulary background. Familiarity with the subject and terminology (meaning background) used in a passage will enable the reader to be fluent and accurate; it may or may not, depending upon his reading purpose, increase his speed.

Locating Information

In locating information, the role of meaning backgrounds may be illustrated by the process of selection of key words to be used in finding references bearing upon a topic. Suppose the topic were the annual cost of malaria to the United States. The individual would be unable to locate complete data unless he had knowledge of the topic sufficiently wide to enable him to select the key words that should be used. Included in this knowledge would be the facts that malaria is a parasitic disease; that it is confined to certain locations; and that the costs are distributed among such items as hospitalization, loss of human resources, and control and eradication of disease.

Following Directions

So essential is a background of meaning to the process of reading to follow directions that the reader who lacks the necessary background soon becomes lost. His pie will never reach the oven. His drowning friend will not be resuscitated. His piece of apparatus will never be constructed. His paint will remain unmixed or will turn out to be the wrong shade.

A high school boy who was constructing a model boat from the manufactured parts recognized very soon that specialized vocabulary and background concepts were necessary to carry out the project. One sentence in the instruction booklet read— *Bend the mainstay to the stempost; run it aft to the mainmast.* In order to read to follow directions, it was necessary for the boy to know the appropriate meaning of many words, such as *stempost* and *aft.*

In other words, more than mere ability to read words is necessary if the individual is to be expected to follow the directions. The individual must have a sufficiently inclusive background of experience so that his reading to follow directions may be understanding reading.

Getting the General Significance of a Passage

For the individual with little or no background of experience, reading a passage to get the general meaning of it would be futile indeed. The process would be hardly more than reading words. There would be little or no meaning. Consider, for example, a passage describing the making of a tunnel through the snow to the barn in thirty-degree-below-zero temperature in order that the live stock may be fed and watered. The general significance of this selection might be the hardship and suffering that a blizzard brings. Such a passage would mean little to a boy who had spent all his days in a southern California city. The boy might recognize all the words; but unless he brought a background of meaning to the reading of the passage, he might not derive an accurate interpretation of its general significance.

Noting Significant Details

Noting the details in a passage dealing with the origin of the names of the states of the United States of America would in all probability be more effectively done by an American than by a New Zealander, even though they might be equally efficient readers. The American would bring to the reading of the passage a knowledge of the names of the states of the United States and, in many cases, knowledge pertinent to the derivation of the various names of the states, whereas the New Zealander would very likely bring a dearth of such knowledge. It is logical to suppose that the reading of the passage by the New Zealander would be relatively more inefficient than that of the American. A background of pertinent meanings is important to effective reading for the purpose of noting details.

Predicting Outcomes

A wealth of meaning background is used by the individual who reads an account of two football teams which gives previous games won and lost; previous opponents; the size, weight, and condition of players; and then predicts the outcome of a forthcoming game between the two teams. A person likewise uses a wealth of meaning when he reads about the past performance of a specific stock on the New York Stock Exchange for the purpose of predicting its future performance. The individual who, as he progresses through a detective story, formulates from time to time his theory of the possible outcome is also using a great deal of meaning background.

The reader in these three situations may be the same individual, but the meaning backgrounds necessary to predict the outcomes are very different indeed. It is apparent that the prediction will be awry in those instances where the meaning background is insufficient to enable the individual to understand the various interrelationships and implications of the factors involved. We might point out that, in spite of a large and adequate background of knowledge and experience, the prediction may still be awry. However, it is more likely to be correct when the backgrounds are present than when not.

Forming Sensory Impressions

Let us suppose that four readers—one a fireman, a second the owner of a large forest of timber, the third an individual who enjoys fires as spectacles, and the fourth one who has never seen a large fire—read the following passage about a fire:

> Few things are more sensational than a fire. Madly leaping and glowing flames, flying sparks, belching smoke, the crackling of burning timber, scorching heat, shrieking fire engines, water that spouts and that chills the bystanders with icy sprays, the odor of burning materials, smothering fumes, crumbling walls, and jostling crowds make fire exciting.[2]

The meanings that the paragraph conveys and the sensory impressions—visual, auditory, olfactory and thermal—for each individual will be dependent largely upon the unique background of experience each brings to the reading. The understanding and appreciation of the passage by the fireman, because of his wide experience in fighting fires, are very different from those of the individual who enjoys fires as

---

[2] White, Wendell. *The Psychology of Making Life Interesting,* The Macmillan Company, 1939, p. 30.

spectacles, while both are different from those of the owner of a large forest. The mere mention of the word *fire* to the latter elicits an apprehensive response. The individual who had never watched a fire might have little sensation in reading such a passage of an actual fire condition as the one given above.

We can easily see from these illustrations that meaning has an important role in determining the effectiveness of the various reading skills and techniques. The fullness and richness of the reading experience are determined in no small measure by the fullness and richness of the background which the individual brings to it.

It seems reasonable to suppose that the meaning an individual will get from a passage is directly related to the meaning he brings to it. For example, an account of an English football game would be meaningless to an American high school football player who did not know the nature of English football. Or, again, the reading of a story laid in the setting of Old Mexico would give the individual a broader and richer experience after he had spent some time in Mexico than before he had had that background or some related generalized background of understanding.

Each individual brings to the reading of a passage a different set of meaning backgrounds. The reading experience of each person will be influenced by these meaning backgrounds. Consequently, the interpretations and conclusions gained from reading a passage will not be precisely alike for any two persons. The reading experience will not recall the same memories, nor will it be colored by the same prejudices, likes, dislikes, fears, hopes, or joys.

Since meaning background is so vital to the improvement of reading effectiveness, a discussion of how meaning backgrounds may be developed seems to be necessary.

THE DEVELOPMENT OF MEANING

Fortunately, the avenues for the development of backgrounds of understanding are very numerous and ever present. Every experience that the high school student has contributes in some measure to the enlargement of these backgrounds. For the sake of convenience in discussion, these many avenues will be grouped into four major categories:

1. *Firsthand experiences,* including all the experiences that the individual has both in and out of school; for example, going on trips and excursions; taking part in organizations, games, sports, and construction activities; holding jobs; participating in music and art; and attending lectures.

2. *Wide reading experiences,* including recreatory reading, reading of newspapers, reading of textbooks, and broad reading to solve problems and get information.

3. *Other vicarious experiences,* including such experiences as listening to the radio; seeing moving pictures, models, and symbolic exhibits.

4. *Vocabulary study methods,* including the use of the dictionary, the use of word drills, the study of prefixes and suffixes, etc.

Through these experiences the student increases, day by day, his understanding of the real world about him. Unfortunately, however, many individuals have not established the habits necessary for a full realization of the background-building possibilities of the multitude of avenues open to them. While one student might derive much from an experience, another student might be almost totally unchanged by it. Each will have brought to the experience a different background, and consequently the gain will be different.

The gain will differ not only in degree, but also in direction and quality. Many and varied will be the interpretations made by a group having a firsthand experience. For example, a group of students might take a trip to a bakery. One student's resulting generalizations and meaning background might be comprised wholly of the mechanical processes involved in the making of a loaf of bread. Another might be interested in the various ingredients and where they were procured. A third might emphasize the part each ingredient played in the making of the finished product. One might speculate as to how so large an amount of bread was marketed, ignoring completely its production. Still another might be interested in the occupational advantages of having such a trade. And lastly, one might be so concerned with the consumption of the product that he came home with a feeling of fullness and complacency from the experience.

Through subsequent give-and-take discussions, both in the classroom and out, of their varied interpretations of the experience, the entire group might derive an extensive generalized background of the baking industry. It is not to be intimated that all the students have or should have increased their meaning background in the same degree or in the same way. Each, on the contrary, will have brought to the experience a different background and will have gained a unique interpretation. However, as a result of the group's sharing their experiences, the backgrounds, meanings, concepts, and generalizations will, for the whole group, become much greater than those of any one individual could have been.

Firsthand Experiences

Firsthand experiences are all experiences in which the individual is confronted with a real situation. In the illustration above, the experience would have been even more of a firsthand nature if the individuals had not watched, but had actually prepared the bread in the bakery. Firsthand experiences undoubtedly produce stronger and more intense meaning backgrounds than do vicarious experiences.

The school's responsibility for developing backgrounds from firsthand experiences is threefold.

First, the school should encourage, establish, and co-operate with enterprises which provide experiences for the students. As a part of the regular school instruction, trips, excursions, construction activities, and tasks in the classroom should be sponsored. For example, consider the opportunities the chemistry teacher has for using trips to build meanings. Trips can be arranged to various commercial plants or enterprises in which chemistry is indispensable. Such commercial plants include cement plants, dye works, paper mills, sewage-disposal plants, powder plants, and rayon and textile mills. Avenues of this sort are open to every teacher. The school itself affords many opportunities for firsthand experiences. Among these are the production of plays, laboratory experiments, parties, games, debates, discussions, and problem-solving. Problem-solving may not seem to be a firsthand experience. The actual experience of taking data, assembling them, selecting the related and rejecting the unrelated, and analyzing them in a valid fashion is as truly a firsthand experience as is going down into a coal mine.

Second, the school should make better use of the experience backgrounds which the students establish. One way of doing this is to foster better interpretations of the experience. The student should be led to approach his varied experiences with the conscious effort to arrive at new and different concepts and generalizations. These new concepts and generalizations should be used as a means of enriching the classroom work and discussions. This will aid the student in clarifying and using his newly acquired backgrounds and will result in the co-operative building of more and broader backgrounds.

Third, the teacher should guide the students to investigate their concepts further by means of wide reading, use of reference materials, and visual and other aids. In addition, the teacher should encourage the student, through these means, to obtain new and related firsthand experiences. Thus, meaning backgrounds lead to further meaning backgrounds.

Wide Reading Experiences

Just as the life experiences of the individual add to his background, so do his reading experiences. Wide reading is recognized to be among the foremost avenues through which the background of the individual can be enhanced or enlarged. Wide reading may be extensive reading either in many or in few fields of human endeavor. Preferably, it should be a wide exploration into many fields, enriched by a more intensive coverage in a limited number of fields.

By the reading of the printed page, it is possible for the student to derive some of the benefits of the author's experiences. Of course, it must be recognized that there is an interrelationship between reading and meaning backgrounds. Reading, on the one hand, adds to the development of meaning backgrounds, while, on the other hand, meaning backgrounds add to the broadness and the depth of the experiences derived from reading. This interrelationship causes a continuous hand-in-hand progression of growth. Thus, the individual adds to his meaning backgrounds and at the same time becomes a more fluent reader who can thereby gain more meanings.

The teacher of a content subject can aid materially in the growth of meaning backgrounds not only by having the students read broadly in his field, but also by stimulating new interests and opening new realms of reading experiences rather than depending solely upon the intensive study of a single text. The teacher, in co-operation with other teachers, should encourage the student to extend his reading out into areas wherein the subject-matter field overlaps others. This, however, does not imply that in some content subjects the reading of a systematic presentation is to be ignored. The teacher should encourage the exploration of the interests or queries so that such a presentation might be measured to some extent by the number and intensity of the interests and queries that the students obtain from it. In the majority of cases the systematic presentation of the subject matter should be given minor emphasis, and the greater part of the reading time should be spent in extensive reading within that and related subjects. This is true because lasting meanings most frequently result from generalized points of view derived from many sources.

The student should be led to approach such wide reading with the conscious effort on his part to notice new and different means of expression, new and expressive words, and new and challenging concepts. A conscious effort on the part of the student can probably best be developed by making it a co-operative enterprise in which each member of the class participates.

The new ideas, words, and expressions form a basis for enriching the classroom work and discussions. In these discussions the student is enabled to use and clarify his newly gained meanings. In addition he adds to them, since each student shares the effect of the experiences of all.

Some of the new ideas, words, and expressions will be faultily or inaccurately used. A student might use a new word in a situation in which that word did not impart or give the meaning that he intended. In such a case he would benefit markedly by hearing others use the word correctly and thus find that this word had several meanings. And then, again, the discussion of the idea or the meaning which a word connotes may increase the depth of meaning the word has for the student. Such oral use of these meanings and concepts tends to make them a functional part of the student's equipment.

The frequent use of various sorts of reference materials should be a significant part of this conscious effort of the student to arrive at clear and distinct meanings. For example, a question might be raised about the validity of the use of a given word or expression. Recourse should be made to an authoritative treatment. Thus the student, in his independent reading, should be encouraged to make frequent use of dictionaries, encyclopedias, and other reference materials.

At times it will be advantageous to study and compare various words and various meanings of a word in order to determine which expresses a given idea the most accurately. A systematic study of words must be made in relation to the concept the word helps to establish. It is wasteful and often harmful to attempt the study of words outside of the content.

Vicarious Experiences

Other experiences of high school students that aid in developing meaning backgrounds include visual and auditory ones of many kinds. Many of these experiences are a result of out-of-school activities. People of high school age attend on an average one moving picture per week.[3] There are radios in the great majority of the homes of the country, and the average time the radio is on is five hours per day.[4]

The moving picture and the radio are powerful forces in building backgrounds of meaning and experience. Both the

[3] Jersild, Arthur. "Radio and Motion Pictures," *Child Development and the Curriculum, The Thirty-Eighth Yearbook of the National Society for the Study of Education,* Part I, Public School Publishing Company, 1939.

[4] Thomas, Lowell. *Magic Dials,* Lee Furman, 1939, p. iii.

radio and the moving picture bring to the individual current news events from all over the world. Both introduce famous people from all walks of life and occupations. Both bring discussions of political and economic issues and problems. The contributions to the development of meaning that these two powerful forces in American life make have not been fully recognized.

Exact data in regard to how the media discussed above may be used to foster growth of understanding are woefully lacking at present. However, few would deny that increasing use will be made of the radio and sound pictures in the schoolroom. There can be no doubt that the experiences which the individual acquires through these media add to and clarify his background of meanings. As research continues, and as more time, effort, and thought are given to them, the radio and sound pictures will become increasingly powerful educational forces.

The use of motion picture films in the science classroom enables the student to gain more accurate concepts about abstract and distant conditions and events. The value of the use of the motion picture in teaching general science was shown in an experiment conducted by Wood and Freeman.[5] A large number of junior high school students participated in the experiment. The experimental groups were taught units on such topics as reforestation, air, water, sand, and gravel by the aid of motion picture films. The control groups were taught the same units, but without seeing the films. The experimental groups made significantly better scores on tests given at the close of the experimental period than did the control groups. In this case, then, the moving picture was

[5] Wood, Ben H., and Freeman, Frank N. *Motion Pictures in the Classroom,* Houghton Mifflin Company, 1929.

found to be a useful visual aid to the teaching of general science.

An unpublished study by Ramseyer, reported by Jersild—

> indicates the value of documentary films in rendering high school children more sensitive to such social problems as soil erosion, flood control, and the like.[6]

The schools are finding increasing use for radios, motion pictures, phonograph records, and other visual and auditory aids in developing meaning backgrounds. In the case of vicarious experiences as well as firsthand and reading experiences, it is essential that the student be aware of the benefits to be derived. The firsthand experience of a visit to a world's fair enables an individual better to appreciate a moving picture depicting a world's fair. Both experiences build meanings necessary to reading with appreciation and understanding news items and stories about fairs.

And, again, the co-operative inspection of meanings, concepts, and generalizations by class groups is an important feature in the building of meanings. These increases in background should make the student a better reader of materials in the field with which the experience deals.

Vocabulary Study Methods

It is frequently necessary to supplement the three natural ways of developing vocabulary and meaning background discussed above by direct vocabulary study methods.

1. *Use of the dictionary.* The training in the use of the dictionary has been started in the elementary school. Not

---

[6] Jersild, Arthur. "Radio and Motion Pictures," *Child Development and the Curriculum, The Thirty-Eighth Yearbook of the National Society for the Study of Education,* Part I, Public School Publishing Company, 1939, Chapter VII, p. 168. Quoted by permission of the Society.

only should this training be continued in the junior and senior high schools, but it should be made an integral part of the study of unfamiliar words in each of the content subjects. Students should receive continuous encouragement in exploring word meanings.

The problem of teaching the use of the dictionary is one of developing an attitude as well as a skill. This attitude may be fostered through (1) example by the teacher; (2) by creating the desire for accurate, precise word knowledge; (3) by developing the desire for a thorough understanding of the printed page; (4) by encouraging the student to speak and write with clarity, forcefulness, and beauty. The student will find recourse to the dictionary an aid in working toward these goals. An attitude favorable to the continued use of the dictionary is likely to result.

As far as possible, the work with the dictionary at the high school level should be a natural outgrowth of other classroom activities. The teacher should be on the alert to aid the student when he is confronted with a unique problem, such as finding the meaning of an obsolete word. At such times the teacher may find it profitable to call the attention of the entire class to a new use of, or a new problem in the use of, the dictionary.

At the outset with a given class, the teacher will find it advisable to give a short pretest of the abilities in using the dictionary. Such a test may include—locating words in the dictionary, kinds of information to be found, meaning of abbreviations, finding of synonyms, determining word derivations, choosing the correct meanings for words in given settings, and determining word pronunciations. The outcomes of the pretest will show which areas need attention.

The following examples indicate some drills that have been found to be useful:

A. List the words in today's lesson that you found difficult and give the appropriate definition for each.

B. Underline the correct meanings of the following words: [7]

  1. psychologist—mind reader, a reader of stars, one who studies the science of the mind, historian
  2. concurs—clashes, agrees, argues, laughs
  3. allusions—false ideas, pictures, dreams, indirect statements
  4. insinuates—hints, burns up, spreads, condemns
  5. maxim—gossip, general truth, behavior, bad manners
  6. affronted—pleased, befriended, offended, confronted
  7. bereavement—loss by death, gift, anger, stupidity
  8. irreparable—torn, sweet, harsh, can't be remedied

C. Look up one of the words in the list below in an unabridged dictionary. Indicate the word you have chosen and give the following information about it: [8]

Pronunciation	Language from which derived
Syllabication	Definition
Part of speech	Plural form (if a noun)

WORDS TO BE LOOKED UP

synonym	unabridged
derivation	etymology
gazetteer	obsolete

D. By use of an unabridged dictionary, find an example of each of the following. Give the name of the dictionary you used and tell on what page you found this information. [9]

  1. An explanation of a foreign phrase.
  2. The name of a character in fiction.
  3. A picture of a machine.
  4. A picture of an animal.

[7] Center, Stella S., and Persons, Gladys L. *Workbook to Practices in Reading and Thinking,* The Macmillan Company, 1940, p. 116.

[8] Ingles, May, and McCague, Anna. *Teaching the Use of Books and Libraries,* The H. W. Wilson Company, 1937, p. 76, by permission of the publisher.

[9] Ibid.

5. A synonym for a word.
6. The dates of the birth and death of a person.
7. The population of a city in your state.
8. A word derived from the Anglo-Saxon language.
9. An explanation of an abbreviation.

E. Using the dictionary, find the meaning of the following abbreviations:

r.t. ——————————   ibid. ——————————
adj. ——————————   abbr. ——————————
pl. ——————————   Gr. ——————————
p. ——————————   Class. ——————————
i.e. ——————————   Obs. ——————————

F. For each difficult word there is a simple and easy synonym. Match them.[10]

contemplate   1. left
rapture   2. feel
apprehension   3. little by little
sepulchre   4. think
illusory   5. joy
egrets   6. fear
ecstasy   7. tomb
imperceptibly   8. joy
palpitate   9. herons
abandoned   10. unreal

Other dictionary exercises may be found in free pamphlet material published by G. and C. Merriam Company. A pamphlet of dictionary exercises is published by The Macmillan Company—*Dictionary Study, A Study Guide to Accompany Macmillan's Modern Dictionary,* by Theodore W. Darnell.

2. *Derivation of words.* Interest in words and word study can sometimes be stimulated by study of the derivation of words. The G. and C. Merriam Company has a set of slides showing in pictorial fashion the derivation of a number of

[10] Center, Stella S., and Persons, Gladys L. *Workbook to Experiences in Reading and Thinking,* The Macmillan Company, 1940, p. 149.

common words. If used to introduce a consideration of word derivations, these slides might well arouse an interest that will motivate students to study the history of many words. Certainly a keen interest in words and how their meanings developed would increase the vocabulary of a student. The study of word derivations, coupled with the policy of being alert to unique meanings of words or picturesque forms of expression, will prove effective in developing vocabulary.

3. *Word lists and individual drill cards.* For some students it may be expedient to supplement the methods suggested above by using some of the more isolated drill techniques, such as word listings, individual drill cards, drill on prefixes and suffixes. For the most part such techniques will produce discouraging results, but there are certain individuals who find them helpful in building word understandings.

An Illustration of the Building of Meanings

Use was made of firsthand experiences, reading, and other vicarious experiences by the Marshall High School,[11] Minneapolis, Minnesota, to enrich the meaning background of some of its students (and, in turn, of all the rest of its students). The following discussion of a project carried on by that school is included here because it illustrates an effective building of meaning backgrounds by initiating, extending, and enlarging experiences—firsthand, reading, and others.

In the fall of 1934 a group of twenty-six eleventh and twelfth graders began a co-operative study of their own community, Minneapolis, to be followed by a week of firsthand study of Chicago.

Each student selected one or two phases of the life of Minneapolis. His choices had vocational or avocational bases or both.

[11] Mason, E. W. "Making School Excursions Worthwhile," *Utilization of the Community Resources in the Social Studies, Ninth Yearbook of the National Counc. for the Social Studies,* Harvard University, 1938, pp. 73-82.

John Jones chose radio engineering because he wanted to explore that field as a possible vocation. Mary Smith made a study of settlement houses, not because she expected to be a social worker, but because she thought it her duty to know something of their activities. Among the phases of Minneapolis life which have been studied by the Marshall High School students since 1934 are schools, public health, public health nursing, radio, politics, government, social agencies, local history, music, art, business and industry, labor organizations, transportation, service groups, newspapers, parks and playgrounds, motion pictures and the stage, youth groups, and women's organizations.

When each student had selected his field or fields for observation, he proceeded to do a substantial amount of background reading of related surveys, reports, biographies, novels, newspapers, and periodicals.

Next, he arranged a series of interviews with leaders in the fields selected. Each student had a dual motive for these interviews—to discover all he could for his own understanding, and to share his findings with the others. In most cases, before an interview was held, the students and the faculty adviser drew up questions bearing on the fields that were chosen. These questions were sent on to the person to be interviewed. Such a method served at least two purposes: first, it gave the interviewee time to frame answers, and second, it showed him that these students had done some thinking in the field.

The students were not interested merely in sight-seeing trips. That is, when a committee on newspapers went to a newspaper office, it was not so much concerned with the quality and amount of paper and ink used each week as it was with the influence of advertisers on editorial policy, the political bent of the paper, the justification of news policies, or the training that editors recommend for those interested in newspaper work. Again, the social work committee was interested in observing the progress of a housing project, and, in addition, also tried to understand certain social and economic factors involved.

Each year since 1934, during the Easter vacation, a group of Marshall High School students has been taking a trip to another city. The first year they visited Chicago. Later, other cities were visited. It is the plan to get a cross-section picture of the Midwest over a period of years. The students expect to observe, at firsthand, communities ranging in size from a farm to cities of several million population. They expect to discover the history of the communities; their cultural, social, and economic problems; and their assets. They feel it desirable to study other communities for comparison with their own. These trips are financed by the co-operative effort of the students.

During the year, before the spring vacation trip was taken, the students gathered printed materials pertaining to the city to be studied in order to increase their background of knowledge. They obtained newspapers of the city and read them carefully for reference to every field in which the group was interested. The students, individually or in groups, listened to radio programs originating from the city. They watched for newsreels related to their study. Certain students were responsible for obtaining materials, others for typing them, and still others for reports and discussions. The group met frequently—once a week early in the school year, and about twice a week after January first.

Every significant area of the community life of the city to be visited during the spring vacation trip was probed. Arrangements had been made previously for various students to confer with leaders of the city. Prominent people in the various cities have proved to be very generous to the students and have been interested in conferring with them. A summary of the progress that has been made during a five-year period by the Midwestern studies group discloses that:

1. The students have shown a tremendous interest in the endeavor. The membership has grown from four individuals to two hundred.

2. The teachers, too, have been increasingly co-operative, so that the project has been an integrated phase of all schoolwork.

3. The students have felt that the experiences have been of inestimable value to them in enabling them to gain a background of understanding of their own city as well as other cities in the Midwest. They have felt that they would be able to participate in a much more intelligent way in the life of the community.

While it would be difficult to estimate the extent and depth of meanings, concepts, and generalizations which are to be derived from such an enterprise, it is obvious that the students had a series of very rich experiences. In the pursuit of these experiences all three major categories—firsthand experiences, reading experiences, and other vicarious experiences—were tapped constantly.

The students had firsthand experiences in interviewing prominent individuals, in visiting plants and industries, in seeing building construction, in seeing city governments at work, and in investigating occupational endeavors. In addition, they had the firsthand experience of preparing for and taking a journey and of meeting obligations in unknown cities. Firsthand experiences also included reporting to the student body in the auditorium.

Reading experiences were many and varied. The students accumulated and digested a wealth of materials. They became familiar with newspapers other than those of their own city.

They read both in preparation for and for further interpretation of their investigations of various phases of Midwestern life.

Radio programs, pictures, and newsreels added to the extensive backgrounds these students were developing. Probably as helpful as any other thing in the development of the meaning background were the many opportunities for cooperative sharing of experiences. In these discussions the students placed a real value on any new or clarified concepts. The students were eager to build up useful backgrounds of meaning. Moreover, there was a constant use of the backgrounds of generalizations which made the learnings a part of each individual's equipment. It is very probable that these students will bring to their future reading well-developed reading techniques and skills and a broad background of meanings, concepts, and generalizations.

SUMMARY

Each and every experience that the high school student has contributes in some measure to the enlargement of meaning backgrounds. Firsthand experiences, such as trips, jobs, sports, musical and art activities, enable the individual to add to his meaning backgrounds. He may also add to his background of experience by wide reading in many fields, enriched by a broad coverage in a limited number of fields. Other vicarious experiences, such as radio, moving pictures, pictures and models, and symbolic exhibits, aid in developing meaning backgrounds. Vocabulary study methods, including the use of the dictionary, the use of word drills, the study of prefixes and suffixes, etc., aid in developing meaning backgrounds.

Three phases of meaning that have an influence upon an individual's effectiveness as a reader are:

1. Simple recognition, in which the individual is able to attach a meaning to a symbol.

2. Extensiveness of meanings, in which the individual is able to associate two or more distinct meanings with a symbol.

3. Depth or vividness of meanings, in which the individual is able to make use of deep and fine appreciations and of broad concepts and generalizations in interpreting a symbol.

Meanings contribute to reading by aiding the effectiveness of the individual as a reader and by influencing the interpretation and appreciation of what he reads.

Selected Bibliography

Dresher, Richard. "Training in Mathematics Vocabulary," *Ohio State University Educational Research Bulletin,* Vol. XIII, November 14, 1934, pp. 201-4.

Eurich, Alvin C. *The Reading Abilities of College Students: An Experimental Study,* College Problems Series, University of Minnesota Press, 1931.

Gray, W. S., and Holmes, E. *The Development of Meaning Vocabularies in Reading,* University of Chicago Press, 1938.

Horn, Ernest. *Methods of Instruction in the Social Studies,* Charles Scribner's Sons, 1937, Chapter 5.

Jersild, Arthur. "Radio and Motion Pictures," *Child Development and the Curriculum, The Thirty-Eighth Yearbook of the National Society for the Study of Education,* Part I, Public School Publishing Company, 1939.

McKee, Paul. "Vocabulary Development," *The Teaching of Reading: A Second Report, The Thirty-Sixth Yearbook of the National Society for the Study of Education,* Part I, Public School Publishing Company, 1937.

Mason, E. W. "Making School Excursions Worthwhile," *Utilization of the Community Resources in the Social Studies, Ninth Yearbook of the National Society for the Social Studies,* Harvard University, 1938, pp. 73-82.

Strang, Ruth, and Rose, F. C. *Problems in the Improvement of Reading in High School and College,* Revised, The Science Press Printing Company, 1940, Chapter III.

Wood, Ben, and Freeman, Frank N. *Motion Pictures in the Classroom,* Houghton Mifflin Company, 1939.

CHAPTER VI

DEVELOPMENT OF READING INTERESTS

When one gives serious thought to ways of developing reading interests, he realizes that wider and more lasting interests are needed than are now usual. While the teachers of English have accepted the responsibility for developing interests and tastes in the reading materials of their courses, the other content subject teachers have been somewhat unconcerned about the developing of lasting interests and tastes in the reading materials of their courses. They are concerned with the establishment of a body of factual knowledge, rather than with the development of permanent interests which would lead the students to continue reading the subject matter after they were no longer given day-by-day assignments by the teachers. The reading material used in the content subjects has been, in general, the somewhat lifeless information collections which do little to stimulate worth-while drives toward further reading.

This chapter will deal with reading interests in their broader sense. There is no intention to minimize in any degree the work in the development of reading interests with which the teachers of English literature have been so wholeheartedly concerned. The purpose is rather to extend that program to include other fields of human experience.

In the following statement Horn points to the need for developing reading interests in the social studies:

Investigations of adult reading habits lead one to suspect that the great majority of adults would not even attempt, of their own free will, to read selections on some of the topics now generally included in books on the social studies. This apathy may reflect either a lack of pertinence of these topics to the life of the common man or a failure of the school to have made the pertinence apparent. Aiding students to develop worth-while interests in the social studies, therefore, would appear to be one of the most important steps toward increasing the quantity and improving the quality of reading.[1]

In our modern highly interrelated world it seems plausible to assume that an average person will develop sustaining interests in a variety of fields. Consequently, he should not confine his in-school or postschool reading to one field alone. And although it is true that many of the better novels, poems, and other works of literature give a broad view of life, still the sciences, social studies, practical arts, and other subjects have much to contribute to the continued well-rounded development of the student. Teachers of these subjects can well afford to inspect the groundwork that has been laid by the teachers of English and to apply some of the bases of this work to the development of interests and tastes in their own subject-matter areas.

READING INTERESTS OF HIGH SCHOOL STUDENTS

The exact status of reading interests of students is very difficult to determine. Much systematic research has been done on this phase of the reading problem, but for many reasons the results must be interpreted with caution. The interests of students are different for each one. Such interests do not lend themselves to quantitative analysis. We have not yet learned to appraise such considerations as depth of appreciation and vividness of imagery. Most of the investigations have been

[1] Horn, Ernest. *Methods of Instruction in the Social Studies,* Charles Scribner's Sons, 1937, p. 177.

limited to the listing of books, magazines, newspapers, and other materials which the students have read. These studies have mainly attempted to determine the types of materials that students of various ages read. Their purpose in doing this has been to estimate in some degree the quality, usefulness, and extent of the students' reading interests.

Certain limitations are inherent in most of these investigations. While it is not possible to overcome these entirely, many of them have been recognized and either eliminated or accounted for by the research workers. One such limitation that enters into the listing of books read is that people tend to remember the titles of the better books that they have read. Naturally, the best books make the most lasting impressions. Another limitation is the fact that people are motivated too strongly by a regard for their own personal worth. Even though an individual may not be required to sign his name to the list of books he has read, he almost inevitably gives a presentation favorable to him. Then, too, it is easier to remember the unique than it is to remember the more commonplace.

Another approach to the study of interests is that of tabulating the books which individuals choose for reading. But the mere fact that an individual takes a book from a library is not proof that he reads it or enjoys it. And, of course, he never has complete freedom of choice.

Reading interests of high school students, as the results of these investigations indicate, are limited and for the most part immature. In spite of their various limitations, the marked similarity in the results of the studies makes possible this assumption. An inspection of the limitations listed above shows that the studies tend to present reading interests in an optimistic light. Reading interests are certainly on no higher a level than the results show. They are probably lower than indicated. The immense number of magazines of an inferior quality that are sold daily give evidence to the fact that people are reading a great deal of inferior materials.

Table V shows the results of a study of the reading interests of entering freshmen at the University of Wisconsin. Questionnaires asking for the amount of voluntary reading done during the previous year were given to 1,980 incoming freshmen.

TABLE V

Books Read Voluntarily by High School Seniors [2]

TYPE OF BOOK	PER CENT OF TOTAL BOYS	GIRLS
Classics	1.5	2.1
Novels of high quality	19.1	28.5
Popular fiction	30.1	33.2
Modern essays	1.3	1.4
Modern drama	3.2	3.7
Modern poetry	1.9	2.5
Detective and mystery stories	5.4	2.4
Western novels	2.0	1.1
Travel and adventure books	7.8	4.4
Biography and history	12.2	10.3
Science and philosophy	5.1	2.1
Educational	6.3	5.8
Technical books	3.3	.7
Religious books	1.1	1.4
Average number of books read	3⅓	5

An interesting indication is that these high school graduates did not report for themselves extensive voluntary reading. The boys reported, on the average, over the period of a year three and one third books voluntarily read and the girls, five books. In all probability, however, these students did not recall all the books read during the twelve-month period.

[2] Byrns, Ruth, and Henmon, V. A. C. "Reading Interests of High School Seniors," *English Journal*, Vol. XXV, January, 1936, pp. 61-64.

One third of the books reported were either popular fiction or detective stories. To be sure, it is not wrong to read these types of material. Yet to have them make up one third of one's reading seems out of proportion to their worth.

Eaton reports a study of the reading interests of the students in a Syracuse high school, which shows that the majority of students are not reading material from science, social studies,

TABLE VI

Percentage of Boys and Girls in a Syracuse High School Reading Books of Various Types [3]

TYPE OF BOOK	BOYS	GIRLS
Fiction	100	98
Short Stories	72	88
Essays and Travel	51	34
Poetry	38	63
History	40	26
Biography	54	58
Science	51	9
Religion	26	42

and academic fields other than literature. As is shown in Table VI, practically all the students were reading fiction, other than short stories, while a large proportion was reading the latter form of fiction. But forty per cent of the boys and twenty-six per cent of the girls were reported as reading history. About half of the boys read science, while only about a tenth of the girls reported such reading. It seems probable that the reading interests of this group of high school students had not been directed toward the academic fields other than literature. Teachers in other academic fields may well follow the lead of the teachers of literature in stimulating reading in their subject-matter fields. The results indicate

[3] Eaton, H. T. "What High School Pupils Like to Read," *Education,* Vol. XLIII, December, 1922, p. 205.

that reading interests tend to concentrate around various sorts of fiction rather than about material from science, social studies, or other academic fields.

Here is a challenge to every high school teacher. It is the task of each one to guide students in their reading so that they may develop new and vital interests. This task cannot be undertaken by one teacher or one department. The teacher of each subject taught in the school must assume the responsibility. In meeting this responsibility, the school can realize one of its greatest opportunities to do something for the student which will be of permanent value to him.

FACTORS AFFECTING READING INTERESTS

There are many factors, both in and out of school, that are related to the development of reading interests and tastes. Many factors composing the environment of the student from his birth and those making up his present environment have affected or are affecting his reading interests and tastes. We shall consider only a few of the more important of these factors.

Reading Environment of the Home

Some students, before they came to the first grade of school, had developed a wide background of general interests as well as reading interests. They came from homes where it is customary to read and discuss books in addition to conversing about current topics of interest. By the time these students reach high school, this cultural environment has probably contributed significantly to their reading interests and tastes. Other students have come from homes where books are rare indeed. And more than likely there has been little else to create strong and lasting reading interests.

In addition to the tremendous variation in quantity of books within the home, there are also great differences in the general quality of the reading. By and large, the homes containing many books will be the ones where the quality of the books is better.

Another significant factor in the development of reading interests is the general attitude in the home toward reading. Some parents are extensive readers and have a great appreciation for the services that reading can offer. On the other hand, some parents do little reading themselves and have little, if any, appreciation of what reading can contribute to their lives and to the lives of their children.

The school should not allow the fact that a student comes from a home where there is little reading or discussion of books to constitute an excuse for the failure to develop reading interests. But it should recognize that in such a case it has an added responsibility and a more difficult task. It is relatively easy to develop broad and wholesome interests and tastes in the student who comes from a home where there is a background of rich and varied experiences, where reading and discussion are an integral part of the family life. It is, of course, a much greater problem to develop the same interests in a student who comes from a more limited home background. The difference in the problem of developing reading interests for each student should be recognized and taken into account.

Out-of-School Activities

There are other out-of-school conditions which influence the reading interests and tastes of students to no small extent. The radio and motion picture may add much to the background of meanings that are necessary for real and vivid understandings and may thereby add fundamentally to the development of interests. The schools should become aware of these two avenues for developing interests and should attempt to make use of their potentialities. In order to do this, they should undertake consumer education in motion picture and radio programs.

The close relationship between the radio and motion pictures and the reading program should be recognized. For example, it is possible for the English teacher to use the interests aroused by the motion picture portrayal of a good book to encourage the student to read that book and others by the same author. Or the science teacher might use a movie depicting the life of a great scientist to develop interest in extensive reading in the field of science. The history of a given period has frequently been made more real and therefore more interesting to the students by seeing the motion picture version of an historical novel. The same outcomes could be derived from the use of good radio programs.

We must realize, however, that the students of today have many interests which detract from the development of the habit of reading. The lives of students are so filled with activities of one kind or another that there is frequently little time for extensive reading. But while such experiences are of much value, time should be saved for reading activities, since reading has a unique contribution to make to the life and personality of the student. This fact should be recognized by the schools in order that they may make provision during school hours for extensive free reading. Reading should become so necessary to the lives of the students that they will include it among their essential out-of-school activities.

Accessibility of Materials

Accessibility of materials is sometimes a help and sometimes a detriment to the development of reading interests.[4] People

---

[4] Washburne, Carleton, and Vogel, L. *Winnetka Graded Book List*, American Library Association, 1926.

tend, naturally, to read the materials that are at hand. If left unguided, students are apt to read for their home reading the materials that are available in the home. Douglas Waples[5] has shown that adults read materials of an inferior type, such as sex novels, romance stories, and cheap detective and western story magazines. Unfortunately, these types of materials are all too likely to be available in the home.

Schools are making their reading materials more and more accessible to the students. In one large city, for example, the school libraries are kept open during the summer vacation in order to make better books immediately available to the students. This service, augmented by the services of the public libraries, enables the students to continue their voluntary reading throughout the summer. Actually, these school libraries are operated in much the fashion of additional branches of the city-wide public library system. The twofold advantage of such a plan is that it makes the books of the school library accessible to the students and that it enables them to continue the habit of withdrawing books established in the school year.

Reading materials in schools are becoming more and more abundant and diversified, are in better format, and contain material of greater intrinsic value to the student. These extensive and worth-while materials in no small measure are aiding in developing broad and adequate reading interests in the student.

Suggestions for Guiding Interests

Allow Students to Read Widely   ●

Several years ago in the junior and senior high school in Negaunee, Michigan,[6] a school-wide experiment in the use

[5] Waples, Douglas. "Community Studies in Reading," *Library Quarterly,* Vol. III, January, 1933, pp. 1-20.

[6] Schoonover, Ruth. "The Negaunee Reading Experiment," *English Journal,* Vol. XXVI, September, 1937, pp. 527-35.

of books was begun. While the English department took the major responsibility for this extensive reading program, all departments of the school co-operated. The major responsibility could just as well have been assumed by any other department of the school. The experiment was initiated because it was felt that the reading of the students had been too regimented.

It was decided that the students be allowed complete freedom in the choice of the materials they read. Many types of reading materials, ranging widely both in difficulty of concepts and vocabulary and in quality, were made accessible to the student body. The students were encouraged to read whatever interested them. If one student declared an interest in "pulp magazine" stories of cowboys and Indians, he had access to many of them. The students were encouraged to read in the field of their greatest interest. In fact, they were encouraged to read anything at all, just so they read.

It was found that, as the amount of the students' reading increased, their reading tastes improved. In a later article referring to the same experiment, Schoonover says:

> Though the final results of the program defy any attempt at exact measurement or evaluation because they are too subjective, enough significant data can now be submitted to justify our belief that pupils of junior and senior high school age will, in general, if given free range and opportunity to choose from a wide variety of attractive books, read voluminously and that their reading tastes and appreciations gradually progress toward a point at which they voluntarily select the better books.[7]

Every student showed a marked increase in the number of books read voluntarily during the period of a school year, and for some students the increase was tremendous. The

[7] Schoonover, Ruth. "The Case for Voluminous Reading," *English Journal,* Vol. XXVII, February, 1938, pp. 114-18.

average number of books read per pupil each year was about fifty-five. It would be interesting to compare after a lapse of ten years the quantity and quality of the reading of these students with the quantity and quality of the reading of a random population of adults of the same ability and age who had not had these free reading activities during their high school years. It is altogether likely that the interests resulting from these extensive reading activities during the six years of junior and senior high school will be so permanent that the reading life of the students will always be abundant and wholesome. It may well be that these students have developed, in addition to lasting interests and tastes, a considerable degree of reading independence and a clear realization of the services reading can perform for them.

Abundant reading will add to the word and meaning backgrounds of the student. These added backgrounds will enable the student to read still more abundantly. The Negaunee experiment lends support to the belief that students will read widely and abundantly when they are encouraged to do so, when materials of their own choosing are plentiful and easily accessible, and when an opportunity is provided for them to discuss their reading interests and to keep account of their reading growth. Enlarging and improving reading interests and tastes naturally accompany the development of meaning backgrounds and extensive reading tastes.

Extensive reading makes for a greater ability to judge the contribution that a selection has to make to the individual. This is especially true when the reading activities of students are to some extent directed and guided by the teachers. La Brant[8] found that in an extensive, though guided, program

---

[8] La Brant, L. L. "An Evaluation of the Free Reading in Grades Ten, Eleven, and Twelve for the Class of 1935," *Contributions to Education*, Vol. 1, No. 2, The Ohio State University Press, 1936.

the students developed criteria for judging the value of their reading.

Build upon Students' Present Interests

Junior and senior high school students whose reading tastes are immature and undeveloped should not be expected to read materials prepared for students of more mature tastes. Formal and informal appraisals should be made to determine each individual's reading interests and tastes. Then the development of interests should begin with the interests the student has and for which he has a word and meaning background. He cannot be expected to be interested in reading materials that are above the level of his meaning background. No individual will be interested in reading materials that deal with concepts entirely outside his realm of experience, and for which he has no background upon which to build an understanding.

People are interested in reading about things that are familiar to them—that are true to life as they have experienced it or that have a sufficient number of elements within their experience so that they can understand the concepts involved. Consequently, reading materials in courses of English, history, government, science, and so forth should include concepts that are within the everyday experience of the students. Upon these concrete, true-to-life concepts may be built the more abstract and remote ones. But the important point here is that the students' present interests and tastes should be taken as the foundation upon which more mature interests and tastes may be built.

It is the real teacher who utilizes the present interests of the students to serve as a background upon which to build new interests. Consider, for example, the case of John, a ninth-grade boy who had failed to enter into the activities of the class. John was a shy and friendless boy. His teachers felt that something had to be done to enable him to make a place for himself in his group. It was known that his dominant interest was in radio construction and that he read omnivorously anything dealing with the construction of radios. The building and rebuilding of his own radio set was a continuous process.

The teachers decided to utilize his interest in the radio to enable John to make his contribution to the class group and also to enlarge his reading interests. Through the guidance of the general science teacher, John was encouraged to expand his reading about radios to include materials on more general aspects of the science of the radio. This led him into the reading of materials in related fields. When the class discussion in general science concerned the radio, John was made responsible for it. He outlined the topics to be considered in the discussion. He prepared reading lists for various classmates. And when the time came for the discussion, John led it. John's interest in the project was very real. During the period of his preparation not only did he read exhaustively on all phases of radio, but he also directed the reading of his classmates. The responsibility for directing this co-operative enterprise gave him a feeling of faith in himself and a degree of respect from the group. In addition, during the semester John wrote a radio dramatization which was presented in the English class. He also prepared a paper tracing the development of radio in America. This paper he read in the social studies class.

When an appraisal was made of John's growth during the semester, it was found that he had actually become an active member of the group. Just as others had co-operated with him in the discussion of radio, so he had co-operated in various other units of the course in general science. His success in leading the unit for which he had been responsible had given him a deep satisfaction.

It was also found that John's reading interests had been extended during the semester. At the beginning of the term his reading had been rather narrowly limited to material about radio construction. But by the end of the semester he had read about the radio not only as a means of communication, but he had so enlarged his reading interests that they included the radio as a service agency in the event of various disasters. He had then become interested in disasters at sea; and this had led to an interest in sea stories in general. It was impossible to predict where this new reading interest would lead him. However, it certainly seemed that, from the point of view of his increased reading interests, the semester had been a profitable one for him.

It can be seen from the above illustration that the growth of interests is developmental in nature. In the beginning the individual has relatively few and immature reading interests. There is a gradual growth in number and depth of these interests. In aiding the student to develop more mature interests, then, the teacher must be aware that the growth will be a gradual one that starts at the degree of maturity which the student already has reached.

It is futile to expect an individual whose interests are narrow in scope and immature in quality to truly appreciate materials which require mature reading interests for their enjoyment. In developing interests, therefore, the work must be started with materials that are at the pupil's interest level. Then the pupils should be encouraged to do extensive reading.

This reading should be guided by the teacher in the specific course in which the interests were evidenced. For example, if the student displayed an interest in reading popularized pseudoscientific thrillers, it is there that the teacher of science might well start in developing reading interest in science. He should guide the student's reading so that the later choices of the student would show developmental growth into such types of books as those concerned with travel, exploration, and the sheer drama of science. Such a developmental growth would be likely to extend over a considerable period of time.

Begin at Students' Reading Level

Just as it is true that the development of reading interests must start at the level of the pupil's interest, so must it start at his reading comprehension level. The student must be able to read a book with some understanding before he can be expected to be interested in it. In the case of many students the lack of mature reading interests can be directly attributed to the lack of ability to read well. Most of the better books in any subject require a higher degree of reading ability than do books of inferior quality. The student with immature reading habits will find the book from which he can easily derive the meaning more interesting than the better book that he is unable to read with comprehension. It seems obvious, then, that in developing reading interests the student must be provided with readable books. Of course, in some fields this task will necessitate a thorough canvassing of the available literature.

The teacher should be cautioned, however, that it is an unsound procedure to keep the student reading at a relatively immature level. It is necessary from time to time to encourage him to read books with which he will have to "tussle," but with which he will have a reasonable chance of winning the "tussle." The fundamental concept is that the student should have material that is fully adjusted to his reading stature and still lends itself toward increasing that stature.

Recognize Students' Reading Strengths and Weaknesses

Since reading is a complex process, and since the individual may not be as advanced in certain techniques as he is in others, and since different types of materials depend upon the use of various reading techniques and their combinations, it is necessary to consider the effects that these varying degrees of ability will have upon reading interests. The individual's specific reading strengths and weaknesses must be recognized, and the materials must be adjusted to them if reading interests are to be developed.

The student who is low in ability to get the general significance of a passage and who has a tendency to note the details will not, in all probability, get much pleasure from the reading of novels. Such a student is like the person who inspects an oil painting so closely that he sees all the brush strokes, but does not view the picture as a whole. The details stand out so markedly that they overshadow for him the significant features of which the details are only a part. The usual novel contributes but little to such a student. On the other hand, materials packed with facts, such as scientific or detailed materials of any sort, are quite likely to be interesting to him.

In order to broaden the reading interests of such a student, it will be necessary to introduce him gradually to materials which demand less noting and remembering of the factual details and more formulating of the general significance of which those details form the pattern. There are novels, such as *A Tale of Two Cities,* by Charles Dickens, in which the factual details must be remembered, but remembered in relation to the general unraveling of the plot. The reading of these novels usually not only proves interesting to a reader who notes details, but is also a means of building up the ability to see the relationship between those details. The step from this sort of reading to that of reading novels in general is a relatively easy one.

Another student who reads at a fast rate but rather superficially might not be able to read material upon current world problems with any degree of interest. But he might find stories based upon the personal lives of world figures interesting. Again, it would be necessary to begin with the reading abilities the student has and progress by easy and interesting steps toward the more extensive interests and tastes that are desired. It is necessary to point out to the student the fact that these two types of material should be read at quite different rates of speed. In order to read with understanding material about current world problems, the individual must pause and appraise the ideas in the light of his background of meanings. The materials that he reads should lead gradually from those that he has found interesting to those of related readings which call for a more critical evaluation.

Another student who has a high degree of comprehension, but a low rate of reading will find it difficult to become interested in a story in which many pages are devoted to the introduction. A student who reads at an average rate of reading might be able to finish the introductory part of the story in, let us assume, an hour of reading time, whereas a slow reader would require a much longer time. In all probability the latter individual would put the story aside after a time because he would not find it interesting enough to challenge him to continue reading. A story, the action of which moved slowly, would for the same reason be uninteresting to the slow reader. For such a student the progression toward the building of more extensive reading interests might be very gradual—from very short stories through compact, fast-moving novels to novels of any sort.

The above illustrations point to the need for adjusting the

reading of an individual according to his varying reading abilities and tastes. Guidance must be given the student in both of these areas if improvement is to result.

The Interrelationship between Interests and Reading Abilities

Improving and extending reading interests is one way of improving reading abilities in general. Broadly speaking, the individual with many and profound interests will be a more avid and voluminous reader than will a reader without those interests. There is also a high relationship between the extent and depth of the reading interests of readers in general and ability in reading. In the chapter on word and meaning backgrounds it was shown that there is a relationship between the amount of reading the individual does and his growth in reading abilities. It was shown that an effective way of improving the understanding of words and the understanding of concepts is to read extensively.

Just as wide reading adds to the individual's store of word and meaning backgrounds, so does it enable him to improve in other aspects of reading development. This is especially true when there is a wise guidance of the reading activities of the individual. Since wide reading is a corollary of many and varied interests, and since it contributes to the development of reading abilities, the assumption that many and varied reading interests also contribute to the development of reading abilities seems to be a sound one.

There is, then, an interrelationship between interests and reading ability. Reading ability, in the first place, makes possible the reading interests, and the reading interests in turn contribute to further development of reading abilities. Instruction should be directed toward the development of both interest and ability in reading.

SUMMARY

Studies of reading interests of high school students indicate that reading interests are limited and immature. An individual should develop sustaining interests in a variety of fields of human relationships. One of the most challenging tasks of the teacher of a content subject is guiding students so that they may develop many new and vital interests.

Factors that affect the reading interests and tastes of students include:

1. The quantity of books within the home.
2. The quality of the reading which is done in the home.
3. The general attitude of the adults in the home toward reading.
4. The use of the radio and the motion picture.
5. The firsthand activities and experiences of the student.
6. The accessibility of reading materials.

Abundant reading is one of the most effective ways of developing reading interests and tastes. Wide reading adds to the word and meaning backgrounds of the student. The interests the student has should be the foundation upon which wider and more mature interests may be built. The reading materials that are chosen for the purpose of developing reading interests should be at the student's reading level. The student must be able to read a book with some understanding before he can be expected to be interested in it. Materials should be adjusted to the student's reading strengths. Reading situations should be so set up as to overcome the student's reading weaknesses.

There is an interrelationship between interests and reading abilities. The ability to read enables the student to develop reading interests, and the reading interests cause the student to read widely, which in turn contributes to further development of ability in reading.

Selected Bibliography

Atkinson, Dora A. "An Investigation of the Reading Habits, Tastes, and Attitudes of Junior High School Students as Revealed in Their Voluntary Reading," *California Quarterly of Secondary Education,* Vol. 9, January, 1934, p. 186.

Betzner, Jean, and Lyman, R. L. "The Development of Reading Interests and Tastes," *The Teaching of Reading: A Second Report, The Thirty-Sixth Yearbook of the National Society for the Study of Education,* Part I, Public School Publishing Company, 1937.

Byrns, Ruth, and Henmon, V. A. C. "Reading Interests of High School Seniors," *English Journal,* Vol. XXV, January, 1936, pp. 61-64.

Center, S. S., and Persons, G. L. "Leisure Reading of New York City High School Students," *English Journal,* Vol. XXV, November, 1936, pp. 717-26.

Eaton, H. T. "What High School Students Like to Read," *Education,* Vol. XLIII, December, 1922, pp. 204-9.

Gray, William S., and Leary, Bernice E. *What Makes a Book Readable,* University of Chicago Press, 1935.

Horn, Ernest. *Methods of Instruction in the Social Studies,* Charles Scribner's Sons, 1937.

La Brant, L. L., and Heller, F. M. "Magazine Reading in an Experimental School," *Library Journal,* Vol. LXI, March, 1936, pp. 213-17.

La Brant, L. L. "An Evaluation of the Free Reading in Grades Ten, Eleven, and Twelve for the Class of 1935," *Contributions to Education,* Vol. I, No. 2, The Ohio State University Press, 1936.

McKee, Paul. *Reading and Literature in the Elementary School,* Houghton Mifflin Company, 1934.

Punke, Harold H. "The Home and Adolescent Reading Interests," *School Review,* Vol. XLV, October, 1937, pp. 612-20.

Schoonover, Ruth C. "The Negaunee Reading Experiment," *English Journal,* Vol. XXVI, September, 1937, pp. 527-35.

Schoonover, Ruth C. "The Case for Voluminous Reading," *English Journal,* Vol. XXVII, February, 1938, pp. 114-18.

Smith, Dora V. "Reading for Fun," *Library Journal,* Vol. LX, July, 1935, pp. 879-81.

Strang, Ruth, and Rose, F. C. *Problems in the Improvement of Reading in High School and College,* Revised, The Science Press Printing Company, 1940, pp. 306-13.

Waples, Douglas. "Community Studies in Reading," *Library Quarterly,* Vol. III, January, 1933, pp. 1-20.

Washburne, Carleton. *The Right Book for the Right Child: A Graded Buying List of Children's Books,* The John Day Company, 1933.

CHAPTER VII

DEVELOPMENT OF A DIFFERENTIATED ATTACK

An Experiment in Speed of Reading Various Types of Materials

Good readers read different types of material at different rates of speed. Some make a conscious effort to adjust their rate of reading to the difficulty and familiarity of the material and to the purpose for which they are reading. Others quite unconsciously increase or decrease their speed in accordance with their purpose and material. But less effective readers seem to have just one reading rate which they use all the time, regardless of what they are reading or why.

As an experiment in speed of reading and some of its implications, one hundred graduate students in a college of education were given selections from four types of material to read. These selections were in the same format; that is, they were in double-spaced mimeographed form. There was no intimation of the sources of the material. After the reading was finished, the students wrote what they remembered of each of the selections.

Material of the Story Type

One selection was a passage from the story *Lorna Doone,* by Richard Doddridge Blackmore, adapted by Jordan, Berglund, and Washburne. This version keeps the vocabulary burden at such a low level that it may be effectively read by immature readers. The average rate at which the students read this simple story-type material from *Lorna Doone* was 374 words per minute. An excerpt from this passage (an average student-minute of reading) follows:

> One November evening, when John was a tall, strong boy of fifteen, he had a great experience. Annie was thirteen, a pretty girl, and a fine help to their mother. The youngest sister, Lizzie, was still only a child.
>
> A great deal of rain had fallen, and the farmyard stream, which was not more than two feet deep in summer, was flooded. It foamed and roared like the waves of the sea and would have been a dangerous crossing for man or animal.
>
> On that evening John and Annie heard a terrible Quack! Quack! among the ducks in the barnyard. They ran out to see what might be the cause of it. There were the ten white ducks and the three brown ones pushing their golden bills here and there and jumping on their three-cornered, webbed feet. Some of them ran along low on the ground, snapping and bending their bills.
>
> "Quack! Quack! Quack! Quack!" Such excitement among the ducks had never before been heard at Plover Barrows farm. Annie called the ducks to quiet them, but they only quacked three times as hard and ran around more wildly than ever. John and Annie began to run after them. Soon the ducks streamed out in a long line, running down the barnyard.
>
> "One, two, three, four, five—" Annie counted. "John!" she cried. "There are only thirteen. One is gone. It is the big old father duck."
>
> It was true, and soon Annie saw her missing duck. The fine fellow was in a sad state. He was caught in the gate which hung by chains across the water. There he rose and fell with the waves, his topknot full of water and his tail washed up and down on the flood. Now and then he gave forth a wild quack. He was a sorry sight.
>
> For a minute John could not help laughing. Then the poor duck's throat got filled up with water, and down he

went. He must surely drown in another moment. Annie was crying and wringing her hands. John was about to rush into the water when a man on horseback came suddenly around the corner of the hedge on the other side of the stream. He rode into [1]

Material from a Shakespearean Play

The second type of material used was a selection from *As You Like It*. The selection was chosen by opening at random a volume of Shakespeare's plays. The average rate at which the students read this literary material was 283 words per minute.

An excerpt from this passage (an average student-minute of reading) follows:

Cel.   No? when Nature hath made a fair creature may she not by Fortune fall into the fire? Though Nature hath given us wit to flout at Fortune, hath not Fortune sent in this fool to cut off the argument?

Ros.   Indeed, there is Fortune too hard for Nature when Fortune makes Nature's natural the cutter-off of Nature's wit.

Cel.   Peradventure this is not Fortune's work neither, but Nature's; who perceiveth our natural wits too dull to reason of such goddesses, and hath sent this natural for our whetstone; for always the dulness of the fool is the whetstone of the wits. How now, wit! Whither wander you?

Touch. Mistress, you must come away to your father.

Cel.   Were you made the messenger?

Touch. No, by mine honour, but I was bid to come for you.

Ros.   Where learned you that oath, fool?

[1] *Lorna Doone* (adapted by Rachel Jordan, A. O. Berglund, and Carleton Washburne), Scott, Foresman and Company, 1938, p. 50 ff.

Touch. Of a certain knight that swore by his honour they were good pancakes, and swore by his honour the mustard was naught; now I'll stand to it, the pancakes were naught and the mustard was good, and yet was not the knight forsworn.

Cel. How prove you that, in the great heap of your knowledge?

Ros. Ay, marry, now unmuzzle your wisdom.

Touch. Stand you both forth now: stroke your chins, and swear by your beards that I am a knave.

Cel. By our beards, if we had them, thou art.

Touch. By my knavery, if I had it, then I were; but if you swear by that that is not, you are not forsworn: no more was this knight, swearing by his honour, for he never had any; or if he had, he had sworn it away before ever.[2]

Material from a College Zoology

A selection from a college zoology textbook made up the third type of material. The average rate of reading this scientific material was 265 words per minute.

An excerpt from this passage (an average student-minute of reading) follows:

DIGESTIVE ORGANS

Teeth are present in nearly all Mammals, but in some they are wanting in the adult condition (whalebone Whales and Platypus). In Echidna teeth are not present even in the young. In some of the Ant-eaters teeth are developed in the foetus and are thrown off *in utero*—the adult animal being devoid of them.

Teeth, as already explained in the general account of the Craniata, are developed partly from the epidermis and partly from the underlying dermis. In the Mammals each tooth is lodged in a socket or alveolus in the jaw. The part of the tooth developed from the epidermis is the

[2] Shakespeare, William. *As You Like It*. Act I. Scene 2.

enamel; the remainder of the tooth—dentine, cement and pulp—being formed from the subjacent mesodermal tissue.

Along the oral surface of the jaw is formed a ridge-like ingrowth of the ectoderm—the *dental lamina.* The position of this is indicated externally by a groove—the dental groove, and from it a bud is given off in the position to be occupied by each of the teeth. This becomes constricted off as a conical cap of cells—the *enamel organ*—which remains in continuity with the dental ridge only by a narrow isthmus. This cap-like form is brought about by the development of a papilla of condensed dermal tissue—the *dental papilla,* which pushes upwards against the enamel-organ. On the surface of this papilla, in contact with the enamel-organ, the cells (*odontoblasts*) become arranged into a layer having the appearance of an epithelium—the *dentine-forming layer.* The cells of the enamel-organ form two layers, of which that [3]

Material from The World Almanac

A passage from *The World Almanac,* entitled "Origin of the Names of the States and Territories," made up the fourth type of material the students read understandingly in the timed situation. The average rate of reading this factual material was 248 words per minute. An excerpt from this passage (an average student-minute of reading) follows:

ORIGIN OF THE NAMES OF THE STATES AND TERRITORIES

Source: State Librarians and other officials

Alabama—Alibama was the Indian name of a tribe in Southern Alabama—a Mushhogean tribe of the Creek Confederacy. Alibamu is from the Choctaw words alba aya mule, meaning "I open or clear the thicket."

Alaska—From "Al-ay-es-ka," or Alakh-Skhak a native Eskimo or Innuit (Aleut) word, meaning Great Country.

[3] Parker, T. Jeffery, and Haswell, William A. *A Textbook of Zoology,* Volume II, The Macmillan Company, 1921, p. 541.

Arizona—From "Arizonac" ("Ari" small and "Zonac" spring) so-called by the Papago and Pima Indians, says State Historian George H. Kelly (1927); and adds: "This state was called Arizona by the Spaniards as early as 1736." A simpler derivation is that given by Prof. John C. Van Dyke in "The Desert," page 208—clipped from "Arida-Zona," meaning the "dry belt."

Arkansas—(Official pronunciation is ar-kan-saw). Algonkin name of the Quapaw Indians.

California—Bestowed by the Spanish Conquistadores, being the name of an imaginary island, near the earthly paradise, in "Las Serges de Esplandian," a romance of chivalry written in the first decade of the 16th century. Another explanation is that the Catalan explorers and missionaries (1769) after long marches in summer near the coast called it the land of oven's heat—"Aixo es calor de forñi de fornalla."

Colorado—Spanish, meaning red.

Columbia, District of—A poetical adoption of the name of Columbus; applied to the territory in 1791 by the Federal Commissioners who laid it out.

Connecticut—Indian, "Quonecktacut," Long River or River of Pines.

Delaware—Named after Lord De la Warr, of England, Governor of Virginia, who entered [4]

Rate of Reading the Four Types of Materials

Some significant facts about speed of reading were disclosed in this experiment. It is interesting to note that every one of the students read the simple story passage from *Lorna Doone* more rapidly than the other types of material. And almost all of them read the passage of factual details about the origin of the names of states and territories more slowly than they did the other materials. For the group as a whole, the rate of reading this factual material was two thirds that of reading the simple story.

[4] Reproduced through the courtesy of *The World Almanac*, 1941, p. 341.

Profile graphs of the rates that the students used in reading the four types of material were prepared. The graphs of the student who read the *Lorna Doone* material at the fastest rate and of the one who read it at the slowest rate are shown in Figure III. Also included in Figure III is a profile of the average rate on each passage. The majority of the students read the four types of materials at different speeds. In other words, most of the students used a differentiated attack to read the different materials. It was a matter of great surprise, however, to find that some read all four of the passages at approximately the same rate. One such profile of a student who failed to differentiate his rate of speed to accord with the difficulty of the material is pictured in Figure III by the dotted line.

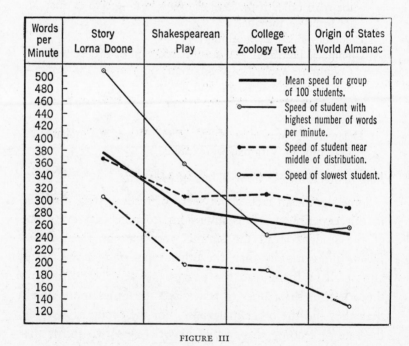

FIGURE III

Graph Showing Reading Rate on Different Types of Material

Comprehension of the Four Types of Materials

As a second phase of the experiment, the students wrote what they remembered of each passage. Their statements of what the passages were about also gave evidence that the students were using a differentiated attack. The statements about the passage from *Lorna Doone* told, in a general way, what the passage was about. They showed that the students were reading to note the general significance of the passage. In writing about the selection from *As You Like It* the majority of the students gave an interpretation which showed that they were reading the material in order to draw inferences. Their discussion of the selection from the zoology text was, for the most part, concerned with an organized presentation of what they had read. The factual reports of the passage about the origin of the names of the states and territories indicated that the students had noted details as they read.

Conclusions and Interpretations

These data bear out to some extent the following:

1. The variation in number of words per minute with which materials may be understandingly read is dependent, in part, upon the difficulty of the material. It seems, however, that there are many high school and college students who have not matured in their reading to the point where they are able to use different rates of speed for materials of different degrees of difficulty. Their reading approximates too closely a generalized rate. Consequently, their comprehension decreases when the material becomes too difficult for them to read understandingly at their generalized rate.

2. The variation in the number of words per minute at which materials may be understandingly read is dependent, in part, upon the general familiarity with the material that the reader

has. As an individual becomes more and more familiar with the material in a specific subject-matter area and gains more and more word and meaning backgrounds, he will be able to read such material with greater ease and at a more rapid speed.

3. It seems also that a student of reading should be taught that, in order to read effectively, he must consciously adjust his reading skills and techniques to the purposes for which he is reading and to the difficulty of the materials he is using to achieve those purposes. He should, for example, adjust his speed of reading to meet the difficulty of the materials. He can and should approach relatively easy material at a much faster reading rate than difficult material. The important consideration is how rapidly he can read and still adequately understand the material.

Adjusting Reading Rate to Suit the Purpose and the Material

Easy material which has few, if any, vocabulary or meaning difficulties can be understood at a relatively high rate of speed. The reader is not obliged to slow down in order to recognize difficult words or to think through difficult concepts. He can afford, therefore, to read such material at a very high rate of speed.

In reading difficult material, on the other hand, it is necessary for the reader to study intently the words which he does not recognize readily and to assemble the meaning backgrounds needed for interpreting a difficult concept. If he approaches such material at a rapid rate, the reader will be forced to skip some important key words or neglect some of the important concepts. Unless he decreases his speed of reading difficult material, he will be unable to comprehend fully what he reads. When the student reads difficult material at a rapid rate, he gets either an incomplete or an erroneous idea of the passage or else no meaning at all. Obviously, then, the student cannot afford to read difficult material at the same rate that he would use in reading simple materials. Therefore, he should adjust his rate of reading to accord with the difficulty he encounters in comprehending the meaning of the passage.

The familiarity of the material to the reader will also determine the speed at which it can be read. Although two students have approximately similar reading ability, the reading material of the various fields, such as biology, history, or philosophy, may represent for each of them different degrees of difficulty. One student, for example, may have had wide experience in the reading of historical materials. He will be familiar with both the terminology and the concepts of that field and will therefore find historical material relatively easy. But if he has done little reading of scientific material, he will be unfamiliar with the terminology and the concepts in this field and will find the material relatively difficult. The other student may have read extensively in the field of science and little in the field of history. He is likely to find the historical material relatively more difficult than the scientific. Therefore, a reader should adjust his rate of reading to accord with his familiarity with the material he is reading.

The purpose also determines the rate at which a passage can and should be read. Certain purposes require a careful, analytical sort of reading; other purposes lend themselves to a more rapid and hurried perusal of the material.

If the purpose of reading is to form a critical analysis of a passage, it is necessary to read carefully and to appraise the concepts. Such reading takes time. The reader must appraise not only the quality and exactness of each idea in respect to his background of knowledge of the topic, but also the relative weights given to the various ideas. He also must determine whether or not all important and related concepts which alter the general conclusion have been included. Such reading should be done slowly and carefully.

If, on the other hand, the purpose is to see whether or not the material is related to a given problem, the passage can be covered in relatively short order. The task here is not determining what is discussed in the passage. The relevance of the material can be determined by isolating and reading a small sampling of the thought units which the passage contains. The value of reading for this purpose is that one can cover the material rapidly. Consequently, it follows that the nature of the purpose alters the rate with which a passage is read.

One of the major responsibilities of the developmental program is to show each individual that he must continuously adjust his rate of reading to meet the demands of both the material and the reading purpose. While it is true for most readers that the desire for adequate understanding of the material controls in some degree the speed at which the student reads, he would probably become a more effective reader if he attempted to keep his speed compatible with the nature of the material and the purpose for which he was reading.

SELECTING THE READING TECHNIQUES TO SUIT THE PURPOSE AND THE MATERIAL

Reading for Different Purposes

The question naturally comes to mind as to whether or not the individual has a number of different "methods of attack" that he may use for different reading purposes and for different types of material. At the present time there is little or no experimental evidence on this question. However, it does seem probable that the reader who has many different reading techniques and skills and many possible combinations of them, would have learned from his many reading experiences to use the techniques and skills in many different groupings.

A good reader works as a good mechanic does. The mechanic is surrounded by innumerable wrenches, pliers, hammers, and drills. To take a tire off a car, he uses one combination of tools; to fix a leak in the gas line, he uses quite another combination. He may use a wrench on both jobs, but one may be much smaller than the other. In order to take the engine head off, some of the same tools may be used, but if so, they will be in a still different combination.

The mechanic has at his command a large number of tools of many sizes and strengths. He selects from his store of tools the appropriate combination. Each tool will be selected of the size, shape, and strength required to accomplish the task at hand. The reader, likewise, has a whole repertory of skills and techniques. For one purpose and one kind of material, the reading skills and techniques and their combination may be quite different from those used in reading for another purpose and for reading material of another kind.

The effective reader may have built up, either consciously or unconsciously, a differentiated attack so that when, for example, he takes *The World Almanac* from the library shelf, he automatically uses an attack suitable to that type of material. He may have another reading method especially suitable for reading modern novels. In other words, some of the effectiveness of a good reader is due to his ability to use his reading techniques and skills in combinations conducive to reading specific materials for specific purposes.

The majority of readers would not read a story like the simplified version of *Lorna Doone* slowly and carefully enough to remember every detail in its proper order. It is conceivable, however, that one who was reading the story for the specific purpose of preparing to tell it to a group of children might read it in just that way. Or, again, it is possible that a teacher of reading who was using the story as material for some immature readers might read the passage slowly, before starting to work with these remedial cases, for the purpose of noting difficult words and concepts. It is frequently true that the techniques an individual uses in reading the same material vary to accord with the purpose for which he is reading.

The reading technique should be well selected to meet the purpose for which the reading is being done. The effective reader selects and assembles those techniques that are appropriate to the tasks at hand.

Let us suppose that the task at hand is to make a comparison of life in the Middle Ages with the life of today. One purpose of reading would be to form an opinion about life in the Middle Ages. In order to do this, the student will need to locate pertinent information. He will then read this material to note the details. Then he will, in drawing his conclusions, continuously use the details noted. Thus, we find that the purpose of this student entails his use of several techniques and a fine balance with at least two of them. The purpose in this case determines the techniques—or better, the combination of techniques—which the reader employs. If the reader does not adjust the techniques carefully to the purpose, his reading will not be effective.

When the individual undertakes a reading task that is new to him or one that represents some added difficulty, he consciously selects and assembles or reassembles the techniques which he feels are suited to the accomplishment of the task. For the most part, the adjustment of the techniques is fairly automatic; but when difficulties are encountered, the process becomes less automatic and the selection of techniques becomes more conscious. This procedure is true of a number of processes. In driving an automobile, for example, the purpose is to get to the destination in safety. The inexperienced driver is aware of all the intricate techniques and skills necessary to driving the car. As he gains experience, the process becomes increasingly automatic. When the driver is thoroughly experienced, driving under usual conditions is almost entirely automatic.

However, when conditions are altered, as when there is ice on the pavement, the experienced driver is immediately aware of the techniques of driving and adjusts them to the changed condition. Again, the experienced driver, when driving through very heavy traffic, finds he must consciously reassemble and readjust his mode of driving to meet the more difficult situation. In reading, when the material becomes more difficult, the reader modifies his hierarchy of techniques, selecting a more analytical and detailed attack upon the material.

Reading Different Types of Material

When there is a change in type of material, the effective reader alters his reading approach to that situation. For example, he does not read a poem in the same way in which he reads a short story. Of course, his purpose in reading both might be to evaluate the material. In both cases he would be likely to skim the material in order to get a general impression of it. Then perhaps he would read for appreciation. But in the case of the short story, the reader might read to note the details of organization, quality, and interest value. And in the case of the poem, he might use oral reading techniques, reading aloud to himself to note the meter and rhythm of the poem as well as the organization, quality, interest value, and meaning. Consequently, in addition to the purpose for which the reading is being done, the nature of the material should suggest to the reader modifications of the reading techniques. It is necessary to help the immature reader select the techniques which are appropriate to the purpose for which he is reading and to the nature of the materials.

REFINING A TECHNIQUE TO MEET THE PURPOSE OR MATERIAL

Different Purposes

Just as it is important for the individual to select a technique to fit his purpose, it is likewise important for him to select the appropriate degree of refinement. By way of illustration let us consider some of the modifications that the individual might make to fit his purpose in the use of one reading technique—reading to organize the material.

In order to simplify the illustration, let us suppose that the passage being read is the quotation from the college zoology textbook, which was used in the experiment described earlier in this chapter; and let us suppose that the individual who is doing the reading is a college student. In this hypothetical illustration three factors—the individual, the material, and the reading technique (reading to organize)—remain the same. The chief variations will be the purpose of the reading on different occasions and the degree of refinement of the reading technique.

First, let us suppose that the individual purposes to read the passage to organize in his mind the facts it contains in such a way that he may understand them and enter into a class discussion of the digestive organs. His organization of the material will very likely be a general one—one that requires only an immature ability to organize.

On another occasion, let us assume that the student intends to organize the material in order to make an oral report to his class upon the subject of digestive organs. This task will require a higher order of ability to organize, since it necessitates a more complete understanding of the subject. In this case the student will organize the material in his mind as he reads, so that the first fact will recall to him the second, and so on. Here the organization of the material will be his own, while on the first occasion the organization, in all probability, was that of the writer of the passage.

On another occasion, the individual may plan to read the material in order to organize it for inclusion in a paper he is preparing on the subject of digestive organs. In this situation the individual will organize the material as he reads it, but he will do so in relation to other materials on the same subject. As he reads the material, he will be organizing it and combining it with materials from the other sources. This will certainly require a higher order of reading ability than was needed on either of the other occasions.

Again, the student may read the passage for the purpose of organizing it in relation to all the material covered during the course as preparation for the final examination. Again the use of the reading technique—reading to organize—is of a different order. This student's purpose may be (and all too frequently is) to read and organize the material so that he may be prepared to answer the specific type or types of questions that his professor is known to include in the examination. This may not be the highest order of organized reading that the student does. Still, combined as it is with some measure of prediction on the part of the student, and motivated as it is with a desire to succeed, it causes the average student on such occasions to do a rather intensive type of reading for the purpose of organizing.

These examples should show how a reader refines a reading technique to harmonize with a reading purpose.

Different Materials

In addition to refining a technique for varying purposes, the reader must also refine it to meet varying degrees of difficulty.

Let us suppose, for example, that the individual in the above illustration, who is reading to organize and prepare the report on digestive organs, is making use of two references. One is a simple, nontechnical presentation, while the other is a highly theoretical and interrelated discussion. The latter would, in all probability, require the greater refinement of ability to organize. It is reasonable to assume that the degree of refinement of a technique which should be employed by the reader is determined by both the purpose for reading and the difficulty of the material he reads.

Summary

The effective reader adjusts his reading to meet the demands of his purpose. This implies that he must use a rate of reading appropriate to his purpose. It also implies that he must select other reading techniques in accordance with his purpose in reading. In addition, he must use the degree of refinement of techniques compatible with his reading purpose. Similar adjustments are necessary as far as materials of varying types and degrees of difficulty are concerned.

It is well to realize that there is a marked interrelationship existing between reading speed, other reading techniques, and the degree of refinement of these techniques. For example, varying purposes require varying rates of speed. Varying refinements of a given technique also are accomplished at varying rates. And, in turn, the speed is determined in no small measure by the specific technique that is being used and by its degree of refinement. *A differentiated attack is the ability to adjust the reading techniques and skills to the purpose at hand and to the difficulty of the materials.*

A combined bibliography for Chapters VII and VIII will be found on pages 195-96.

CHAPTER VIII

DEVELOPMENT OF ABILITY IN READING THE MATERIALS OF THE CONTENT SUBJECTS

The discussion of a differentiated attack in relation to the content fields will be based upon several generalizations which have grown out of material presented in previous chapters. These generalizations are:

Each field of human experience, such as science, social science, and literature, places a unique burden upon the student's reading abilities. Each has its own specialized vocabulary and background of meaning. In addition, the student who reads in any given subject must approach his reading with the purposes requisite for reading in that field. While it is true that there is a degree of overlapping among the reading purposes in various fields, yet it is likewise true that each field stresses certain of these purposes more than it does others. And, too, not all the purposes for reading are required for any one field. The reading techniques and various balances among them are determined, in no small measure, by the specific purpose for which the reading is done. The ability to adjust the various techniques to the purposes and materials is a differentiated reading attack. Since each field sets up its own purposes for reading, and since each has its own reading materials, each content field can contribute markedly to the establishment of a differentiated attack.

The reading of factual prose is the type of reading that is met in the usual academic-subject textbook. The technique used most frequently is that of getting the general significance of the passage. There are many skills and abilities that are useful in reading the textbooks in the various academic subjects. However, in addition, there are required in each content subject specific reading techniques as well. While it is recognized that there is an overlapping, the discussion of reading in any one content subject will consider techniques and purposes typical of many of the reading situations in that subject.

General Procedures Helpful in All Content Fields

The teaching of reading necessary to any one field can probably be most effectively and efficiently taught by the teacher of that field, who is aware of the purposes for which the students are reading and the backgrounds necessary for understanding what they read. Students do most of their reading in connection with problems arising in the content fields. Therefore, the teachers in these subjects are better able to know the day-by-day purposes for which the students are reading than any specialized reading teacher. It follows, then, that every teacher should be concerned with the contributions his field can make to the reading program. In order that the content teacher may enter into the developmental reading program in an effective way, he must be aware of the reading needs of his subject.

Steps in Guiding the Reading of Students

One of the teacher's first steps toward guiding the reading of the students in a content field is to consider how he himself reads for the various purposes in his field. He should, in addition, consider the demands that the materials common to his field make upon his own reading abilities. Undoubtedly he has often considered the vocabulary and meaning backgrounds with which the student must be familiar in order to read within the subject. His interest in and preparation for the teaching of the subject have contributed to his acquisition of wide backgrounds of meaning. And his interest in and preparation for teaching have probably contributed to his becoming an efficient reader of that subject. Very likely, then, he is the one who is most able to teach the student how to do the reading the subject requires.

A second step in guiding the reading of the students within a subject-matter field is to analyze the day-by-day purposes for which the student is reading. In this analysis the teacher should make an appraisal of the reading techniques which can be most effectively used in achieving each purpose. The teacher must envisage himself in each reading situation and determine what techniques he uses in meeting the reading purposes.

The third step in guiding the reading of the student is to show him how he can most effectively read for the purposes at hand. This guidance, based upon the teacher's own experience, will give the student insight into the effective adjustment of his reading techniques. For the majority of students this guidance will be sufficient to develop the degree of differentiation needed to meet the given purpose. A continuous guidance of this sort will effectively aid the student in establishing the differentiated attack needed for the subject.

A fourth step is to appraise the kind of purposes for which each student is an ineffective reader. The teacher should not only show the student how to read more effectively for his purposes, but also give him many opportunities to experience such reading. This entails setting up reading situations which demand the type or types of reading which the student finds difficult. These situations, however, must be so adjusted that the individual may be reasonably prepared to meet them successfully. As a matter of fact, the teacher will find that the general classroom work offers ample situations for developing differentiated reading. It is essential that guidance and instruction in reading be done at the time when they are needed. Students need help in adjusting these reading techniques to meet the new demands which the content subjects are continually making upon them. The very pressure of these demands throws them into a state of confusion, so that they approach their reading, if they are unguided, in inefficient ways.

It can be seen that teachers have a real opportunity, as well as an obligation, to contribute to the knowledge of reading in relationship to content subjects in the high school. It is quite possible for teachers to analyze carefully the reading abilities needed by small units of a given subject, to provide instruction in those abilities, and to measure the outcomes of such instruction

Motivating Voluntary Reading

Effective reading in any content subject is dependent upon the interest that is developed in the materials of that subject. Well-formulated procedures designed to stimulate the students to read widely in any content field have been productive of results. It is the responsibility of each teacher to encourage the reading within his field. The following teaching procedures have been used with more or less success in all the content subjects to motivate voluntary reading.

1. *Calling attention to passages, chapters, or books.* Few indeed are the students who have not been motivated to read and enjoy books to which their attention has been directed by enthusiastic readers. Teachers have used many ways of bringing material to the attention of their students.

One such method is frequent reference to books in class. New books are brought into class and displayed. Brief selections are read either by a member of the class or by the teacher. A brief résumé may be given either by a student or by the teacher. Books upon a specific topic of interest to a group or an individual are recommended. Students are encouraged to suggest readings to one another and also to be able to state what in the material prompted them to make the suggestion.

2. *Calling attention to pictorial and tabular materials.* Interest in a book or passage can be stimulated by showing its pictorial illustrations. A discussion of tabular materials leads to reading the verbal content relating to them. For example, a statement of the relative position of a city in the "Goodness" Table of Cities contained in Thorndike's *Your City* is sufficient to motivate many listeners to read the entire book.

3. *Calling attention to current materials.* Material pertinent to topics under consideration in various subjects is appearing daily in newspapers and magazines. Reference to current materials leads students to be alert to them. The teacher who puts newspaper and magazine clippings on the bulletin board soon finds it necessary to take them down in order to make room for materials the students have clipped and brought to class. Response of this kind indicates the extent of voluntary reading of current materials that the students are doing.

4. *Calling attention to the presentations of a topic by two or more authors.* Students may be led to read and evaluate discussions of a topic by more than one writer. It is important for high school students to realize that there are differences in points of view, in moods, in prejudices, as well as in purposes and that the reader should analyze the statements in the light of such factors when comparing and critically evaluating two or more presentations of a topic. They should learn that there is much to be gained by reading several points of view. Comparing the editorial comment about a current happening in two newspapers whose editorial policies are different helps a

student sense how unlike the same facts may appear when the writers' purposes are unlike. A comparison of the presentation of a battle in the War between the States in a history textbook used in a Pennsylvania high school with that in a textbook used in an Alabama high school helps a student sense the way in which a writer's point of view colors his presentation of a topic.

There is today a constant and continuous bombardment of the adult through sight and sound communication processes wherein divergent and contradictory points of view are expressed. One minute a sponsored radio program tells him one thing; the next minute from another program he hears something quite different. Totally contradictory, too, are two advertisements in the magazine an individual thumbs through as he listens to the radio. In a world where nonprofit-making institutions, such as schools, churches, and governments, as well as profit-making ones, such as corporate and individual enterprises, deliberately make use of propaganda techniques to mold public opinion, human beings need to develop an ability to evaluate and weigh the words they hear and see. Training in reading critically and in formulating opinions prepares the student to solve his social and personal problems. Such training should be given by teachers in each of the content subjects. An understanding of the need for reading several presentations of a topic obviously makes for more extended reading.

5. *Encouraging discussion, reports, and debates.* Participation in panel and informal discussions in the classroom motivates students to read widely on the subject under discussion. Such participation is very worth while. The student gets experience in locating pertinent information, in reading, evaluating, and organizing it, and in verbalizing it. For the same reasons, student debates and reports are activities produc-

tive of learning in the various content fields. There are few other classroom activities which will encourage reading as much as these.

Many teachers have found that clubs, such as science clubs, current events clubs, literary clubs, debating clubs, develop new reading activities and expand reading interests. Such clubs are especially effective at the high school level because the adolescent student enjoys these types of group activities. The reading situations growing out of club activities set up purposes that are very real to the student and result in noticeable gains in reading.

6. *Formulating problems that require reading.* The formulation of problems, rather than the assignment of a definite body of reading, makes for more worth-while and extensive reading on the part of students. The teacher's responsibility is threefold: (1) he must make the classroom situations such that the students have an opportunity and an incentive for formulating their own problems; (2) he must guide the students toward the selection of problems that are of intrinsic worth and, at the same time, aid in extending reading experiences; (3) he should, upon occasion, take the initiative in assigning specific problems that lead the students into areas of new interests.

READING IN THE SOCIAL STUDIES

The authors of this book agree with the thesis set forth by Horn in the following quotation; namely, that the teaching of reading is an important responsibility that must be accepted by the teacher of social studies and in the social studies class:

> So intimately is reading bound up with learning in the social studies that inferior reading ability on the part of students who have completed courses in these fields is clear

evidence of the slovenliness of the teaching of the subjects themselves. For the efficient teaching of the social studies requires, and to a considerable extent will develop, all of the four main types of abilities indispensable to the efficient use of references: (1) the location of information; (2) the understanding, appraisal, and selection of data; (3) the organization of what is read, especially when several sources are used; and (4) the provision for future use. ... When the students' efforts are frustrated by poor reading ability, the teacher cannot use part of the class period in social studies more profitably than in the removal of these disabilities. Both evidence and common sense indicate that time thus spent, far from detracting from scholarship, increases accomplishment in the subject itself. This is to be expected, for as the student grows in his ability to read, his study becomes more effective.

That one cannot depend upon the ordinary teaching of social studies to develop the reading abilities essential to accomplishment in these subjects is indicated by the fact that students who have completed both the elementary and secondary courses in these fields have, on the average, a rather low level of reading ability. Even teachers who are otherwise superior often fail to give as much attention as they should to this important aspect of their work. Special periods are therefore useful not only to serve as a reminder of the importance of such skills but also to practice them intensively. These periods may be set aside out of the time assigned to the social studies or they may have a separate place in the program. In either case, the exercises should be closely integrated with the work in the social studies; that is, they should be motivated by needs made apparent in the social studies class, and such abilities as are developed should be immediately reapplied. When related in this manner and when properly conducted, these special periods bring about a steady improvement of all of the reading involved in learning the social studies.[1]

[1] Horn, Ernest. *Methods of Instruction in the Social Studies,* Charles Scribner's Sons, 1937, pp. 202-5.

Difficulties that students have in reading social studies materials include:

1. *Difficulties of vocabulary.* Students should have many contacts with a word in order that they may be prepared to read it understandingly in various settings. The students should at all times be aware that they are building a social-scientific vocabulary. They should be taught to use word recognition techniques so that they will be able to work out the meaning of new words. After a new word has been recognized and understood in its setting, the student should make use of it in other settings.

2. *Difficulties of specialized meanings.* Such specialized meanings of words as "taking the fort by *storm*" and *"grants* of land" are encountered in the printed materials of the social sciences sufficiently often to cause difficulty. Students soon learn that there may be many connotations of any one word and that an individual never completes the adding of specialized meanings of words to his knowledge of them. Extensive reading of social studies materials enables one to build a background of understanding of the vocabulary used in them.

3. *Difficulties due to contractions.* Many of the ideas discussed in books on the social studies are presented in so condensed a form that they can be understood only by an individual who already has a fairly complete understanding of the ideas. Sometimes the contraction difficulty is due to the fact that too many ideas are said in too few words. At other times the difficulty results from a complex idea being presented too briefly. Again, extensive reading is a cure for the difficulty. In such cases it is profitable for the students to study various phases of the problem or problems and to pool the learnings they have acquired individually in their class discussions. Such poolings of learnings should help to broaden the understanding of each member of the class group.

4. *Difficulties of ideas.* As Horn has pointed out, "many of the data of history, geography, and other social studies are far removed from the experiences of the students."[2] And yet, "ideas must be built by the student out of the materials of his experience."[2] Consequently, "the gap between the experience of the child and the realities that he is expected to understand is so wide that it can be bridged only with great difficulty."[2] The teacher and students co-operatively must build up the background necessary for understanding the ideas, however difficult. Suggestions for building a background of understanding are given in Chapter V.

5. *Difficulties of sentence length.* Sometimes a complex sentence is the easiest way of expressing a complex idea. Since inevitably there are complex ideas in social science materials, it follows that students must learn how to read complex sentences understandingly. When students are taught to read from the standpoint of meaningful reading, they do not find long complex sentences difficult to understand.

6. *Difficulties of abstraction.* Social studies materials are filled with abstractions, such as those represented by the words *mobs, society, relationship.* The introduction of abstract concepts should be gradual. By means of class discussions, concrete illustrations, and collateral reading, such abstractions gradually come to be understood.

7. *Problems of organization.* Each of the social studies is organized in a sequential way. Just as textbook writers and curriculum makers have problems of selection, elimination, and organization in building up their presentations of any one subject, so does a student have difficulty in organizing his knowledge of it. Strang has stated that in reading history materials—

[2] Horn, Ernest. *Methods of Instruction in the Social Studies,* Charles Scribner's Sons, 1937, p. 130.

Students can be taught to read history as an account of the evolution of ideas and institutions, to see cause-and-effect relationships, and to detect erroneous statements and implications. They should seek to discover how the present grew out of the past and how various persons and forces have influenced the "shape of things to come." [3]

The learning of the student should proceed in an orderly fashion so that he may build up a systematic, scientific background of knowledge.

8. *Difficulties of reading critically.* Critical reading calls for a weighing and evaluating of the statements in the passage in the light of what the reader has read and knows about the subject. Frequently students read materials from the social studies critically just as they do other scientific materials in order to formulate an opinion as to the authoritativeness and accuracy of them. The task of evaluating the several collateral readings of a course unit, when such critical reading is both demanded and taught by the teacher, enables students to grow in the ability to read critically.

9. *Difficulties in locating material.* Students have difficulty in locating materials pertinent to a topic in the social studies just as they do in other subject-matter areas. As was pointed out in Chapter IV, the ability to locate information is made up of a hierarchy of reading skills, including the use of such helps as card catalogues, encyclopedias, indexes, and tables of contents. McKee believes that the most effective means by which the ability to locate information can be improved lies in the manner of teaching the content subjects. He states further:

History, elementary science, geography, and hygiene should be taught in such a way that the pupil is required to

[3] Strang, Ruth. *Improvement of Reading in High School and College,* The Science Press Printing Company, 1938, p. 110.

locate information if he succeeds in realizing his assignments. The procedure in teaching these subjects should
require him to use the index, the table of contents, footnotes, and all the important printed parts of a book, as well
as many different books, rather than a single text. In the
higher grades it may well involve the use of the library card
file, and, in fact, to a more or less degree, all suitable and
appropriate sources of information if such are available.[4]

Adults, constantly confronted with problems of living in
our society, are continually grateful for having learned the
reading abilities which make it possible for them to solve such
problems. One contribution of lasting value that a course in
social studies may make to a student is that of building techniques of locating information about a topic in which he is
interested. The tendency to assign the next ten pages in a
textbook does not enable the student to grow in ability to
locate information. Opportunities should be provided that
will cause the students to gain experience in using reference
materials in the social studies from both the school library
and other available libraries.

10. *Difficulties in reading maps, graphs, and other pictorial
materials.* The reading of maps is an integral part of courses
in history and geography. Bowman has said:

Maps are a kind of shorthand description of the earth,
a way of looking at distant places "as if they were on the
palm of your hand" as a Chinese map maker has put it.[5]

Included on maps are many symbols that the student must
learn to read if the maps are to have meaning for him. He
must be taught how to read maps and other pictorial materials

[4] McKee, Paul. *Reading and Literature in the Elementary School,* Houghton
Mifflin Company, 1934, p. 373.
[5] Bowman, Isaiah. *Geography in Relation to the Social Sciences,* Charles Scribner's
Sons, 1934, p. 2.

just as he must be taught to read the more verbal materials in the social studies. Discussions of the reading of pictorial materials are included in Chapters IV and IX.

READING IN LITERATURE

The fundamental purposes of teaching literature, as stated by McKee, are:

1. to enable the child to re-experience what the poem or prose selection has to tell, and to extend and enrich his experiences; and
2. to develop proper tastes and permanent interests in good literature.[6]

The latter purpose, that of developing proper tastes and permanent interests in the subject-matter area, is a fundamental purpose of every subject in the curriculum. As has been stated in Chapter VI, wide reading of material appropriate to his reading level develops and extends the reading interests of the individual. When a passage, chapter, or book in which a student is interested is so easy that it can be read without difficulty, the student is more likely to complete it and additional reading as well. New interests gained from such reading stimulate more reading, which reading in turn broadens and strengthens the newly gained interests.

It is unfortunate that material in high school courses of study in English is oftentimes unsuitable. As stated by Gates:

Much of the material, especially in the upper grades and high school, is unsuitable in two respects. It is altogether too difficult. It is also unsuitable in substance; it would capture little interest even if it could be understood. It is literature suitable not for boys and girls with I.Q.'s from 80 to 110—a range including about 80 per cent of those

[6] McKee, Paul. *Reading and Literature in the Elementary School*, Houghton Mifflin Company, 1934, p. 515.

struggling with it; not for adults within this range of intellect; not indeed for the typical adult of higher intelligence, even those who are graduates of Yale and Vassar, but for a select list of literary specialists. It was about 50 years ago when a group of such specialists selected a list of classics judged to be good for youth in school. They were profoundly wrong in their judgment, but amazingly potent in their ability to secure followers to support their errors for a half century. Some of their disciples, even now, are so convinced of the infallibility of this classical tradition that they would rather throw two-thirds of the pupils out of school than toss two-thirds of the chosen classics out of the course of study. I am convinced, however, that this doughty group, clasping the Atlantic Monthly to their breasts as shields, are soon to be put to rout.[7]

Many teachers of English have found that it is possible to create and maintain in their students the desire to read books voluntarily. At times the voluntary choices of some of the students include poorly written, sensational types of material. But under wise guidance the students learn to select more worthy materials and develop a prejudice against cheap writing. Reading is encouraged when a wide range of materials—varied both as to reading difficulty and as to content—is easily accessible. Among the methods that have proved successful in stimulating wide reading are: book-club days, periodic panel discussions, reading clubs, book reviews. Students, thus challenged, explore widely topics of interest, formulate judgments, and participate in give-and-take discussions. Cumulative records of books read during each month of the year stimulate extensive reading in a class group.

Certain difficulties in enabling the student to re-experience what the poem or prose selection has to tell are at once appar-

[7] Gates, Arthur I. "Intelligence and Artistry in Teaching Reading." Reprinted from *The Elementary School Review*, April, 1940, by special permission. Copyright, 1940, C. C. Certain.

ent. McKee, in discussing this purpose of teaching literature, says:

> The approach to literature must never be analytical or critical. Such attacks destroy experience-getting. Instead it must be a creative activity in which the child puts past experience together to feel what the author has to tell, and in which there is a sympathetic sharing of experience.[8]

The student must learn to form sensory impressions of the experiences related in the material. He must see the pictures, hear the sounds, feel the temperatures and movements, experience the tastes and smells that are described. Whatever blocks such reliving is harmful and should be eliminated if permanent interests in good literature are to be created.[9] From his meaning background the reader selects and recombines experiences that enable him to understand and appreciate the beauty and meaning of the prose or poem. The understanding and appreciation of the reader whose background of experience is barren will be correspondingly barren. For an understanding of material of whatever sort, the reader must have had experiences or knowledges that are related to its content.

The types of reading abilities used in a literature class are, thus, quite different from those used in a class in science, in social science, or in mathematics. In a general science class, for example, the student reads frequently in an analytical and critical fashion. He reads also for the purpose of getting information to remember. In a literature class, on the contrary, the reading is done for appreciation and for sheer enjoyment. Analytical, factual reading destroys the beauty of the experience. One would not read the following stanza, analyzing

[8] McKee, Paul. *Reading and Literature in the Elementary School,* Houghton Mifflin Company, 1934, pp. 517-18.
[9] Ibid., p. 517.

thoroughly the facts presented in order that their accuracy might be appraised and, if judged correct, remembered:

Elegy

The Curfew tolls the knell of parting day,
The lowing herd wind slowly o'er the lea,
The plowman homeward plods his weary way,
And leaves the world to darkness and to me.

THOMAS GRAY

Rather he would see the pictures, feel the movement, hear the sounds. He might read it orally or to himself to appreciate its beauty. He might not wish to remember and organize the facts contained in it, but rather to remember it as a whole so that he could recall it at will to re-enjoy and re-experience it or simply to remember that it provided a pleasing emotional experience.

When the junior and senior high school students reach adulthood, the reading experiences in the field of literature of the majority of them will be recreational. Such matters as style, structure, development of plot and theme and character-ization will concern them little or not at all. Consequently, in the reading of literature during their school days, such matters should receive little time and attention. Instead, the emphasis should be upon enabling students to re-experience what the selections have to tell.

The task of a teacher of literature is a difficult one. As Gates has written:

> To enrich and enliven literature for a boy or girl with-out disturbing the free spirit of a recreational enterprise is a difficult and subtle art. . . . To add to the understand-ing and enjoyment of literature as the musicians and actors in an opera increase the significance and appeal of the li-bretto—this should be the accepted objective of the teacher

of literature. That this requires effort and talent cannot be denied. Is there any real job for the teacher of literature? In my opinion, no assignment in the entire school curriculum calls for more intelligence and artistry than the teaching of reading and literature.[10]

READING IN MATHEMATICS

Reading mathematical materials requires, among others, the following abilities: noting details and weighing them, following directions, and organizing factual contents and drawing inferences from them. Comprehending such materials demands careful reading. In other words, such reading must be slow and interpretative.

Students who have not yet learned to attack such materials slowly must be taught to do so. They will find it expedient from time to time to pause in their reading in order to relate previous material to that which is being read, and to predict what will follow. A student must learn to differentiate his reading speed so that he consciously uses a rate that enables him to comprehend fully what he is reading.

Work-study reading techniques are among those most highly related to achievement in mathematical subjects. The teacher of mathematics should contribute to the developmental reading growth of his students by training them in these techniques. At the same time he will be helping his students read the materials of the course. Students trained in the use of work-study reading techniques will be better prepared to achieve in the mathematics course itself.

Difficulties that students encounter in reading mathematical materials include:

1. *Difficulties of vocabulary.* Included in mathematical materials are words and meanings of words unique to those

---

[10] Gates, Arthur I. "Intelligence and Artistry in Teaching Reading," *The Elementary English Review*, Vol. XVII, No. 4, p. 162.

materials. While it is true that a mathematical term has precisely one meaning in that science, it may be used with other meanings elsewhere. Students must learn the precise meanings of such words in order to understand mathematical materials. For example, the italicized words and expressions in the following sentence illustrate the difficulties of mathematical terminology:

The *squares* of the *periodic times* of the several planets *vary* as the *cubes* of their *mean distances* from the sun.

In order to read this sentence with understanding, the student must know that in it the *periodic time* of a planet is the time it takes the planet to make one revolution, that *vary* means that the squares of the periodic times of any two are directly proportional to the cubes of their mean distance from the sun, and that *mean distance* means the average of all distances from the sun at each position it occupies while making the revolution. When this sentence is put into algebraic language it means

$$\frac{T_1^2}{T_2^2} = \frac{D_1^3}{D_2^3}$$

where T_1 is the periodic time of one planet and D_1 is the mean distance of this planet, and where T_2 is the periodic time of the other planet and D_2 is its mean distance. Writing the sentence in the equation form is like following directions. They both need the same kind of careful reading.

Context clues will be of little value in getting the meaning of the *italicized* words from the rest of the sentence, and unless the relationship is understood the sentence cannot be written in the equational or shorthand language illustrated above. The word *vary* cannot be understood unless there is direct instruction through introducing the word in many precise and concrete situations. It is the task of the student with the aid of his teacher gradually to build the mathematical vocabulary needed and the ability to see the relationship in the statements read.

2. *Difficulties due to giving the wrong word the preponderance in a sentence.* Students fail sometimes to read and, consequently, to do correctly a problem in arithmetic because they fasten their attention upon some one word in a problem and give it undue weight. This reading difficulty is illustrated by the following problem:

> In the blank spaces write the result of each of the four fundamental operations on the numbers 2 and *10*.

This problem was given to a group of one hundred college students. Thirty-eight per cent of these teachers-in-training responded to the words *four fundamental operations* rather than to *result*. Their answers were either $+ - \times \div$ or *add, subtract, multiply, divide* rather than *12 8 20 5*. It is evident that these students failed to weigh the words properly as they read the problem. Inaccurate reading of this type and similar types explains a large number of inaccurate solutions to arithmetical problems.

3. *Difficulties due to failure to distinguish between relevant and irrelevant facts.* In solving problems, students undertake to use all the numbers given in them even when some of the numbers are extraneous to the solutions. It is not necessary to know the son's age to solve the following problem; yet the answers many students obtain in solving it indicate that they fail to realize the irrelevancy:

> A father can dig a ditch in 20 days. His 12-year-old son can only do one half as much as the father. How many days will the assistance of the son cut down the time required by the father?

One teacher of mathematics, when his students give answers that indicate the use of irrelevant facts, shows the students how he reads problems. His procedure in reading a problem is to:

a. Read it through rapidly to get a general impression.

b. Read it to put the facts in the proper relation one to another.

c. Read it again to check the organization of the interrelationships.

4. *Difficulties due to failure to include all the necessary steps.* Sometimes the failure to include all the necessary steps in solving a problem is due to the fact that the student skips over pertinent material in reading the problem. When questioned, students are likely to say, "I did not see that statement when I read the problem." Specific drill in reading problems is helpful. Answering questions such as the following gives the student training in reading arithmetical problems: (1) What facts are stated in the problem? (2) What question or questions does the problem ask? (3) What arithmetical operation must be used in doing the first step of the problem? (4) What steps are needed for its solution? (5) What approximately should the answer be? At other times, of course, failure to include all the necessary steps is due to lack of understanding the mathematical processes involved.

5. *Difficulties due to the wrong mind-set when reading a problem.* If, for example, the word *of* has been used in several successive problems to mean *times,* students are likely to continue to read the *times* meaning of it when some other connotation is needed. Thus, six per cent *of* 120 means .06 *times* 120, while in the statement "the sum of 20 and 26 is 46," the word *of* does not imply multiplication. Yet frequently students use the former meaning of the word *of* when asked to find the sum of two numbers. Experience in reading to note and weigh details overcomes this difficulty.

6. *Difficulties due to inability to relate pictorial, tabular, and verbal materials.* One must be able to read pictorial and tabular materials before he can be expected to get meaning from them. One must know how to get the meaning from the verbal materials that discuss the pictorial or tabular material. But that is not all. In addition, one must be able to relate the verbal material with the pictorial or tabular, or both. Geometry, statistics, and other mathematical subjects call for high ability in all three of these types of reading. Training in preparing pictorial material from its tabular or verbal presentations helps students to relate the three. It is also helpful to prepare discussions of the meaning of tabular or graphic materials. Exercises in matching verbal material with its graphic or tabular presentations enable students to learn to relate one with the other.

7. *Difficulties due to failure to relate previous material to that being read.* In developmental subjects, such as geometry, later lessons grow out of earlier ones. Failure to understand the earlier lessons makes the reading of later ones well nigh impossible. Consider the following theorem:

> Two triangles are congruent if three sides of one are equal respectively to the three sides of the other.

The proof of this theorem can be read understandingly only by a reader who has understood the postulates and the proofs of the preceding theorems.

READING IN SCIENCE

The study of the sciences can make a distinctive contribution to the development of reading skills. Reading scientific materials requires, among others, the abilities to use a specific vocabulary, to locate materials, to note details, to see relations, to organize facts, and to form generalizations. All the preceding skills require slow, careful, and critical reading. As instruction progresses, the teacher from time to time will find it expedient to give the students training and practice in the reading abilities needed for performing a specific problem or for reading a specific unit of work.

Difficulties encountered in reading high school science materials, in addition to some already discussed in the sections on mathematics and the social studies, include:

1. *Difficulties of vocabulary.* One of the objectives of the science courses in high school is to build a scientific vocabulary. Much of the time and effort of students and teachers is used in achieving this objective. This is as it should be since scientific materials use many words in other senses than they connote elsewhere. In physics, for example, the word *force* is used to mean that which is capable of doing work, as in the sentence, "The *force* needed to run a washing machine is 250 watts." In biology the word *culture* has a meaning that is far different from that used in the social studies. While the meaning of each word of the terminology of each science is precise for that science, this very precision requires that a sufficient vocabulary be built for each science.

While it is probably true that high school textbooks in science should be so written that the vocabulary burden would be far less than it is at present, yet until they are so written the students should be given every opportunity to read present scientific materials. Technical words that are needed should be meaningfully defined and explained. New terms should be introduced slowly so that the students continuously increase their vocabulary.

2. *Difficulties due to inability to locate materials.* One of the objectives of science teaching is to develop a scientific attitude in students. Encouraging them to ascertain, by carefully consulting several authorities, what propositions are facts and

to base their conclusions on known facts will aid in developing this attitude. Accordingly, the need for extensive reading of scientific materials is evident. It is also apparent that the students need the means through which the evidence concerning a given proposition can be located.

The bare knowledge of the mechanics of using dictionaries, encyclopedias, indexes, etc., while essential, is not sufficient to enable a student to locate scientific information rapidly and effectively. He needs, in addition to the foregoing knowledge, an understanding of the sorts of reference materials that are most reliable for science. He must be shown the sources that the teacher has found to be helpful in locating scientific information. Then the student should be given practice in using these sources in his problems and his topics for study.

When a student brings items of interest to the attention of the class, or when he reports his findings on a given topic, often it will be helpful to the whole class to have him tell how and where he located his information. Such a practice strengthens the ability of the students to locate information independently. The current policy of requiring the pupils to read "the next ten pages" of a textbook does not put the needed premium on the ability to locate information, nor does it give any practice in doing so. While there is a place for a systematically organized textbook in the study of any science in the high school, there is an essential need for wider and more independent reading.

3. *Difficulties due to inability to follow directions.* A laboratory manual in any of the sciences presents the difficulty of reading to follow directions. The description of an experiment must be read slowly and thoughtfully so that the sequential order of the steps described may be followed step by step. For example, note the careful reading which the following instructions for a laboratory experiment entail:

a. Place about 3 c.c. of clear barium hydroxide solution in the bottom of a clean beaker and leave it exposed to the air for half an hour or more (?). Barium hydroxide $Ba(OH)_2$ behaves towards carbon dioxide like limewater, but, being more soluble than calcium hydroxide, its solution is more concentrated and a more copious precipitate can be obtained. Explain the result, and write the equation for the action.

b. Blow air from the lungs through a straight tube into 5 c.c. of limewater (?).

c. Fill two bottles with water and invert them in the trough. By means of a tube, fill one with air from the lungs immediately after drawing a breath. Fill the other with air after the lungs have been almost emptied. Slip a glass plate under each bottle and set both upright on the table. Light a taper and plunge it into one bottle and then into the other. Explain the result.[11]

4. *Difficulties due to failure to read formulas fully.* The formula—

$$NaNO_3 + KCl \rightleftarrows KNO_3 + NaCl$$

means: one molecule of sodium nitrate when mixed with one molecule of potassium chloride will form a molecule of potassium nitrate and a molecule of sodium chloride, and the process is reversible. That is, it is in equilibrium. In order to read materials in the sciences, the student must learn how to work out the meaning of many different formulas. Teachers of science and mathematics must teach this reading skill and must provide their students with many experiences in reading formulas.

5. *Difficulties due to failure to note essential details.* The understanding of scientific materials requires careful, exact, and thorough study. Every detail of such material needs to

[11] Kendall, James. *A Laboratory Outline of General Chemistry,* D. Appleton-Century Company, 1927, p. 89.

be noted, weighed, and either rejected as not being essential or retained as being necessary for understanding the concept under consideration. Such reading cannot be done hurriedly. If accuracy is to be maintained, it must be done slowly and thoughtfully.

Swenson [12] found that as the difficulty of scientific material increased, unless the speed of reading was appropriately decreased, the accuracy of reading was impaired. Scientific material is among the most difficult that the high school student is expected to read. So, if accuracy is to be maintained (and it is essential that accuracy be maintained in reading science), rapid reading is neither to be expected nor desired. This does not mean, however, that the student should be allowed to become an indolent reader, but that he should make a vigorous effort to read accurately and only as rapidly as is compatible with the accurate noting and appraising of the essential detail.

6. *Difficulties due to inability to see relations among facts and from them formulate accurate generalizations.* The reading of scientific materials entails more than the retention of facts relevant to a given concept and the rejection of others. It includes also the ability to see the relationships among the related facts and through their relationships to form a tentative generalization. It includes also the ability to check the reasonableness of the generalization by relating it to the reader's firsthand experiences and to his previous reading.

Difficulties in formulating accurate generalizations often result from accepting conclusions that the facts do not justify. The tendency to reach a conclusion on insufficient data, to neglect to take into account the underlying assumptions, or to allow prejudices to color an interpretation of facts results in a faulty generalization.

[12] Swenson, Esther. "The Relation of Ability to Read Material of the Type Used in Studying Science to Eighth Grade Achievement," unpublished master's thesis, Graduate School, University of Minnesota, Minneapolis, Minnesota, 1938.

Another difficulty in reading to generalize results from the failure to generalize when a generalization is tenable. The student should be taught to look for relationships and to arrive at a generalized conclusion whenever possible. While he should avoid overgeneralizing, he should know that the facts of science can be remembered in a functional fashion when they are a part of his generalized knowledge.

Extensive reading of scientific material for the purpose of clarifying definite concepts of importance to a student will aid him to develop this highly important but troublesome ability. The students of a class will be helped by discussions of the merits of generalizations and of the possible weaknesses.

Summary

Various teaching procedures that have been used with more or less success in all the content subjects to motivate voluntary reading were discussed.

Difficulties students have in reading social studies materials include difficulties of vocabulary; of specialized meanings; of contractions; of ideas; of sentence length; of abstractions; of organization; of reading critically; in locating materials; in reading maps, graphs, and other pictorial materials. Suggestions were made for overcoming these difficulties.

The teacher of literature is primarily interested in enabling the child to re-experience what the poem or prose selection has to tell, to extend and enrich his experiences, and to develop proper tastes and permanent interests in good literature. These fundamental purposes were discussed.

Difficulties students encounter in reading mathematical materials include difficulties of vocabulary; giving the wrong word the preponderance in a sentence; failure to distinguish between relevant and irrelevant facts; failure to include all the necessary steps in solving a problem; having the wrong mind-set when reading a problem; inability to relate pictorial, tabular, and verbal materials; failure to relate previous materials to that being read. Exercises and procedures for overcoming these difficulties were presented.

The following difficulties encountered in reading science material were discussed and suggestions made for overcoming them: difficulties due to vocabulary, inability to locate materials, inability to follow directions, failure to read formulas fully, failure to note essential details, inability to see relations among facts and from them formulate accurate generalizations.

SELECTED BIBLIOGRAPHY

Blank, K. J. "Improving Reading in Biology," *School Science and Mathematics,* Vol. XXXII, November, 1932, pp. 889-92.

Bond, Elden. "Tenth-Grade Abilities and Achievements," *Contributions to Education,* No. 813, Bureau of Publications, Teachers College, Columbia University, 1940.

Bond, Eva. "Reading and Ninth Grade Achievement," *Contributions to Education,* No. 756, Bureau of Publications, Teachers College, Columbia University, 1938.

Bowman, Isaiah. *Geography in Relation to the Social Sciences,* Charles Scribner's Sons, 1934.

Gates, Arthur I. "Intelligence and Artistry in Teaching Reading," *Elementary English Review,* Vol. XVII, April, 1940, pp. 133-38.

Horn, Ernest. *Methods of Instruction in the Social Studies,* Charles Scribner's Sons, 1937.

Jacobson, Paul B. "The Effect of Work-Type Reading Instruction Given in the Ninth Grade," *School Review,* Vol. XL, April, 1932, pp. 273-81.

Leggitt, Dorothy. "Measuring Progress in Working Skills in Ninth-Grade Civics," *School Review,* Vol. XLII, November, 1934, pp. 676-87.

Lyman, L. R. "The Enrichment of the English Curriculum," *University of Chicago Monographs,* No. 39, January, 1932.

McCallister, James M. "Determining the Types of Reading in Studying

Content Subjects," *School Review,* Vol. XL, February, 1932, pp. 115-23.

McCallister, James M. "Reading Difficulties in Studying Content Subjects," *The Elementary School Journal,* Vol. XXXI, November, 1930, pp. 191-201.

McCallister, James M. *Remedial and Corrective Instruction in Reading,* D. Appleton-Century Company, 1936, Chapters 11-15.

McKee, Paul. *Reading and Literature in the Elementary School,* Houghton Mifflin Company, 1934.

Shores, J. H. "The Ability to Read Historical Materials as Related to Eighth-Grade Achievement and General Reading Abilities," unpublished master's thesis, Graduate School, University of Minnesota, 1938.

Shores, J. H. "Reading and Study Skills as Related to Comprehension of Science and History in the Ninth Grade," unpublished doctor's thesis, Graduate School, University of Minnesota, 1940.

Simon, Donald L. "Developing Desirable Reading Habits in Studying Citizenship," *School Review,* Vol. XLII, June, 1934, pp. 447-58.

Strang, Ruth, and Rose, F. C. *Problems in the Improvement of Reading in High School and College,* Revised, The Science Press Printing Company, 1940.

Swenson, Esther. "The Relation of Ability to Read Material of the Type Used in Studying Science to Eighth-Grade Achievement," unpublished master's thesis, Graduate School, University of Minnesota, 1938.

Tinker, Miles A. "The Relation of Speed to Comprehension in Reading," *School and Society,* Vol. XXXVI, July 30, 1932, pp. 158-60.

Wesley, Edgar B. *Teaching the Social Studies,* D. C. Heath and Company, 1937, pp. 194-95.

CHAPTER IX

DEVELOPMENT OF INDEPENDENCE IN READING

A TRIP TO THE LIBRARY

Let's listen to the conversation of three members of a ninth-grade group, known to one of the writers, as they enter their classroom.

Charles: "We're going to build a tennis court in our side yard this spring. Then we won't have to sit around all the time waiting for a court. We can play on our own court any time we want to. While we're in the library this period, I'm going to find out how big a court should be and how to make it. What are you going to do, Harold?"

Harold: "I have some words to look up. I found them in this book. If I get that done in time, I'm going to get another book about Buffalo Bill. Boy, if you haven't read this one, you ought to! There's an Indian fight on every page!"

Robert: "Maybe we'll see where Buffalo Bill was buried when we go on our trip to California this summer. We're going to go right after school is out. That's what I want to do this morning—find out some interesting things we can see on the way. I think it's a good idea to read about the country before you go through it, don't you? It makes the trip more interesting. I'm going to find out how far it is between the places we want to stay all night, too."

That day a trip to the library had been planned for the reading period. The practice of devoting two periods a week to the improvement of reading techniques and skills had been inaugurated in the school attended by the pupils mentioned above. Most of the students had entered wholeheartedly into the project because they were eager to improve their reading. Already there were many evidences of improvement. The knowledge that they were becoming abler readers inspired them to increase their reading skill still further. In the previous reading period, it had been agreed that each student would spend the time in the library, using reference books for the purpose of locating information about something in which he was interested.

This special library period had been arranged to enable the teacher to observe the students as they used reference materials and to appraise informally the ability of each to locate information; but primarily the teacher wished to find out how independently each student could do his reference work.

Before the group passed to the library, the teacher was pleased to learn that most of the students had well-defined reading purposes. That fact showed that the students were achieving a certain amount of independence and that their reading interests, too, were being increased and stimulated. Although the teacher knew that many of the pupils were much too dependent upon the help of someone else, he hoped that from his observations that hour he would learn how they, both as individuals and as a group, might improve their habits of independence.

The Librarian Co-operates

The librarian planned to co-operate by observing how the members of the class used reference materials. She sought to find indications of dependence or independence in the different phases of reference work. Her observations were recorded on a sheet of paper. At the end of the day, she gave her record to the classroom teacher so that the latter might have her impressions of the developmental level of independent reading of the various members of the class.

As the librarian waited for the group to come to the library, she recalled some of the reading techniques she had seen used in previous years. She knew that the new school-wide developmental reading experiment was enabling the students to make a fuller and better use of the library than was true in former years. She felt that not only were the students using the school library to advantage, but that they were also building the types of reading habits that would enable them to use more fully the library facilities the city offered.

One of the incidents the librarian recalled was the time she had watched Ruth, a ninth-grade girl, look up several words in the dictionary. Ruth had stood before a standard, unabridged dictionary. First, she had looked at the word at the top of the page and noted the first letter; then she had gone through the dictionary, page by page, until she came to the first letter of the word she was looking up. Next, she had looked at her list to determine the second letter of the word she was looking up, and she had laboriously found it in the dictionary. Continuing this letter-by-letter method, she had finally located the desired word and painstakingly copied the definition. Then she had closed the dictionary. Next, she had consulted the list of words for the first letter of the next word to be looked up. She had reopened the dictionary to the first page and again had begun the process of paging through it. The librarian remembered that it had taken a relatively short time for Ruth to become proficient in finding words in the dictionary after she had been taught the technique of doing so.

She recalled watching a boy page through several issues of

Popular Mechanics as though he were searching for some article. She recalled, too, his incredulous look when she had told him that there was a table of contents in which he might find the location of his article in a very short time without trouble. On several subsequent occasions, the boy had taken the trouble to stop and tell her how useful he was finding tables of contents in looking for current information on topics which interested him.

Results of the Visit to the Library

The students for the most part, upon entering the library, had set about their own tasks in a businesslike manner. Harold had gone immediately to the dictionary and had efficiently found the meanings of the words in which he was interested. Robert had used an atlas to find information about the country through which he was to pass on his forthcoming automobile trip. Charles had copied from an encyclopedia a drawing of a tennis court with the dimensions noted upon it. He read the entire article about tennis courts and jotted down other facts which would be useful in constructing a court. The other students had undertaken to realize their purposes, some effectively and others not so effectively.

Both the teacher and the librarian had made records of the areas in which instruction would enable certain students to work more independently. As a result, the teacher was able to formulate problems to help the students who needed help gain experience in independent reading.

THE MEANING OF INDEPENDENCE IN READING

The newborn infant is almost wholly lacking in independence. He depends upon those who care for him to satisfy most of his wants. He is so dependent upon others that if he were not cared for, he would die. Soon, however, the young child learns how to make his wants known; and it is not long before he is able to provide for more and more of them.

The process of achieving independence is developmental. The child constantly becomes more independent as he grows older. During adolescence the majority of children increase in independence to a marked degree. This is especially true of those who receive wise supervision and guidance which put responsibility upon the individuals for the enterprises they undertake. One of the most pronounced characteristics of the adolescent is the drive to become emancipated from parental and other types of supervision. This desire to be free to do things for himself is a motivating force which is very useful in helping the individual achieve independence in many aspects of his life.

From the very first lesson on, a primary purpose of instruction is to enable the learner to work in an independent fashion. The beginner learns to hold a book and to page through it by himself. He is thus prepared for holding and paging all books of similar format. He has achieved a measure of independence. He soon learns how to recognize a new word so that he can determine its meaning independently. He develops word recognition skills so that he can derive independently the meaning of other words. With the development of the various reading techniques and skills comes a developmental growth in reading independence.

When the individual enters high school, there is an increased need for a differentiated reading attack. As he grows in ability to differentiate his reading attack in accordance with new and complex purposes and materials, he also grows in reading independence. The adolescent, as we have noted, is eager to do things for himself. When he sees the relationship in the uses of the various techniques and skills in achieving goals independently, his satisfaction is real. The individual should grow in reading independence during adolescence so that, when he can no longer depend upon the school to guide him, he can continue to increase his reading efficiency. As a result of his developing ability to read independently, he will be better able to use his reading in realizing such purposes as reading for enjoyment, for solving problems, and for keeping informed on current happenings.

An individual's independence in reading is his ability to rely upon his own resources to locate and use printed materials for the purpose of meeting a goal.

THE NEED FOR INDEPENDENCE IN READING

Inasmuch as reading is a complex process and inasmuch as no two students' reading development is the same, much reading instruction must be individual in nature. But one cannot conceive of a wholly individualized developmental program in which the teacher gives individual attention to some forty-five students who are altogether dependent upon her. The amount of guidance the teacher is able to give will be governed in no small measure by the degree to which self-reliance is developed. In teaching reading to a group of students who have not developed a fair degree of independence, much of the teacher's time and effort is likely to be dissipated in the task of keeping the students at work.

Effective Class Management

A teacher can liberate himself from many classroom management and disciplinary tasks by developing the spirit of cooperative independence. This may be achieved by encouraging the attitude on the part of the class that each student must be a responsible contributor to the group enterprises. To be this, the student must be aware of his obligation to collect the information required for an understanding of his phase of a group problem.

The attitude of co-operative independence rightfully transfers the responsibility of keeping the class busy from the teacher to the members of the class. The teacher's responsibility, then, is to guide the group enterprise and work individually with students when they are in need of help. The students' attitude toward co-operative independence enables the teacher to devote his time and effort to constructive guidance in reading.

Individual Growth

The student who is self-reliant in hunting material and in getting meaning from the printed page is better prepared to solve his problems or to read for enjoyment than the student who does not have this ability. Many a student is unable to formulate clearly the steps which must be undertaken in achieving a desired outcome. Such an individual is frequently unable to determine the areas in which he should read. He is even less able to locate the materials within these areas. He is not likely to use reading as an aid to meeting his needs, whether they be recreational or otherwise. Even though his reading abilities other than independence may be of high order, the individual without self-reliance would be unlikely to do extensive reading unless that reading were well plotted for him.

In many situations the teacher assumes the responsibility for determining what is to be read in school. Under these conditions the students who lack independence will probably confine their reading to what the teacher prescribes. Since extensive out-of-school reading will not be typical of these students, they will have limited reading experiences. They may not develop in other aspects of reading as rapidly as could otherwise be anticipated. The development of areas other than independence, such as those of interests and tastes, meaning backgrounds, and critical reading, are likely to suffer. The development of self-reliance is, therefore, essential to continued growth in reading.

The ability to rely upon oneself adds to the security of an individual in reading just as it does in most phases of human achievement. The student who is frequently obliged to ask help of the teacher in meeting his reading problems or in determining the use that should be made of reading in solving his problems cannot avoid feeling a sense of inadequacy. Since he finds it very discouraging to be obliged to seek aid at each new step in a problem, the insecure student is inclined to avoid reading. He thereby becomes less able to read and in turn even more insecure. The school can do the student a real service by showing him how to meet various reading situations unaided.

Reading in Adult Life

Every literate adult has many purposes in reading. In fact, reading is a part of a great majority of the activities in which he engages—whether it be reading an advertising folder in order to select a furnace, reading the ballot in order to vote according to his wishes, locating and reading informative material in connection with his business, reading a theater program to acquaint himself with the cast of characters, reading a contract before signing it, or reading a novel for recreation. The life of a person who does not read is far more barren and less effective than it would be if he did read. He would greatly increase the richness of his life if independence, interest, and ability in reading were added to his other powers.

The many diverse daily reading activities of the adult must, for the most part, be done independently. The individual who is no longer in school does not have the opportunity to turn to someone else for guidance in reading. The adequacy with which he meets these various reading purposes depends greatly upon the training in reading independence that he had in school. Training in this reading ability is rightfully one of the big areas of teaching reading in the junior and senior high school. It is during these school years that most people receive their last formal training in reading. Consequently, reading instruction should be directed toward enabling the students to become as able and independent readers as possible.

THE ENCOURAGEMENT OF INDEPENDENCE IN READING

Successful achievement in the development of reading techniques, differentiation, vocabulary, and reading interests will make for a self-reliant reader. There are, however, certain additional learnings necessary for growth in independence. It is these learnings we are to consider. Among the practices which would, if used, encourage the development of this reading ability are: (1) freeing students from day-by-day textbook assignments; (2) enabling the students to set up their own goals for reading; (3) encouraging the use of library facilities; (4) giving instruction in the use of libraries; (5) developing the ability to read to achieve a goal; (6) making provision for the use of what is read; (7) appraising the use of reading through intrinsic means.

Freeing Students from Day-by-Day Textbook Assignments

One of the most serious deterrents to the development of self-reliance in reading is the day-by-day textbook assignment which is so prevalent in the high school. Many students rarely, if ever, find it necessary to depend upon their own resources to locate the material upon a topic. Too frequently the student's only responsibility in reading is simply to learn the facts contained in the "next ten pages." In order that the student may become independent, he must, for a part of his reading, be released from teacher-selected material. He should be expected to make, from reading material of his own choosing, contributions to the solution of class problems. It is through such experience that he will learn to rely upon his own abilities. And it is through such experience that he will have an opportunity to use reading in becoming an independent learner.

Enabling Students to Set up Their Own Goals for Reading

A self-reliant reader analyzes the reading situation and sets up for himself the right sort of reading purposes. Sometimes the reading purposes are determined for him, as is often the case in school life. There the teacher usually outlines so clearly the reading approaches to the solution of situations that many students achieve but little ability in appraising situations for themselves and in establishing appropriate plans of procedure. Those who do not develop these powers are most unfortunate, since the majority of adults are frequently obliged to meet and appraise situations in order to determine the reading approach which they must use.

A better instructional procedure is one in which the teacher places the student in situations which demand reading and shows him how to analyze these situations in order to set up for himself the right sort of reading purposes. The teacher should in this case place an increasingly greater responsibility upon the student so that he may gain independence in appraising situations and establishing appropriate plans of procedure. A reading unit such as the following, given by Center and Persons, provides experience in reading for a specific purpose:

PROBLEM-SOLUTION PATTERN

Reading is thinking, and reflective thinking, according to John Dewey, is problem-solving. This pattern of thinking and writing is used when the author pursues a line of thought requiring close reasoning. A situation is presented. There is a difficulty of some kind. The thinker tries first one way of removing the difficulty, then another. Finally, the solution seems to be at hand; it is tested, and if it removes the difficulty, it is accepted as the answer. These are the steps in solving a problem:

1. Experiencing a felt difficulty
2. Stating the question clearly
3. Experimenting with ways of removing the difficulty
4. Selecting one way that seems to solve the problem
5. Testing the accepted way to prove that it is the real solution

Authors sometimes employ this pattern of thinking. When they do, the reader should follow the same pattern of reading. Such close partnership of author and reader means that the two minds move with rhythmic precision to the same goal or end.[1]

The writers' and readers' purposes and the procedure in reading a selection are set up as follows:

The writer's purpose: To offer the solution of a problem.
The reader's purpose: To find the author's solution and to note the steps advanced in the solution.
Procedure: The pattern of the author's thinking is clearly defined.
  First: Discover the main argument.
  Second: Discover the plan of action which the author proposes.
  Third: Consider the evidence and supporting data presented.

[1] Center, Stella S., and Persons, Gladys L. *Problems in Reading and Thinking,* The Macmillan Company, 1940, p. 504.

> *Fourth:* Review the entire line of thought and consider its soundness.[2]

When several such units have been completed, the student should have many more in which he locates materials illustrative of the "problem-solution" type of writing. In other words, the teacher should be aware at all times that too great a dependence upon prepared exercises can limit the development of independence on the part of the student. Nevertheless, the prepared exercises are effective in the preliminary stages of learning the skills necessary for independent reading.

Encouraging the Use of Library Facilities

It is often said that the most important room in a school is the library. This statement is true only when the teachers and students recognize it to be true. The library facilities should be made as adequate as is possible with considerable time and effort expended in the selection of the materials to be added. Quite as fundamental a problem is, however, that of using more completely the facilities which are available. It is the rare school that makes as complete a use of the library as it should. This condition is prevalent because of the presence of stereotyped instruction such as the textbook procedure cited earlier. The independent reader is one who has become acquainted with and made extensive use of one or more libraries. One aspect of independence is familiarity with the many uses to which library facilities can be put.

Giving Instruction in the Use of the Library

Encouragement in the use of the library will not in and of itself develop for all students the ability to locate material inde-

[2] Center, Stella S., and Persons, Gladys L. *Problems in Reading and Thinking,* The Macmillan Company, 1940, p. 516.

pendently. Systematic instruction in the use of the many aids available must be provided. The library is apt to be, for the untutored, a labyrinth through which he cannot find his way. At times, then, the library rather than being a source of aid becomes a source of confusion. It is necessary that instruction be given to enable the student to make thorough independent use of the library facilities.

For this undertaking the teacher should enlist the services of the librarian. Necessary also are the trips to the library where specific problems, such as those indicated in the following inventory, adapted from Bennett, are carried forward:

PERSONAL INVENTORY

1. Explore your library, noting the location of:
   a. The card catalogue.
   b. The delivery or charging desk.
   c. Reference books.
   d. Indexes and guides.
   e. Bound periodicals.
   f. Current periodicals and newspapers.
   g. Reserve books.
   h. Reading room or rooms.
   i. Any special features, such as books, pamphlets, and clippings on local history.
   j. Note the arrangement of books or other materials referred to in *c, e, f,* and *g* above.
2. Explore the stacks, noting the sequence of numbers and the general location of books in different subject fields.
3. Read carefully the regulations for:
   a. Circulating books.
   b. Reserve books.
4. Choose a current topic or problem in which you are interested. Locate a reference to a magazine article on this topic in the *Readers' Guide to Periodical Literature.* Copy the entry as it is given there, interpret each item in the

entry, using the H. W. Wilson Company pamphlet, "Cataloguing and Indexing Service," for assistance if needed. Locate the magazine article.

5. Locate several of the reference books in your library and secure the following information about each:

    a. Scope of the work as revealed on the title page and introduction.

       Limitation or specialties claimed.

    b. Editor.

    c. Arrangement:

       (1) Alphabetical by word?

       (2) Alphabetical by subject?

       (3) Any other type of arrangement?

    d. Are there cross references?

    e. Are there bibliographies?

    f. Is there an index? If not, why?

    g. Is there a table of contents? If not, why?

    h. Date of publication.

    i. Copyright date.

    j. Publisher.

    k. Is it the first edition, or has it been revised?

    l. Number of volumes.[3]

Developing Ability to Read to Achieve a Goal

The student must have a well-developed repertory of techniques and skills in order to read effectively. In addition, for independent reading he must have insight into the most advantageous adjustment of these techniques and skills to accomplish the purpose at hand. Such an insight comes as the result of a continuous growth in differentiation. This is accomplished by reading many types of materials and for many different purposes. It is most important that the student understand the adaptation of reading skills and techniques to the purpose for which he is reading.

[3] Bennett, M. E. *College and Life,* McGraw-Hill Book Company, Inc., 1933, pp. 165-66.

Making Provision for the Use of What Is Read

The independent reader uses what he reads. He is the reader who reads for a purpose and uses his reading to realize that purpose.

All too frequently the high school makes no provision for the student to utilize what is read. He is supposed to read and store the concepts and generalizations for use at a later date or for the passing of a test. The use to which he should put reading may be to aid in the selection of a class play, to bring some information into the class on a given problem, to enjoy a novel, or to add to his own growing concepts of radio.

Let us consider two diverse purposes and see how the school can develop independence by making it possible for the student to use what he reads to achieve these purposes. A purpose might be the reading of a poem for enjoyment. Instruction can be so carried forward that various students read, enjoy, and share their enjoyment. The important thing is that provision be made for that sharing. Thus, one builds an ability to read, enjoy, and share with others. In such a case it might well be that the student would select one from a number of poems he had located and read independently to be read to his classmates. A classroom enterprise of this type, when expertly conducted by the teacher, enables students to develop confidence in their ability to select and read materials so that others may enjoy them.

Again, let us suppose that in a class discussion a question of national parks arose. One student volunteered to write for information pertinent to the discussion. It was necessary for him to determine to whom and for what types of materials to write. In an independent fashion he must set about the task of determining to whom to write. After the material has been procured and use has been made of it, the student, as well as other members of the class, will have a better appreciation of the fact that reading can be used for the independent solution of problems.

Appraising the Use of Reading through Intrinsic Means

Just as the day-by-day assignment restricts the development of independence, so do some of the current practices of appraisal. Those appraisals which test factual memory of a set assignment rather than functional knowledge limit the student's independent reading. The appraisals of reading should be made in part by observing the type of material read, the uses made of reading, and the extent of independent reading.

AN ILLUSTRATION OF DEVELOPING INDEPENDENCE IN READING GRAPHS

Rarely in the past has there been a positive approach to the teaching task of providing opportunities for the students to develop independent methods of reading. The following description of a positive approach used by a teacher to enable his students to grow in reading independence illustrates what can be accomplished when the teacher is aware of the problem.

One day in a ninth-grade class in general mathematics, a student expressed the answer to a problem in pictorial form. Other students in the group were interested in this use of a graphic presentation of one of their own homework problems. Several students experienced difficulty in reading the graph. All the boys and girls wanted to prepare and read pictorial presentations of number. In order to have such experiences, they realized that it would be necessary for them to learn how to use pictorial methods for the purpose of presenting facts.

Questions formulated as a result of group discussion included the following: How long has man used pictorial means to describe quantitative experiences? In how many of the occupations of the world are graphs used to present factual data?

How many facts and how much meaning can be conveyed by a graph? How many types of graphs are used today? What principles should one follow in setting up a graph in such a way that it will tell its story clearly, accurately, and concisely?

After the purposes of the co-operative enterprise were clearly defined, each student assumed the responsibility of contributing to its solution. Immediately the teacher was besieged with such questions as: Where can I find out about . . . ? How can I locate . . . ? Has anything ever been written about . . . ? Thirty-five pupils at the same moment clamoring for the attention of the teacher! It was apparent that it would be necessary for each student to locate independently the reading material needed for his phase of the project. The pupils recalled that several reading methods and techniques had been helpful in carrying out a co-operative enterprise on a previous occasion. These were discussed in relation to the present endeavor. Material about the previous topic had been located in such reference aids as dictionaries, encyclopedias, magazine indexes, as well as the card catalogue. These aids would be useful in the present project. Also every book, magazine, and newspaper was a potential source of information since graphic presentations are widely used in all types of printed materials. In fact, as one student stated, "A large number of the books I have read, not even excepting novels and detective stories, have had graphic pictures of one kind or another."

Possible sources of material dealing with man's early use of graphic methods included histories of mathematics as well as histories of man's development in early times. Reading the graphic illustrations in the textbooks and reference materials used in all their classes would provide experience in getting the meaning from graphs and would show also some of the ways by which graphs convey meaning.

When the class in general mathematics next convened, it

was found that many graphs had been located and that a great deal of information about graphic methods had been ferreted out by the students. One student brought into class illustrations of the four types of graphs shown in Figure IV. Data, such as shown in these and other graphs examined by the class, can be strikingly presented in a relatively small space. The significance of the relationships among number concepts of magnitude can be more nearly comprehended by the graphic method than when those relationships are given in verbal form only.

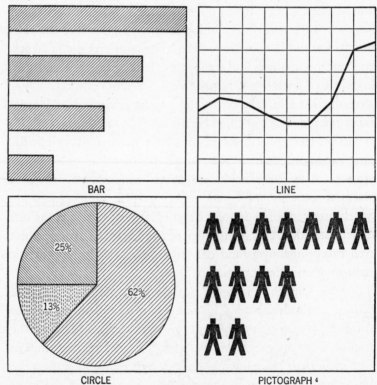

BAR

LINE

CIRCLE

PICTOGRAPH [4]

FIGURE IV

Four Types of Graphs

[4] By permission of Pictograph Corporation, New York City.

The ability to interpret maps and graphs is indispensable to good reading. They are integral parts of the textual material, frequently serving the purpose of making the verbal material more comprehensible. Good students pay more attention to graphs than do poor ones. The poor student passes over them, hurrying on to the less exacting reading of the text. The good student, on the other hand, reads them quite as thoroughly as he does the verbal materials.[5] These and other concepts were discussed by the students.

Many experiences in the reading and preparing of graphic materials were provided. An informal appraisal of the reading of several types of graphs, made several days later, showed that the members of this co-operative enterprise had profited from their experiences. The results of the appraisal indicated growth in the ability to locate, read, and use graphic materials independently, as well as growth in information about graphs.

SUMMARY

An individual's independence in reading is his ability to rely upon his own resources to locate and use printed materials for the purpose of meeting a goal.

Instruction in independence should be directed toward enabling the student to set up reading purposes which are intrinsically important, and toward developing his ability to locate materials, his ability to apply the various reading techniques and skills, and his ability to make use of what he reads.

SELECTED BIBLIOGRAPHY

Bennett, M. E.   *College and Life,* McGraw-Hill Book Company, Inc., 1933.

Broening, A. M., and others.   *How to Use the Library: Practice Ex-*

[5] Pressey, S. L., Janney, J. E., and Kuhlen, R. G.   *Life: A Psychological Survey, Laboratory Workbook,* Harper and Brothers, 1940, p. 11.

ercises in the Use of the More Important Library Tools, Nobel and Nobel, 1936.

Carpenter, H. S. "Reading with a Purpose in the School Library," *Wilson Bulletin,* Vol. IX, May, 1935, pp. 471-75.

Feagley, F. M. "The Teacher and the Library," *American Library Association Bulletin 28,* March, 1934, pp. 116-23.

Ingles, Mary, and McGogue, Anna C. *Teaching the Use of Books and Libraries,* H. W. Wilson Company, 1937.

Johnson, B. L. "Teacher and Librarian Co-operation," *Wilson Bulletin,* Vol. X, March, 1936, pp. 449-52.

CHAPTER X

APPRAISALS OF READING ABILITIES

At the first class meeting of a new group of students, one alert teacher was troubled with uncertainties. Meeting with him in this first class period were some thirty-five to fifty eager and interesting personalities. En masse, the group of individuals was much like the one he had been privileged to work with the previous semester. But how different had been his knowledge of the different individuals in the class after a semester of daily association and co-operation with them from his knowledge of them on the first day! His class had seemed only a "group" to him at the beginning of the last semester. But the sad truth was that he had taught them as a group, not only the first day but for several weeks. It was only during the closing weeks of the semester that in his thinking he had substituted "Sally Smith" and "Jim Brown" for "My 9:45 class."

As he surveyed his 9:45 class today, his first consideration was whether or not the room was large enough and sufficiently well equipped for the class. Next, he counted and recorded the exact number of individuals in the group. As he did these things, he focused his attention momentarily upon each student to see if he recognized any of them. "Yes, there in the back of the room is Jim Brown. I recognize him and am relieved to find that I am able to call him by name. I remember, too, that his classroom behavior was always satisfactory. He contributed from time to time to class discussions, co-operated in class projects, and passed the course with a 'C,' I believe.

Well, at least there is one student I know—one less name to learn." At this point in his thinking, doubts and uncertainties pressed in upon the teacher. He was all too keenly aware that being able to recognize, call by name, and generalize about the relative standing of a Jim Brown was far from knowing him.

The customary survey continued. The students filled in cards with name, date, age, sex, major, previous courses in the subject-matter area, and special interests. As they did this, the teacher continued to recall anecdotal observations of Jim Brown. He remembered, for example, that on one occasion he chanced to observe Jim at work in the library. Jim was reading from a book and copying down its contents practically verbatim. His studying appeared to be mechanical. He read, reread, and then copied each paragraph almost in its entirety. From time to time he had to force himself to return to his reading, since he frequently found himself dreamily gazing out the window.

The teacher had, at that time, controlled the impulse to ask Jim for the central thought of the material he was reading and his evaluation of it. He felt that Jim did not know how to study. His estimate of Jim's reading ability was confirmed at a later time when Jim gave a report to the class. His report seemed to be the result of reading and copying material with little interpretive thinking. It might well be that Jim's achievement this semester would be greater if it were possible to help him gain increased skill in various reading abilities used in this subject-matter area.

The teacher had become convinced that it is a sound policy to include standardized measures as a part of the original survey of a group of students. He felt that the informal observations which he had made on previous occasions should be continued since they had proved to be very useful as a part of the normal classroom work. But he believed that to these observations should be added the administration of tests of mental ability, reading abilities, and initial knowledge of the subject matter under consideration. Fortified by this knowledge of abilities and achievements of the individuals with whom he was working, a teacher would be more intelligent and constructive in guiding his students than he could possibly be without such accurate and specific appraisals.

Purposes of Measurement of Reading Abilities

Just as reading is an integral part of every phase of scholastic endeavor, so is appraisal of the reading abilities of students an integral part of the teaching process. Consequently, in order that learning and teaching in any subject-matter field may proceed in an orderly and intelligent fashion, appraisals must be made of the students' present achievements in reading.

Among the more important purposes of the measurement of reading, from the point of view of the teacher in the high school, are:

1. To improve instruction in reading by
   a. Determining the nature of instruction
   b. Adjusting instruction to individuals
   c. Determining the readiness to undertake the learning of advanced reading abilities
   d. Testing the effectiveness of instruction
2. To improve instruction in the content subjects by
   a. Determining the nature of instruction
   b. Adjusting instruction to individuals
   c. Determining the readiness to undertake a new area of subject matter or a new phase within an area of subject matter
   d. Testing the effectiveness of instruction
3. To aid in the selection of materials
4. To aid in the guidance of students
5. To contribute to research in education

The Use of Appraisals in Improving Instruction in Reading

Appraisals play an important role in any program designed to improve the reading abilities of students. The appraisals may be of many types. They may include standardized and teacher-made tests and questionnaires, informal observations, interviews, and reports. These appraisals define the problems which will confront the teacher and show him the direction which his attempts to improve reading abilities must take. They also delineate the obstacles which must be overcome. They show him the interests of the students and thereby guide him into the areas in which most pronounced progress can be expected. Appraisals may show the amount of individual attention which must be given to the students. Hence, they further indicate the extent of the program that may be profitably undertaken. If the appraisals are made at regular intervals, the effectiveness of various instructional practices can be determined from them. The results of such appraisals show the level of reading growth at which the instructional program must be initiated, and they also predict the rate of progress which may be expected.

Using Appraisals to Determine the Nature of Instruction

Appraisals of a given group aid in planning the nature of instruction by indicating the abilities in reading which should receive primary attention. They indicate the amount of time and effort which should be expended in promoting adequate growth in reading. For example, one group might show a fairly consistent and advanced development in the five areas with which the reading program concerns itself. Another class group might show an equally advanced development in all areas except those of adequate interests and tastes and of independence in reading. Obviously, the amount of time and effort spent by the teacher would be somewhat different for the two groups. The first group, with high interests and the ability to work independently, could be expected to continue to develop their reading abilities with a minimum of guidance from the teacher. The second group, on the other hand, although equally high in reading skills, would demand a considerable amount of the teacher's time and effort. It should also be noted that the emphasis in the first group would be placed upon the continued development of a balanced reading program; in the second group, special emphasis would rather be placed upon awakening new and vital interests and upon developing independence in reading. The nature of instruction is determined, therefore, from the results of the program of appraisals.

Using Appraisals to Adjust Instruction to Individuals

In addition to formulating the nature of group instruction, the results of the appraisals are of value in adjusting instruction to the individuals of the group. It is in this respect that appraisals make perhaps their greatest contribution to the improvement of instruction and to the adjustment of the individuals of the group. By knowing the reading strengths and weaknesses of a student, the teacher can better guide him into becoming an effective contributor to the group enterprises. The adjustment of instruction may take the form of improving the reading efficiency of the normal or superior reader, which may mean giving added emphasis to the one phase of reading in which a generally good reader is slightly deficient. Or the adjustment may take the form of remedial instruction for an individual who is markedly low in one or more aspects of reading.

In the development of an able performance in any skill, it is necessary to appraise ability in various phases of it as well as in the skill as a whole. The following story illustrates the use of appraisals in adjusting instruction in a field other than reading: Since Adair wanted to enter the city tennis tournament in August, he was concerned about his tennis game. Despite the fact that in the past month he had spent many hours playing tennis, it seemed to him that he had made no progress toward the purpose that had been motivating him to practice so continuously. To achieve any success in the tournament it would be necessary for Adair to improve rather markedly within the next few weeks. How might improvement be achieved? The mere playing of the game hour after hour had proved to be ineffectual.

Adair decided to talk the matter over with his friend, Mr. Nelson, who was an excellent player. Mr. Nelson suggested that a careful study be made of the degree of skill which Adair had achieved in the various abilities which go into the game of tennis. It might prove helpful, too, to make careful observations of the ease and facility with which Adair differentiated his attack in various situations. At times, Mr. Nelson pointed out, it is necessary to hit the ball deep into the back court, and at others it should be just lifted over the net.

After the careful appraisals had been completed, Adair used the results to help him in improving various parts of his tennis game and, therefore, his tennis game as a whole. Before these accurate measurements had been made, Adair had been aware, in a general way, of certain faults in his game. He knew, for example, that frequently a backhand shot ended in the net. But he had not known his relative ability in each part of the game. The survey of his tennis game gave him information about his developmental progress in each of the abilities which go to make up the game. This enabled him to make a better use of these abilities in his future tennis playing. As you might expect, he made great improvement in playing tennis during the succeeding weeks.

The abilities and techniques may be thought of as "strokes" in the game of reading. They are an integral part of the game. The systematized appraisal of the various strokes in Adair's tennis playing proved to be helpful in improving his game. Measurements of reading are useful in improving instruction, both in specific reading skills and through them reading development as a whole.

Using Appraisals to Determine Readiness to Undertake the Learning of Advanced Reading Abilities

Since the development of reading abilities is a continuous process, it is important at all times to know how far advanced each individual is in each ability. The teacher, therefore, should continually be making appraisals of each individual's growth in various reading abilities. This procedure is necessary in order to determine the readiness of the individual to undertake the learning of more advanced phases of these abilities. For example, one would not expect a student who had not developed the ability to use an index to locate a bit of information in a large reference book. If the teacher determines through observational methods that the student is deficient in the use of the index, he should develop this ability first by using a less cumbersome and complicated index. If a student cannot read the simple mimeographed directions of classroom procedures, one would not expect him to be very efficient in following the directions required to work out a complicated experiment in physics or chemistry.

Using Appraisals to Test Effectiveness of Instruction

Another use for reading appraisals, when given at regular intervals, is for testing the effectiveness of reading instruction. For example, a teacher might be concerned with the development of more adequate interests and tastes. He wants to know which of two methods is the more effective in developing appreciation of poetry. The two methods considered might be intensive reading of poetry as opposed to extensive reading of poetry. The teacher uses two of his class groups in the project. He measures the appreciation of poetry at the start of the experiment by having the two groups rate poems of different degrees of literary merit. After one group has pursued a program of extensive reading of poetry and the other of intensive reading of poetry, the teacher again makes an appraisal of their appreciation of poetry. If the two groups were approximately equal on the first test, the second appraisal will indicate the effectiveness of either method when compared with the other in developing an appreciation of poetry.

Another teacher might be interested in appraising the effectiveness of his adjustment of material to the reading ability of a high school boy whose general reading proficiency was about equal to that of a sixth grader. The appraisal might, on the one hand, be made by simply noting the interest with which the boy reads the material and the adjustment which he makes to the class situation; or it might be made by determining the gain which he makes in reading ability. It is apparent that the effectiveness of instruction can be determined only by making some sort of appraisal of the outcomes of that instruction. It is evident also that test results should be supplemented by other types of appraisals.

The Use of Reading Appraisals in Improving Instruction in the Content Subjects

Each of the content subjects makes demands upon the reading abilities of the students. Appraisals are necessary in order to know whether these abilities are sufficiently developed to meet the demands of the content subjects. Such reading appraisals contribute to the improvement of instruction in the content subjects by (1) giving indications of the nature and scope of the subject-matter instruction for the class group as a whole, (2) aiding to formulate instructional procedures which will meet the needs of individual students, (3) aiding to determine the students' readiness to undertake a new area of subject matter or a new phase within an area of subject matter, (4) providing accurate measures which will contribute to the testing of the effectiveness of instruction in the content fields.

Using Appraisals to Determine the Nature of Instruction

Appraisals of reading abilities are significant factors in determining the nature of endeavor on the high school level. The use of informal appraisals of one kind or another before a unit of work is undertaken is so common that we fail frequently to appreciate their value. Before the excavation of the basement of a house, for example, appraisals are made of the slope and drainage of the land, the quality of the soil, etc. These factors determine to some extent the nature of the excavation. The housewife, too, is constantly making appraisals and from the results determining the nature of endeavor. It is very likely true that as often as cakes are baked, just so often an appraisal is made, as the following illustration indicates.

At the outset one who is baking a cake surveys the store of foods in the cupboard to determine the kind of cake that she may make. She decides upon a crumb cake when she has ascertained that the quantity and quality of the various ingredients in the supply closet will be sufficient for making a cake of that kind. Next, she takes from the cupboard the various pots, pans, and cutlery which are to be used in mixing and baking a crumb cake and puts them upon the worktable ready for use. By the selection and elimination of utensils, she has made an adjustment to the purposes at hand. The last time she baked a crumb cake, the new stove seemed to brown the cake on top, but left it doughy in the middle. She therefore adjusts the stove so that the process of baking will be slower and consequently more thorough. The art of baking a cake is one which requires appraisals of the materials and tools, together with a wise and experienced interrelation of each step in the process in terms of the end result desired.

Quite as truly are appraisals of reading abilities an integral and significant part of the determination of the nature of instruction, whether that instruction consists of an entire course or of a small unit of it. An inventory of the reading skills which are on hand and available for use will indicate the kind and quality of instruction that may most profitably be used. Use should be made of the books and equipment which will lend themselves to the instruction. Instruction should progress at the rate at which it will reach the desired outcomes. A general deficiency on the part of the entire group of students in any reading ability will signify need for adjustments of various sorts in the method of instruction.

By knowing something about the students' present stages of development in reading comprehension, it is possible to judge, to some extent at least, how well able they are to read the materials of the course with understanding and to adjust the materials to their abilities. By knowing the students' present scores in speed of reading the materials of the course, it is possible to adjust to their capacities the amount of material they may legitimately be expected to read for any one class period. By knowing the developmental stages which have been reached in various other reading abilities, the teacher and the students are more able to direct learning in the subject than would be possible without such knowledge.

In order to set up situations which will help the student develop and refine these various reading techniques and skills, it is necessary to know the progress that he has already made in the acquisition of each. From the previous discussion it is evident that both a knowledge of the students' status in the various reading abilities and the use of this knowledge provide fundamental bases for determining the nature of instruction in such a subject, for example, as science in the high school.

Using Appraisals in Reading to Adjust Instruction in Content Subjects to the Individual

Appraisals of reading provide knowledge which may be used in adjusting instruction in the content subjects to the individual. This fact is well illustrated by the classroom procedure of an eleventh-grade class in economics. This group of students was undertaking a consideration of the topic "The Development of Industry in the South." They had found co-operative discussions during the class hour, augmented by independent work on the part of the students outside the class hour, to be productive of desirable learnings. Both the teacher and the students felt the development of co-operative independence to be a major objective of the class in economics.

Complete and careful appraisals were made of the reading abilities of the students from time to time, as well as of their progress in various aspects of economic thought. The students were fully acquainted with the results of these various appraisals. It had become the custom—a procedure which had proven very effective in motivating study—for a student to correlate the task of gaining experience in the reading ability or abilities in which he was deficient, with the task of securing information that would contribute to the topic which the class was planning to discuss the following day.

As one might expect, during the course of each class discussion questions would be raised which would have to be held in abeyance until the students could acquire items of information, illustrations, and accurate knowledges. If the reading skill to be used in the acquisition of such information was that of skimming through a large amount of material in order to locate an isolated fact, a student who was deficient in that skill would volunteer to do the reading; because in addition to being able to contribute to the class discussion the following day, he would also have practice in the reading skill in which he was deficient. The teacher suggested materials of a nontechnical nature on a topic under consideration to those students who were not yet able to read the more technical discussions. The reading of the more complicated and technical materials would be undertaken by those students who had achieved greater developmental proficiency in reading.

Using Appraisals to Determine Readiness to Study New Areas or New Phases within an Area of Subject Matter

Before a new area of subject matter is undertaken, appraisals of reading abilities are useful in determining the readiness of the students as a group and of students individually to begin a consideration of the new material. Appraisals of reading abilities, combined with other appraisals, are useful also in determining the readiness of the students to undertake a consideration of a new phase within an area of subject matter.

One would not begin the study of correlation in a course in statistics when one was aware that the students of the group could not read algebraic formulas with understanding. It would be necessary for the group to receive instruction in the understanding and reading of mathematical materials before the instruction in statistics could be undertaken.

Frequent halts should be made in the orderly sequence of instruction in any one subject-matter area in order to enable students to assimilate and review the previous learnings. Many times the determination of the students' readiness to study a new phase of a subject is based upon the teacher's judgment.

Sometimes the judgment of the teacher is supplemented by subjective or objective appraisals of the students' ability to think and generalize in the phases of the subject which precede the new one. To these appraisals should be added one of determining the readiness of the students to do the reading in the new phase of the subject.

Using Appraisals to Test the Effectiveness of Instruction in the Content Subjects

Measurements of reading abilities are useful in testing the effectiveness of instruction in the content subjects. One of the major objectives of science teaching is to help the students learn to think in a scientific fashion. Among other things, this objective implies that the student must learn to read and evaluate scientific literature and that he must also increase his knowledge of the meanings of scientific words. Consequently, measurements of size of scientific vocabulary and of ability to read and evaluate scientific material at the beginning and at the end of instruction, which is directed toward helping the student learn to think in a scientific fashion, will give one indication of the effectiveness of such instruction. Naturally, measurement in the field of science will give other indications of the effectiveness of instruction. But since reading is an integral part of the instruction in all subject-matter areas, measurement of improvement in reading the materials in those areas should form a part of a systematic evaluation of the results of instruction.

The Use of Appraisals in Reading to Aid in the Selection of Materials

A wise choice of materials should take into consideration the reading interests and achievements of the students who are to use them.

In all types of activity materials must be selected that are appropriate to the user and to the purpose for which they are to be used. A climber, for example, would not climb a snow-capped mountain peak if he had only tennis shoes. On the side of a peak, tennis shoes not only are useless in climbing to the summit, but they also constitute a hazard in reaching the goal. It is necessary to have strong, sturdy leather boots with eleven calks in the toes and five or so in the heels in order to assure a reasonably smooth, safe ascent.

We can no more expect the child with inadequate reading habits to reach the heights of literature than we can expect a mountain climber with tennis shoes to reach the summit of the peak. Some few, with laborious effort and much endurance, may be able to accomplish the feat, but the hazard is too great. Besides being ineffective, inappropriate reading materials in a specific subject have a detrimental effect. Frequently a dislike for a certain body of subject matter on the part of one or a group of students can be traced to the fact that the materials of the course were too difficult for the students to read with comprehension.

The Use of Appraisals in Reading to Aid in the Guidance of Students

The guidance of the individuals who make up the population of the high school is an important function of education. In order that a wise and appropriate counseling of an individual may be achieved, complete data about the individual must be available to the counselor. Since good reading ability is essential to adequate educational adjustment and is highly related to personal and emotional adjustment, appraisals in reading make up a significant part of the data the counselor uses in guiding an individual into a fuller educational, vocational, and emotional development.

THE USE OF APPRAISALS IN READING TO CONTRIBUTE
TO RESEARCH IN EDUCATION

If progress is to be made in education, research is necessary. Appraisals are a fundamental part of research. In the previous discussion of the use of evaluation in reading many indications of possible areas of research have been evident. But despite the fact that the volume of research in reading is great, there are many gaps in our knowledge of reading in the high school.

Teachers can make a valuable contribution to the teaching of reading by formulating new procedures which can be used in the classroom, by using them, and by making appraisals of the outcomes of such procedures. This implies, of course, that they make reports of their research.

Teachers are contributing to research in education in a second way—by making it possible for trained research workers to come into their classroom in order to conduct researches of one kind or another. Some have made it possible for the research worker to do the teaching in a specific subject-matter area for an experimental period; in addition they have co-operated with a pretesting and final testing period. Others have co-operated by undertaking the teaching themselves, using the procedures prescribed by the experimenter. In these and many other ways the classroom teacher, through understanding and untiring efforts, has helped make it possible for research in education to be undertaken. There is a need in education for an increasing amount of co-operative experimentation to be made in the classroom by the teacher and a trained research worker. Although laboratory experimentation is productive of results which are useful in teaching, experimentation within the classroom itself is even more productive of applicable results.

Reading Outcomes That Should Be Appraised

Appraisals should be made of reading achievement in each of the five areas of reading instruction. In the first of these—reading skills and techniques—it is necessary to measure the extent of the student's developmental progress in the various abilities which are used in the high school. The less mature skills, such as phonetic analysis, use of context clues, and orientation, do not ordinarily need to be measured. But if it is found from the measurement of general development in reading that a student is seriously retarded, an appraisal of the progress in the beginning reading skills should be undertaken. This appraisal would constitute a problem of measurement which should be considered in the remedial program. Thus, in the majority of cases appraisals are made to determine whether or not a student has an adequate repertory of basic skills, rather than to break these basic skills down into their fundamental reading habits. Appraisals in this area—reading skills and techniques—should include:

1. Measurements of comprehension, such as sentence, paragraph, and story comprehension, and power of comprehension

2. Measurements of vocabulary, including word meanings and pronunciation

3. Measurements of rate

4. Measurements of oral reading

The second area of instruction in reading is the development of vocabulary and background concepts. The appraisals which may be made are twofold:

1. Measurements of word meanings in various content-field areas

2. Measurements of background of understandings in various content-field areas

The third area of instruction in reading is that of developing reading interests and tastes. Since this type of development is as truly a growth process as is development in other areas, the appraisals should be in the nature of determining the maturity of the interests and tastes of the students. The following sorts of appraisals should be made:

1. Appraisals of the quality and extent of independent reading in various areas, such as content-subject fields, field of literature, current events •

2. The determination of any specialized interest

The fourth area of instruction in reading is the development of independence. Appraisals which may be made of growth in this area should include:

1. Testing the ability to locate information, such as finding material in a book, using an index, using general reference material, recognizing common abbreviations, using the card catalogue

2. Testing the ability to find meanings; for example, ability to use the dictionary, the encyclopedia, and footnotes

3. Determining the actual level of the student's independence in reading

The fifth area of instruction in reading is developing a differentiated attack. The appraisals which should be made of the degree of ability in differentiating the attack should consist of locating the level of growth in differentiation, rather than of determining the factors responsible for the inability to adjust the reading to the purpose and material at hand. The latter phase—that of determining the factors responsible for difficulty in this area—is a function of the diagnostic and remedial program. Among the appraisals which should be made are the following:

1. Determination of the ability to comprehend the material in the various subject-matter fields, such as literature, science, social science, mathematics

2. Determination of the ability to read for a variety of purposes, such as reading to organize, to interpret the general meaning, to follow directions, to note significant details, to memorize material

3. Determination of the ability to read various types of material, such as story and study types, maps, graphs, and other tabular data

TESTING PROCEDURES

Selection of Instruments

The effectiveness of a reading program is, in no small measure, the result of an adequate functional program of appraisals. Although it is true that the teacher is constantly making appraisals of the reading abilities of her students, the need for a systematized program of appraisals is apparent. A brief inspection of the complexity of reading and the numerous outcomes which are desired from it shows that it is difficult and often cumbersome to make adequate appraisals. The program should be thorough and so well organized that overlappings with resultant waste may be avoided.

In order to eliminate waste in the testing program, it should be designed so that each student is measured only as extensively as necessary in order to know his reading strengths and weaknesses. For most students this knowledge can be obtained by means of group tests, inventories, and other group methods of appraisal, supplemented by informal observations, reports, and interviews. For a limited number of students, however, more precise appraisals are needed. This chapter will limit its discussion to the appraisals which should be made of the reading abilities for the group as a whole; the individual appraisals necessary for students of limited reading ability will be discussed in the chapter devoted to diagnosing reading disability—Chapter XII.

In the selection of the appraisals to be used, the cost of the instruments and the testing time must be given careful consideration. In order to avoid overlapping in the testing program, the available instruments should be thoroughly investigated so that a careful choice may be made. The Appendix gives a list of tests suitable for high school use. The nature of the outcome of instruction which is being measured must be considered in the selection of the type of instruments that should be used. For example, in the measurement of reading comprehension, a standardized test is probably the most effective instrument. On the other hand, the determination of the reading tastes of students probably can be best judged by informal appraisals made by the teacher.

Types of Appraisals

Inasmuch as the teacher has a very important place in the program of appraisals, a brief, nontechnical discussion of types and purposes of appraisals follows:

I. GROUP TESTS

a. *Standardized tests.* Standardized tests are tests which are objectively scored and which have a means of comparing the performances of a student or of a group of students with a sampling of students of like groups. These comparisons are usually made by means of norms which are furnished by the author of the test. The norms indicate the average performance of students of like age or grade level and tell the teacher how well her class, or an individual member of that class, compares in the ability measured with the average of a large group of students.

The results of a battery of tests indicate the strengths and weaknesses of an individual or a class group in the various aspects of reading which are measured by that battery. These tests are usually designed to measure the maximum of outcomes in a minimum amount of time. The ease of scoring and interpreting the results is also a factor in the construction of a standardized test. The tests are so organized that they may be easily scored and interpreted.

b. *Teacher-made tests.* Teacher-made reading tests are tests which the teacher constructs to measure specific outcomes of her reading instruction. Such tests are an important addition to the more formal standardized tests in that they can be applied to the measurement of the outcomes of narrower limits of instruction. In order to achieve the results desired, teacher-made tests must be carefully constructed in line with the outcomes to be measured. For example, if the instruction at any one time has been directed toward determining the sequence of events in a given story, the test should measure whether or not that objective has been realized.

c. *Questionnaires.* Questionnaires differ from the two previously discussed group measures in that they lend themselves to determining the individual's impression about his own performance. They reveal the student's opinion of his progress, his attitude toward reading as well as his memory of the books read, and his interests.

2. OBSERVATIONAL METHODS

a. *Informal observations.* The teacher's observation of the student in reading activities of the day is a rather continuous one. He observes the student as he sets to work at a specific task and notes his growth in study habits and in independence. The teacher sees the student in the library and study hall and notes the type of book that he is reading and the degree to which it is sustaining his interest. As the student enters the classroom with a book under his arm, he frequently pauses to comment upon his enjoyment of it, and the teacher makes an informal appraisal of the reading interests of the student. Just as the teacher is accustomed to suggest for reading current books and materials pertaining to the subject at hand, so do the students bring to the classroom clippings, magazines, and books for the teacher to read. All these activities and many others provide the teacher with opportunities to judge in an informal way the development of the student's interests, values, meanings, concepts, and the realization of the services reading can perform for him.

Teachers sometimes keep anecdotal accounts of such incidents, not trusting to their memory to form a final appraisal of a student's growth in these areas of reading. In guiding and planning the reading experiences of students, teachers find that these anecdotal records of informal observations of an individual's reading abilities are very helpful in understanding his reading strengths and weaknesses. It is not possible for a teacher to remember all the facts pertinent to the reading development of all the students he teaches. Anecdotal and other records are useful since they enable the teacher to review the reading history of a student in a few minutes.

The teacher who makes frequent use of various observational techniques gradually becomes more expert in using them. Hence, his appraisals become more and more accurate and reliable. Rating scales are frequently used in order that the teacher's judgments of students in relation to one another may be more consistent. Rating scales also enable the teacher to compare the rating of the past performance of an individual with the rating of his present performance. They are useful in enabling the teacher's judgment of students to become a part of the permanent cumulative record of the student.

b. *Interviews.* A considerable proportion of the high school teacher's time should be devoted to conferences with students. It is often during this time that the teacher may do some of his most effective teaching. Especially is this true when it is possible for the teacher so systematically to organize his thinking about the student that the conference may serve as a means of enabling him to understand and guide the student as fully as possible. During such interviews some of the most accurate appraisals of the student's interests and tastes in reading and appreciation of reading can be made. Often the real purpose behind a student's scholastic ambitions can be determined in the interview. The result of this sort of appraisal is of fundamental value in enabling the teacher to make better use of the student's interests and to adjust instruction to differences in personalities.

c. *Reports.* Oral and written reports of the students often afford the teacher considerable insight into their reading development. The number and kinds of books a student reads and the quality of his reports indicate his growth in various areas of reading instruction. These reports and discussions may serve as informal measures of the student's ability to organize material, to do independent thinking in a specific area, and to apply the meanings and concepts of material read.

It is possible for the teacher to design report forms for the students to follow that will reveal to each of them the degree to which specific reading purposes have been achieved.

ADMINISTRATION OF TESTS

The responsibility for the standardized testing program will depend upon the facilities within the school system. It may be possible for the high school to have a co-ordinator of the reading program. If provision is made for such a person on the teaching staff, it would be his responsibility to select the testing instruments, administer them, and make the results available to each classroom teacher. A discussion of the co-ordination of the reading program appears in Chapter XIV.

In those schools where neither a reading co-ordinator nor a school psychologist is available, a teacher, teacher-committee, or an administrative officer of the school may be designated to carry forward the standardized testing program. In any case, regardless of who administers the testing program, each teacher should assume some responsibility for scoring the tests. No matter how the testing program is organized, it is essential that some system be devised which will make it possible for the tabulated results to be available to the classroom teachers. The system that will prove most expedient will depend upon the size and the administrative setup of the school. A system that proved to be a functional one in one high school is the following:

1. During the first week of school a battery of standardized tests was administered.

2. Each teacher scored and tabulated his quota of the tests.

3. The results were assembled and mimeographed for distribution to the class teachers.

4. The administering, scoring, and recording of the tests designed to measure reading ability in the content subjects were the responsibility of the teacher of each content subject.

A record form should be worked out to fit the needs of the high school in order that a record of development in reading may be kept. These record forms should be mimeographed or printed so that every teacher will have a form for each student in his classes. An illustration of a usable record form is given in Table VII. The teacher should record the results of the standardized tests on the profile chart at the top of the form. There is a place on the form for recording the results of teacher-made tests, the results of reading tests in the content fields, and for jotting down appraisals made from time to time by the teacher as a result of interviews, observations, questionnaires, and ratings.

TABLE VII

Reading Appraisal Record Form

Name.........................Grade.......Date..............

Age.........Date of Birth.........Intelligence Quotient..........

GRADE OR PERCENTILE SCORES

Compre-hension	Rate	Vocabu-lary	Locating Information	Organi-zation	Study Skills	Content Field Reading Skills

Standardized Tests Used

Teacher-Made Tests

Reading Tastes and Interests

Evidences of Independence in Reading

Evidences of Growth in Meaning Background

Evidences of Appreciation of Reading

Evidences of Faulty Habits

(Report anecdotal records or comments on results of conferences on reverse side with date of each.)

The time required to keep this record of development in reading up to date is small in relation to the uses which may be made of it. With these records at hand it is possible for the teacher to become aware of the reading strengths and weaknesses of the students as a group and as individuals almost at the outset of instruction. Then the instruction, including the assignment of materials, may proceed adequately and intelligently. It is possible for teachers to use the records mentioned above to make an accurate and careful selection of students who will profit by remedial instruction in reading.

It is quite as much the duty of the teacher of a content subject to teach the student to continue the study of that subject through reading and other means as it is to teach factual knowledge. Consequently, all teachers should understand the principles of reading instruction and should continually be making appraisals of the student's growth in the reading abilities to which their subject contributes most.

Summary

The results of appraisals of reading abilities may be used to improve instruction in reading and in the content subjects by aiding in determining the nature of instruction, in adjusting instruction to individuals, in determining the readiness to undertake the learning of new areas of subject matter, and in testing the effectiveness of instruction. The results of appraisals of reading abilities are useful also in selecting appropriate reading materials; in guiding students into a fuller educational, vocational, and emotional development; and in contributing to research. Each of these uses of appraisals was discussed.

The appraisals that should be made in the five areas of reading instruction were considered. It was shown that the teacher has an important part in the program of appraisals. It is the

teacher who makes the most complete use of reading appraisals.
Several of the more important types of appraisals were discussed from the points of view of what the appraisal is, how
it is made, and its function. Group measurements (including
standardized tests, teacher-made tests, and questionnaires) and
observational methods (including informal observations, interviews, and reports) were discussed.

The administration of a program of reading appraisals depends upon the facilities within the school system. A system
that might be a functional one for many high schools includes: (1) the administering during the first week of school
of a carefully selected battery of standardized tests; (2) the
scoring and tabulating by each teacher of his quota of the
tests; (3) the assembling and distributing of the results to the
teachers; (4) the administering, scoring, and recording of tests
designed to measure the reading ability in a content subject
by the teacher of that subject; (5) the making of informal
appraisals and observations by the teachers from time to time
during the school year.

Selected Bibliography

Barr, A. S., Burton, W. H., and Brueckner, L. J. *Supervision,* D.
Appleton-Century Company, 1938, Chapters 6-10.

Betts, E. A. *The Prevention and Correction of Reading Difficulties,*
Row, Peterson and Company, 1936, Chapter 5.

Gates, Arthur I. "The Measurement and Evaluation of Achievement
in Reading," *The Teaching of Reading: A Second Report, The
Thirty-Sixth Yearbook of the National Society for the Study of Education,* Part I, Public School Publishing Company, 1937.

Harris, Albert J. *How to Increase Reading Ability,* Longmans, Green
and Company, 1940.

Hawkes, H. E., Lindquist, E. F., and Mann, C. R. Editors. *The Construction and Use of Achievement Examinations,* American Council
on Education, Houghton Mifflin Company, 1936.

McCallister, J. M. *Remedial and Corrective Instruction in Reading,* D. Appleton-Century Company, 1936, Chapter 4.

Strang, Ruth, and Rose, F. C. *Problems in the Improvement of Reading in High School and College,* Revised, The Science Press Printing Company, 1940, Chapters VI and IX.

Wesley, E. B. *Teaching and Social Studies,* D. C. Heath and Company, 1937, Chapter XXI.

Witty, Paul, and Kopel, David. *Reading and the Educative Process,* Ginn and Company, 1939.

SECTION III

THE PROGRAM FOR THE RETARDED READER

CHAPTER XI

READING DISABILITY

The preceding discussion has been concerned solely with a program that is designed to help all students continue their growth in reading. Such a program is called the developmental reading program. In the junior and senior high school reading growth will result from instruction in reading given in a general reading period, supplemented by special instruction in reading given as an integral part of each content subject.

However, since the present spread in reading abilities is as large as investigations have found it to be, there is needed special remedial work for that small group of students who require such instruction in addition to that given in the developmental program. But when a thoroughgoing developmental program shall be pursued through the elementary and high school years, the present frequency of reading disabilities in the high school will be lessened. Less often, then, will remedial help be needed.

Selection of Remedial Cases

As an illustration of the spread in reading ability discussed above, a percentage distribution of the grade scores in reading ability of a group of students[1] who were finishing the tenth grade in a Midwestern city is shown in Table VIII. Included in the table are the results of three tests: *Gates Reading Sur-*

[1] The same group of high school students was discussed in Chapter I, pages 19-22.

vey,[2] *Iowa Silent Reading Tests,*[3] and the *Traxler Silent Reading Test.*[4]

The *Gates Reading Survey* test measures vocabulary, power of comprehension, and reading speed and accuracy. This test furnishes grade norms from about grade 1.5 (middle of the first grade) to grade 13.0 (end of the twelfth). Because it furnishes a wide range of accurate norms, this test gives the teacher reliable information about the pupils in her class, including the extreme cases. In other words, these norms tell the teacher the approximate grade level at which the various members of her class are reading in the aspects of reading that the test measures.

The *Iowa Silent Reading Tests* measure sentence and paragraph meaning, vocabulary, paragraph organization, and ability to locate information. The scores on these aspects of reading are combined to make a total comprehension score. The tests also furnish a reading rate score. They are useful because they give a profile indicating a student's relative position in a variety of reading abilities. The tests have grade norms for total reading comprehension and for reading rate that range from 8.0 (end of the seventh grade) to 14.0 (end of the sophomore year in college). Percentile scores for the various sub-tests are also furnished.

The *Traxler Silent Reading Test* measures vocabulary, paragraph and story comprehension, and speed. The total score represents all these combined. Grade norms are provided for the total score. These norms range from 7.0 (end of the sixth grade) to 10.9 (end of the tenth grade). This test is a useful

[2] Gates, Arthur I. *Gates Reading Survey for Grades 3 to 10,* Bureau of Publications, Teachers College, Columbia University, New York City, 1939.

[3] Greene, H. A., Jorgensen, A. N., and Kelley, V. H. *Iowa Silent Reading Tests, Advanced,* Revised, World Book Company, 1931.

[4] Traxler, Arthur E. *Traxler Silent Reading Test,* Public School Publishing Company, 1934.

instrument because it is set up in such a way that it avoids artificiality.

The grade scores that appear in Table VIII include: vocabulary, power of comprehension, and speed on the *Gates Reading Survey* test; total comprehension score on the *Iowa Silent Reading Tests;* and total score on the *Traxler Silent Reading Test.*

TABLE VIII

Percentage of Cases by Grade Level of a Tenth-Grade Group on Three Silent Reading Tests

Number = 225

Grade Score	Gates Reading Survey			Iowa Silent Reading Total Comprehension	Traxler Silent Reading Total Score (Comprehension, Rate, Vocabulary)
	Comprehension	Vocabulary	Speed		
Above 12.9	1	3	4	16	
12.0—12.9	20	13	6	18	
11.0—11.9	30	24	17	20	30 [5]
10.0—10.9	25	17	8	15	18
9.0—9.9	19	24	16	16	24
8.0—8.9	3	8	19	9	16
Below 8.0	2	11	30	6	12

[5] Above 10.9 grade score.

The students comprising the group whose scores are pictured in Table VIII were finishing the tenth grade when they were measured. They should have been reading, therefore, at a grade score of 10.9 (end of the tenth grade). The table shows that many of them were somewhat retarded. Usually students retarded less than two years in reading ability receive sufficient reading instruction in the developmental program without participating in the remedial program.

An inspection of the table shows that the percentage of students who are retarded two years or more in reading varies for different attributes. For example, in the Gates Comprehension Test only 5 per cent are retarded two years or more, while on the Gates Vocabulary Test the per cent retarded two years or more is 19, and on the Gates Speed Test, 49. Since the per cent of those retarded in speed is so large, the developmental program should at the start undertake instruction in those types of reading which will tend to increase the speed.

It should be noted that 28 per cent are two or more years retarded according to the total score on the Traxler test. Since this score includes measurements of rate and vocabulary (in both of which the students demonstrated low ability on the Gates tests), it seems reasonable to suppose that both rate and vocabulary are operating to raise the percentage of students who are retarded two years or more. The problem of speed is evidently an all-school problem. Hence special instruction designed to improve the rate of reading should not be limited to the remedial program alone.

Further investigation shows that some of the students who were retarded two years were reading as effectively as could reasonably be expected, since their reading ages and mental ages were about the same. Consequently, such students could not rightfully be called remedial cases. They should receive instruction in reading in the developmental program. However, this instruction should be designed to fit their needs.

Figure V shows the case of a girl, more than two years retarded in reading, who probably should not be considered a remedial case. In all measures of comprehension this student's reading grade is superior to her mental grade. She can probably best be served by the developmental program. It is necessary, however, for her teachers to realize that she is somewhat handicapped by her low background of word meaning and that her rate of advancement will be somewhat slower than that of the average student.

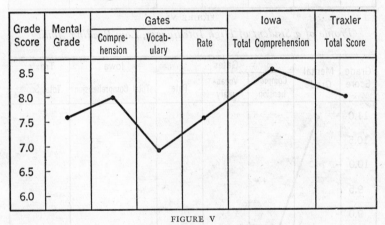

FIGURE V

Profile of a Student Two Years Retarded in Mental and Reading Grades

Figure VI charts the reading grade scores of a boy with superior intelligence. While his reading ability is only approximately a year below his grade level, it is on the average fully two years below his mental grade. Undoubtedly this boy would profit considerably from remedial instruction. Very likely some habit or lack of technique is interfering with his reading development. The need for remedial work with him would likely be of short duration.

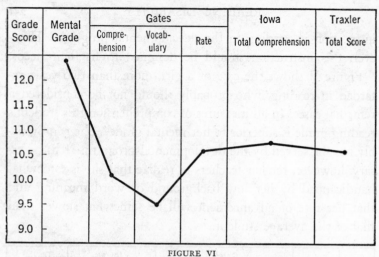

FIGURE VI

Profile of a Student of High Intelligence, Low Reading Ability

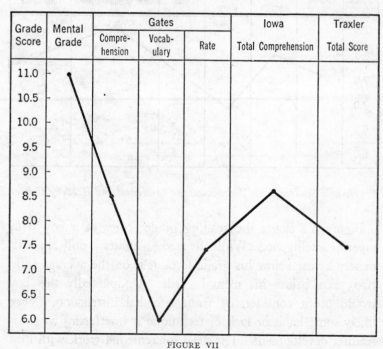

FIGURE VII

Profile of a Student Deficient in Reading Ability

The reading and mental grade scores of a girl who should undoubtedly be given remedial instruction in reading are recorded in Figure VII. The profile shows that this girl is well over two years retarded in all the measures, and five years retarded in vocabulary. Such a student would profit little from the developmental program unless it was augmented by remedial instruction.

Selection of the cases to be included in the remedial program must be done on an individual basis. The three profiles reproduced here, combined with the 222 other profiles of reading and mental grade scores of the students in this 10A group, indicate this clearly. Other factors, such as interests, attitude toward reading, and degree of independence, should be considered in selecting the remedial cases.

CAUSES OF READING DISABILITY

Although it is understood that the extreme disability cases form not a distinct group but simply the lower end of a distribution, it is still both interesting and important to determine possible factors which might be responsible for these differences. It should be noted, before a discussion of the causes of reading disability is undertaken, that the case is rare indeed in which reading disability can be attributed to one single isolated factor. Rather it is due to a combination of several factors.

The causes of difficulty in any one case are usually very subtle. In addition to the subtle nature of the causes of reading disability in general, there is the added fact that the disability of a high school student might have had its beginning at any point in the entire developmental reading program. One student's disability might have had its roots during the initial lesson, while another student might have got into difficulty in the fourth grade. A third student might have seemed to progress satisfactorily to an even higher grade. In any one of these cases, the cumulative effect of the disability might have been such that reading retardation would have been difficult to detect until the reading program made demands upon the student which he could not meet.

In order to understand a reading disability thoroughly, it is necessary to ascertain when it began and what factors led to it. In formulating remedial procedures, it is always helpful to know how persistent and firmly entrenched the disability has been. The student who has had reading difficulty for many years presents a somewhat different problem from the student who has had difficulty for a comparatively short time.

Consider, for example, the twelfth-grade girl whose father is opposed to reading in artificial light. Since this girl's day is filled with school and recreational activities during the daylight hours, there is little opportunity for out-of-school reading. Obviously, such a person will have a very limited experience with reading. It will not be surprising to find that this student is an ineffective reader, even though her intelligence is relatively high. Such a student might progress satisfactorily in reading development as long as the reading of the majority of her peers is confined to the daylight hours. But during the high school years, this student probably fell behind her class group because she did not have the chance to have her full share of reading experiences.

It is not possible for a student who, for any reason, must confine his reading experiences to school hours to get enough experience with reading to develop at the normal rate. Unless the material in the reading program is adjusted to the rate of such a student's learning, he may find the reading materials of the classroom too difficult to read and will, therefore, fall behind even more rapidly. Consequently, he loses not only the experiences he should have had in reading outside the classroom, but also much of the benefit he might have derived from in-school reading.

Although the case cited on page 254 is unusual, there are students whose out-of-school reading is limited by such things as work, lack of materials, and lack of incentive. Whenever this difficulty can be attributed solely to the lack of experience in reading, an effective developmental program throughout the junior and senior high school years may, for the majority of cases, completely overcome its effect.

To say that the reading disability in the case described earlier was caused by lack of experience does not take all the factors into account. If the school had adjusted the reading materials to the developmental level of the students and had enabled this particular student to gain a wide range of reading experiences, it is reasonable to suppose that her disability could have been avoided. In the case discussed earlier, the teacher's task should have been that of establishing a rapport between the school and home so that they could have been working toward a common purpose. It is obvious that the task of the teacher in such a case is quite different from what it would be in working with a student whose reading disability could be attributed to faulty techniques which were established in the early grades, and which, through practice and use, had become firmly entrenched in the reading pattern of the student. In any therapeutic work it is important to correct or make adjustments to the factors which are causing the difficulty.

If an effective remedial program is to be outlined for any one individual, it is advisable that the causes of reading disability be known, even though they are often subtle and deeply rooted. It is only through such knowledge that the therapeutic work can be adjusted to the causes rather than to the symptoms.

The causes in a given case of disability are hard to determine because of their subtle nature and because of the complexity of the reading process. The interrelationship between the factors which may be responsible for disability makes it difficult to discover which of these factors or what group of them is most frequently responsible for reading disabilities. It is probably because of the complexity of the problem that there is some disagreement among the workers in this field about the relative weight of the various causes of disability.

It is safe to assume, however, that reading difficulty is not due to a single or simple cause, but rather to many factors, either singly or in combination. It is more frequently the case than otherwise that the factors responsible operate in groupings rather than individually. Nevertheless, for the sake of simplicity, it is advisable to discuss separately some of the more common causes.

Intelligence

Intelligence is highly related to reading efficiency. Those students who have high intelligence may, on the whole, be expected to read well. They will, by and large, have more reading interests, and increasingly more clearly defined word and meaning backgrounds; they will display more independence; and they will find more uses for reading than will students of less intellectual ability. This, however, does not mean that every individual of high intelligence is necessarily an effective reader. And it is just as incorrect to assume that, because a student is an ineffective reader, his intelligence is low. This is true because of the many causes of reading disability other than low intelligence.

The remedial reading program should concern itself with the students who have wide discrepancies between their mental ability and their reading ability. It is common practice for school systems to undertake remedial work in reading for students who are low in both mental ability and reading ability. But unfortunately it is assumed in these schools that the students who are low in reading ability but have high mental ability will be able to achieve passing marks in their school subjects through the sheer force of their intelligence. This, of course, is a faulty generalization. The mere achievement of passing marks is not all that should be expected of students with high intelligence. The more crucial problem is that of so improving the student's effectiveness in reading that he is able to do work in keeping with his mental ability.

While it is true that something can be done for the poor readers of low intelligence, much more can be accomplished with the students of high intelligence who are low in reading. They constitute the real reading problems. It is the discrepancy between reading and mental ability which should determine whether or not the student, in addition to receiving reading instruction in the developmental program, should receive remedial instruction. Where there is no large discrepancy, the individual can probably best be served in a developmental program which is adjusted to individual rates of learning.

Since intelligence is such an important factor in both the selection of the reading disability cases and the adjusting of instruction in the developmental and remedial programs, the mental ability of the students should be determined. It is expedient to use group intelligence tests for the initial survey of intelligence. Of course, since group intelligence tests usually require some reading, they do not give poor readers ample opportunity to demonstrate their intelligence. They must, therefore, be supplemented by individual measurements for all poor readers in order to give even an approximate indication of their true mental ability. Even such an instrument as the

Stanford-Binet Test of Intelligence, the most widely used individual intelligence test, somewhat handicaps the poor reader.[6] This handicap may amount to as much as twenty points in the intelligence quotient. In interpreting Binet results, it is safe to assume that the intelligence of a poor reader is probably no lower than that demonstrated and that it is quite likely to be somewhat higher.

There are students in the high school who do not have the mental ability necessary to cope with high school materials. The problems of the high school teacher are to develop the reading of these students as much as possible and to find suitable and adequate materials which the students can be reasonably expected to read. The problem, then, is that of adjusting the instructional methods and materials to the mental ability of the students. Much can be done in the developmental reading program for the students of low mentality.

If it were possible to raise the intelligence of high school students, remedial measures would be of more value in this area than in any other of the school curricula. But since this is not possible, it is necessary to accept the facts as they are and adjust instruction to these students. The only hope for the low intelligence group at present is to recognize the causes of their difficulty and keep instruction at the level of their ability.

Meager Background of Experience

Students' backgrounds of experience are as varied as their intelligence. These variations are the result of differences in environment or susceptibility. The concern of the teacher is not only how wide the backgrounds are, but how well he can supply materials for reading suitable to them. For example,

[6] Bond, Elden A. "Some Verbal Aspects of the 1937 Revision of the Stanford-Binet Intelligence Test, Form L," *The Journal of Experimental Education,* Vol. VI, March, 1938, pp. 340-42.

the student who comes from an isolated rural community may not be as well prepared in backgrounds to read social studies materials of urban life as the student who has lived in an urban society all his life. On the other hand, the child who has spent his entire life in a highly industrialized city may not be as adequately prepared to meet initial reading lessons concerning the farm as will a child who has spent his life on a farm.

At any grade level the instruction in reading must lean heavily upon the meaning backgrounds of the students. If at any time the student has a poor background of meanings, he may get into difficulty; and in turn his background will become increasingly meager. Consequently, the poor reader in high school, regardless of the primary cause of reading disability, probably has a meager background of the type derived from wide reading experience. For this reason it is difficult to determine whether the poor reading is caused by the limited background of meaning or the limited background is the result of poor reading. But in any case the background of meaning can and must be improved.

Inadequate Meaning Vocabulary

Inadequate meaning vocabulary may be a primary cause of reading disability. When children enter school, they show marked variation in the number of words which have meaning for them. This is true at all stages of development. The student who has but few word meanings at his command is quite likely to find it difficult to read and understand materials which depend for their meaning upon words with which he is not familiar. Such a student would probably not be inclined to turn to reading as an activity. The fact that extensive reading is one of the ways in which vocabulary can be enlarged has a cumulative effect in causing reading disability. Again it should be noted that poor reading brought about by any other cause would tend to limit the meaning vocabulary of a student by the time he had reached the high school.

Aside from lack of experience in reading, there are many conditions which bring about meager meaning vocabularies. For example, the child brought up in a home in which the vocabulary was limited or conversation at a minimum might not have the opportunity to build as extensive a vocabulary as would the child who came from a home of rich and varied verbal experience.

An extreme case encountered by the authors is that of a fourteen-year-old boy who was the only child of deaf mutes. This boy had not built up a very extensive background of word meanings and had not used effectively the background that he did have. Although he was relatively sociable in playground activities, he was likely to shrink from conversation. At the outset he had difficulty in learning to read. By the time he reached junior high school, his vocabulary was very immature. If this developing condition had been recognized earlier, the problem would have been less severe. After a year of instruction designed to develop word meanings and give experience in reading materials for which he had adequate word meanings, this boy had gained two full years of reading ability. It was felt, in addition, that a more adequate basis for his continued improvement had been established.

Incorrect Placement in School

Incorrect placement in school may come about from a variety of causes and may have various effects on reading disability. It might be, for example, that the student was placed too high at all times for his reading development, in which case he would find the reading materials and purposes too difficult. If the reading program had been adjusted to his level of development, his difficulty would have been of little consequence. When too rapid advancement is not accompanied by the proper adjustment of instruction, the student is likely to fall behind in reading development and to become a reading disability case. In the majority of such cases the answer is not that of retardation, but of adjusting the reading program to each individual.

Incorrect placement can also come about in the grades as a result of advancing too slowly for reading development. This is likely to be true of the bright students. One student may be kept so long on one phase of reading development that he overemphasizes this phase to the extent that interfering habits are created. Another student may lose interest in all phases of schoolwork, including reading, because the work is monotonous to him. Or a student may make seemingly satisfactory progress without reading by merely attending to classroom discussions.

Sooner or later, however, students come to a point in their schoolwork where they can no longer proceed satisfactorily without being able to read. At such a time those who read too inefficiently find themselves in trouble. If they had been given an opportunity to advance a little more rapidly, or if the program had been enriched, this would not have occurred.

Double promotion, school absences, or a change in schools may cause faulty placement because areas of instruction may be omitted. Since reading is developmental in nature, any omissions may have deleterious effects. It is often difficult to determine whether the cause of reading disability is the gap in instruction or the fact that the instruction was not altered for the individual so that he might adjust to the new circumstances.

Defective Vision

The child with poor vision will not inevitably be a poor reader. Although it is true that defective vision is a primary cause of reading disability, many children with poor vision progress normally in reading.[7] Still, it is undoubtedly more difficult to learn to read if vision is defective. For example, it takes keen visual ability to distinguish the difference between *house* and *horse*.

It is reasonable to suppose that a child with poor vision may have other attributes which can overcome the increased effort he must expend in reading. He may, for instance, have such an interest in reading that he is willing to put forth the effort necessary to compensate for the visual handicap. A large background of experience may prove to be a sufficient force to enable the child with poor vision to learn to read at what appears to be a normal rate. In either of these cases, of course, learning to read might have progressed more rapidly if vision had been normal.

In all cases of reading disability, the visual abilities should be measured; and whenever a defect which can be corrected is located, the correction should be made. Among the more common visual defects are nearsightedness, farsightedness, muscular imbalance, astigmatism, and lack of ability to fuse or combine the images from the two eyes.

In most cases these defects can be corrected. However, a student with a reading disability who has had a persistently uncorrected visual defect cannot be expected, simply by having his vision corrected, to overcome the faulty habits he has formed. The correction of vision is the first step in remedial work for such cases, but it must be followed by careful training in reading. If his vision had received attention early, it is likely that faulty habits would not have been formed or necessary techniques omitted.

[7] Fendrick, Paul. "Visual Characteristics of Poor Readers," *Contributions to Education,* No. 656, Bureau of Publications, Teachers College, Columbia University, 1935.

Auditory Defects

Defective hearing may be a primary cause of reading disability. This is especially true under methods of instruction which depend for their effectiveness upon oral presentation by the teacher or oral reading and phonetic analysis by the students.[8] If a pupil is exposed to the oral types of instruction, auditory ability appears to be a factor of importance in relation to reading ability. If, however, the pupils are taught by methods which are predominantly visual in nature, auditory factors do not appear to be so significantly related to reading disability.

It seems reasonable to suppose that a child who is hard of hearing may well get into difficulty if his hearing defect is not known to the teacher. If such a student does not have a favorable location in the classroom, he may miss much of the instruction and as a result fail to build up the backgrounds necessary on the high school level. Teachers often do not seem to be able to recognize that the child's hearing is not perfect, but they attribute his behavior to listlessness, inattentiveness, or lack of interest. Consequently, adequate measures of hearing ability must be made for all reading disability cases.

If a competent otologist finds it impossible to correct the hearing loss, adjustments of instruction must be made. Even though the hearing loss is corrected, instruction must begin at the level of the student's reading ability, and inappropriate reading techniques must be altered or eliminated.

Speech Defects

The relationship between speech defects and reading disability is rather complex. It is obvious that a student handicapped by a speech defect will have difficulty in oral reading, even

[8] Bond, Guy L. "Auditory and Speech Characteristics of Poor Readers," *Contributions to Education,* No. 657, Bureau of Publications, Teachers College, Columbia University, 1935.

though his silent reading ability is very good. And it seems logical that if the instruction in silent reading depends on the use of oral reading, the student handicapped by a speech defect may experience difficulty in both fields. If, however, the instructional techniques do not depend upon oral reading, the student with speech defects can be expected to have little if any more trouble with silent reading than any other student.[9]

Since oral reading is an integral part of the reading ability of any given student, the relationship between speech defects and oral reading should be recognized. Obviously, the speech cases should be given speech correction. This is the function of the speech department.

However, all teachers in the reading program should be aware of the detrimental emotional effects which may accompany the oral reading of a student who has defective speech. This does not imply that the speech case should not do oral reading, but rather that the purposes and the materials should be adjusted so that he will be able to read successfully. He should be given ample time to familiarize himself with the materials so that reading difficulties will not add to any possible confusion.

Emotional and Other Personality Disturbances

Most workers in the field of reading are aware of a high relationship between reading disability and factors of personality adjustment. Gates,[10] after studying the case histories of one hundred reading disability cases chosen at random, found that ninety-two out of the hundred demonstrated inadequate personality reactions and that only eight had established ade-

[9] Bond, Guy L. "Auditory and Speech Characteristics of Poor Readers," pp. 37-40. (See Footnote 8 on page 263.)

[10] Gates, Arthur I. "Failure in Reading and Social Maladjustment," *Journal of the National Education Association*, Vol. XXV, October, 1936, pp. 205-6.

quate compensatory reactions. It is a moot question whether disability in reading is a cause or a result of personality disturbances. It is reasonable to assume that the child who enters school with emotional and personality disturbances probably will become a reading disability case. It is also reasonable to assume that the child who experiences severe emotional or personality disturbances at any subsequent time in his school career will likewise experience difficulty in reading. It is likely, too, that the child who experiences difficulty in reading for any other reason may become so confused and frustrated that he frequently displays emotional and personal disturbances. The following quotation from Monroe brings out this point:

> Whether the reading defect is caused by unfavorable behavior or personality, or vice versa, is sometimes difficult to determine. A child may be resistant to learning through negativism and unfavorable emotional attitudes. In such a case reading would undoubtedly suffer along with other scholastic achievements. On the other hand, and probably more frequently, a child may develop the emotional and personality problems as a result of failure in learning to read. The emotional attitudes may develop through the child's failure and then, in turn, may aggravate still further the retardation in reading.[11]

The vast majority of reading disability cases are behavior and emotional problems. Consider, for example, the case of Charles, a thirteen-year-old boy of above average intelligence who had failed miserably in learning to read. Charles was a very large boy. He had spent the first six years in a small rural school and had transferred to a large consolidated junior high school. His reading grade was 3.5 (halfway through the third grade). Obviously he could not read the materials of the seventh grade —the grade to which he was assigned.

[11] Monroe, Marion. *Children Who Cannot Read*, University of Chicago Press, 1932, p. 105.

When Charles was confronted with reading material, he complained of headaches and said that his eyes hurt him after reading less than two minutes. He said that if he could bring his father's glasses to school, he would be able to read with little trouble. This boy, whose vision was very good, could work for long periods of time on puzzle type material, which called for the matching of figures similar to words, without any indication of visual difficulty. Soon after attempting to read, however, he would get sick headaches, vomit, and ask to be allowed to go home.

This emotional problem seemed to be a direct result of the difficulty with reading. The results of remedial work confirmed this belief. Charles was given a year of individual instruction in reading. After a good rapport was established between the remedial worker and Charles, a thorough explanation of the reading problem was given to him. He was given interesting material at his reading level and, as his reading improved, the reading level of the material increased. There were no more headaches and no more vomiting spells. At the end of the year, Charles was able to read the material of the seventh grade with relative ease, and the functional physical disturbance had disappeared.

The case of Charles indicates that poor reading can cause personality disturbances. When he first entered junior high school, his tense, disturbed condition in a reading situation was quite obvious.

The emotional concomitants of poor reading are not always so apparent, but they are frequently present in reading cases. Albert, for example, was a twelve-year-old boy of superior intelligence who had also failed to learn to read. He had worked out for himself a very satisfactory defense. Whenever he found himself in a reading situation, it was his custom to say, "I do not care to learn to read because books are make-believe. I want to live in a world of reality, to sail boats, go on trips, and really experience things." Because he could not read, he would do everything possible to avoid reading and frequently became very obstinate.

In both of these cases poor reading seemed to bring in its wake emotional and other personality disturbances. This causal relationship may be just the reverse. An emotional or other personality disturbance may be a primary cause of reading disability. The case of Betty and Anne, twin ninth-grade girls, was one in which an emotional condition seemed to be the cause of reading disability for one of them. Anne was an intellectually gifted girl who learned to read easily and who had done excellent work throughout her school life. Betty was of average mental ability. She did not learn to read with the facility of her twin sister. Her progress in the beginning was very much like that of other children in the group. However, the parents of these girls, realizing that Betty was not getting along as well as Anne, began to coach Betty in reading at home. Betty was forced to spend time reading, while Anne was allowed to engage in any type of activity which interested her. Frequently, of course, she read for recreation at the same time when Betty received lessons in reading. The parents made comparisons between the reading ability of the two girls in the hope that Betty would be shamed into putting forth more effort.

At first, in grades one and two, Betty's progress in reading was about like that of the majority of the class. But since her parents and teachers constantly compared her progress in other subjects in school as well as in reading with that of her sister, Betty had a continuous sense of failure, even though she was progressing satisfactorily in terms of her own mental ability. During the later years of the elementary school, she grew to dislike school intensely. It was not long before it was apparent that this girl, who had progressed satisfactorily in learning to read during the first two years of school, was failing to continue that satisfactory progress. Indeed, by the time she entered high school, she was severely retarded in reading ability.

Betty was given a Stanford-Binet Test of Intelligence soon after she entered the ninth grade. The examiner, endeavoring to establish rapport, began by talking about the fact that he knew her twin sister Anne, and that she was a very fine girl. It was apparent to the examiner that Betty, from that time on, was extremely negativistic. The intelligence quotient, on the basis of this examination, was found to be 57, which would place Betty in the moron group in intelligence. The examiner, however, wrote on the front of the Binet blank, "Re-examine this child. This is not a true measure of ability."

Another form of the Stanford-Binet Test of Intelligence was given to Betty after a sufficient lapse of time. This time no mention was made of her sister. The intelligence quotient, on the basis of this examination, was 109, which placed her in the normal group in intelligence. Subsequent measurement and work indicated that this latter test was the more accurate.

Betty was given remedial instruction in reading. She made such good progress that before the year was over, she was able to read as well as the majority of her peers. Betty's parents and teachers were told that any comparison between the two sisters should be strictly avoided. One can only estimate what the effect of the remedial work would have been if the teacher had not known about the emotional problem which had resulted in the reading disability and had selected a story about twins as suitable material for the first remedial lesson!

In working with reading disability cases, the remedial teacher must be aware of the students' emotional reactions to reading. Whether the reading disability of a student is the result or the cause of emotional or other personality disturbances, the remedial teacher, in order to proceed wisely, must have a complete developmental history of the student. And at the outset any antagonistic attitude toward reading must be overcome. Remedial reading teachers frequently report that when the student feels that he *can* learn to read and actually wants to *try,* the task of teaching him is well begun. In some reading deficiency cases a fatalistic attitude toward reading is so engrained that the remedial teacher must exercise patience, and the instruction must at first proceed very slowly.

Inappropriate Teaching

In the ultimate analysis it might be said that, in the majority of cases, inappropriate or faulty teaching is a primary cause of reading disability. Even those children who have borderline mental ability, sensory limitations, physical handicaps, or emotional problems can learn to read if the instruction is adjusted to their needs. This does not mean, however, that the teachers are always responsible for reading disability cases.

Many factors contribute to make the teaching less adjusted to the needs of the students than it might be under more favorable conditions. One such factor is that teachers have such heavy schedules that it is impossible for them to do as good work as they otherwise could. The teacher who has five different classes to teach every day, in addition to other teaching duties, does not teach any one of them as well as he is potentially able. Frequently, too, classrooms are overcrowded and poorly equipped. Under such conditions there is little wonder that instruction is faulty or inadequately adjusted to the needs of the students.

Another factor which frequently makes the teacher's task more difficult and contributes to faulty or inappropriate teaching is that the reading materials used are not suited to the needs of the class. One teacher may have relatively few reading materials; another may have materials which are inappropriate or too difficult for the use of specific students within a group. In either case poor reading development is likely to be the outcome.

An almost inevitable result of carrying forward a school program with inadequate reading materials is a large number of disability cases. It is often possible for an efficient teacher to prepare materials to supplement a minimum of materials; but if the child is to learn to read effectively, he should have the opportunity to read extensively from materials suited to his level of development.

Use of the group method of teaching may be a primary cause of reading disability. Instruction, in order to be effective for all students within a group, must be adjusted to the needs of the individual students. When instruction is designed to enable the middle group of readers to progress in a somewhat normal fashion, but takes little account of the very good readers or very poor readers, students at either extreme may fail to develop satisfactorily in reading ability and, as a consequence, may become disability cases.

The young, inexperienced teacher is very likely to adjust instruction to the needs of the majority of the class and to give little or inappropriate instruction to the very good and very poor readers. As the teacher gains experience and the task of teaching becomes an easier one for him, he usually undertakes to individualize instruction. Some teachers, however, during the course of their entire teaching life, teach groups rather than individuals. This mass instruction is one of the reasons for poor reading ability among high school students.

A rather common result of group methods of instruction is the failure to detect the mistakes of the student at the time they are made and to arrange for their correction. Relatively unimportant mistakes in reading, if allowed to continue, may develop into firmly entrenched habits which will be difficult to overcome or correct. This failure to detect a student's mistakes may be a contributing factor to disability at any point in the reading program. If, for example, a student with faulty vision makes errors of discrimination which go undetected, he may soon find that the material is becoming too difficult for him to read. This might well take place in the early educational experience of the child, but its influence may be felt when he gets into the more difficult materials of the junior and senior high school.

Group methods of instruction may cause such faulty habits as using a spelling attack for the recognition of words, using head movements, pointing, skipping unfamiliar words or phrases, and reading all material at the same rate. Under group teaching methods such habits are likely to remain undetected. While they may not impede the student's progress in the initial reading instruction, such habits will sooner or later prove detrimental to effective reading.

Disability cases resulting from faulty habits are relatively frequent on the high school level. One such case, for example, was that of a tenth-grade boy who read very poorly. Diagnosis showed that this boy's only means of recognizing unfamiliar words was that of spelling a word aloud. If the unknown word was *felicity,* for example, he would say aloud to himself, "*f-e-l-i-c-i-t-y, felicity,*" and then proceed with the sentence. This boy was depending for word recognition on a faulty and time-consuming technique. It is small wonder that he found reading both uninteresting and difficult.

The overemphasis of a skill or technique frequently results in reading disability. The ability to read is the result of a fine balance between numerous skills and techniques. If for any reason one of these skills or techniques is overemphasized at the expense of others, reading disability may result. This overemphasis may result from instruction which is not individualized or which places too much stress upon one technique. Overemphasis on reading for details, for example, might make the entire group approach all their reading in a slow and laboriously detailed fashion. This would definitely impede the students' progress in developing a differentiated attack.

An individual within a group may overemphasize a given technique, although the reading program in general is fairly well balanced. A child who learns readily to separate the word into its phonetic elements may have acquired a sufficient degree of that ability long before the other members of the class. However, under group instruction, it is likely that he will continue to receive instruction in syllabification. As a result, he may learn the lesson too well and become an overanalysis disability case. For him words will fall into syllables and he must reassemble them. This will result in a slow, word-by-word reading performance, which might go undetected for many years. One such case was a senior in college. This student was exceptionally able in such courses as mathematics and science, which do not make as great demands upon speed of reading as English and the social studies, but he found the latter subjects extremely difficult.

Inadequate Motivation

Throughout the discussion of the developmental program, the role of purpose in reading has received much attention. It has been stated that the purposes for which the student is reading determine, in no small measure, the way in which he will read. If the purposes are inadequately or faultily defined, the resulting reading may be ineffective.

Inadequate or inappropriate motivation may cause reading disability. The student may be in a home environment where there is little motivation to read. Or he may be inappropriately motivated in the school environment. For example, poor incentives of one kind or another may prove to be faulty motivation for some students. The remedial worker must determine the reasons for which the student is or is not reading. The student may not be reading, for example, because he finds that he can obtain the same information with less effort by other means. Or perhaps he feels that the content of the material is of little intrinsic worth to him and therefore has no real motive for reading. If adequate purposes, motives, and incentives for reading are established and if the materials and methods are adjusted to the student's needs and abilities, the great majority of students may be expected to learn to read with little difficulty.

SUMMARY

Usually students retarded less than two years in reading ability receive sufficient reading instruction in the developmental program without participating in the remedial program. Students who are retarded two or more years in reading ability, in most cases, should receive remedial instruction in addition to the regular instruction in the developmental program. The selection of the cases to be included in the remedial program must be made on an individual basis. Factors such as reading interests, attitude toward reading, independence in reading, degree of discrepancy between reading age and mental age should be considered carefully in selecting the remedial cases.

Difficulty in reading is usually brought about by a combination of several factors. The case is rare indeed in which reading disability can be attributed to one single, isolated factor. It is advisable to ascertain the causes of the reading disability, if possible, even though they are often subtle and of long standing.

Some of the more common causes of disability in reading are: (1) low intelligence; (2) meager background of experience; (3) inadequate meaning vocabulary; (4) limited home environment; (5) incorrect placement in school resulting in too rapid advancement, too slow advancement, gaps in instruction; (6) defective vision; (7) defective hearing; (8) defective speech; (9) emotional and other personality disturbances; (10) inappropriate teaching due to inadequate teaching, inappropriate materials, group methods, failure immediately to detect and remedy mistakes, overemphasis of a skill or technique; (11) inadequate motivation.

Selected Bibliography

Barry, L., and others. "Reading Difficulties of High School Pupils," *School Review*, Vol. XLVI, January, 1938, pp. 44-47.

Bond, Elden A. "Some Verbal Aspects of the 1937 Revision of the Stanford-Binet Intelligence Test, Form L," *The Journal of Experimental Education,* Vol. VI, March, 1938, pp. 340-42.

Bond, Guy L. "Auditory and Speech Characteristics of Poor Readers," *Contributions to Education,* No. 657, Bureau of Publications, Teachers College, Columbia University, 1935.

Fendrick, Paul. "Visual Characteristics of Poor Readers," *Contributions to Education,* No. 656, Bureau of Publications, Teachers College, Columbia University, 1935.

Gates, Arthur I. "Failure in Reading and Social Maladjustment," *The Journal of the National Education Association,* Vol. XXV, October, 1936, pp. 205-6.

Gray, W. S. "Reading Difficulties in College," *Journal of Higher Education,* Vol. VII, October, 1936, pp. 356-62.

Harris, Albert J. *How to Increase Reading Ability,* Longmans, Green and Company, 1940.

Monroe, Marion. *Children Who Cannot Read,* University of Chicago Press, 1932.

Ryans, David G. "Some Questions Pertaining to Reading," *School and Society,* Vol. XLIII, April, 1936, pp. 572-74.

Strang, Ruth, and Rose, F. C. *Problems in the Improvement of Reading in High School and College,* Revised, The Science Press Printing Company, 1940, Chapter VI.

Witty, Paul, and Kopel, David. *Reading and the Educative Process,* Ginn and Company, 1939.

Wrenn, C. Gilbert. "Aiding the Fit," *Journal of Higher Education,* Vol. VI, October, 1935, pp. 357-63.

CHAPTER XII

DIAGNOSING READING DISABILITY

As a result of the general testing program, it is possible to select those students who are in need of remedial work. This selection, however, must be done on an individual basis. The question that must be answered in each case by the co-ordinator or person responsible for the remedial program is, "Is there any indication that some factor or factors are operating which must be cleared up or overcome before the student can develop in reading at the rate at which he is capable?"

It must be realized that remedial cases do not form a distinct group. A person who is very slightly retarded in reading development, of course, would profit from the more highly individualized instruction in the remedial program. It is probable, however, that the remedial program can accommodate only those cases that are most severely handicapped, and that through the individualization of the general developmental program, the cases of less severity can be effectively taught. The diagnostic and remedial program should concern itself with the relatively small number of severely retarded cases, since diagnostic and remedial work is comparatively expensive, and the returns must justify the expense. It is the severely retarded case that is most in need of the remedial instruction. And it is the severely retarded case who will profit most from remedial instruction.

Purpose of Diagnosis

After the cases to be given remedial work have been selected, it is necessary to make a thorough diagnosis of each case. *Diagnosis consists of measuring and studying the symptoms and determining the causes in order to understand the nature of the disability.* The nature of the disability must be understood if appropriate remedial instruction is to be applied. Remedial instruction cannot be undertaken effectively until the factor or factors responsible for the reading disability are known. Remedial work that is not based upon a thorough diagnosis is likely to be very wasteful of the time and effort of the student and the remedial teacher. Moreover, remedial work undertaken without adequate diagnosis is likely to fail completely. A student who has had difficulty with reading is already inclined to be insecure. A further failure in the remedial program would prove to be very detrimental indeed. The person responsible for the remedial program should be aware of the possible outcomes of failure and should make every effort to insure that each student will succeed in that program.

The adequacy of the diagnosis determines in no small degree the success of the remedial program. Since reading is a complex process, there is no one single or simple cure for reading disability. The remedial training that will be effective for one case might prove detrimental or wasteful for another. It is only through an understanding of the underlying factors of disability of any given case that an adequate remedial program can be formulated. For example, two students are having difficulty with reading. The appraisals show that both are low in reading comprehension. Further analyses of the difficulty indicate that one student is low in comprehension because of an inadequate recognition vocabulary. The other student is low because he is a word-by-word reader who is so conscious of words that he is unable to group them into thought units. The first case needs remedial work which builds up his consciousness of words and ability to inspect them. Obviously such a procedure would be definitely detrimental to the second case.

It is only through a knowledge of the needs of the reading disability case that remedial work can be adjusted to the individual. The diagnosis is undertaken to make the remedial work more effective and to lessen the hazard of failure.

The Program of Diagnosis

Practical Considerations in Planning the Program

Certain practical considerations have been taken account of in organizing the program of diagnosis described in this chapter. In the first place, the program was set up in order to enable the diagnostician to obtain a rather complete inventory of the factors associated with reading disability. This inventory, therefore, includes those measurements and appraisals that seem to be essential in diagnosing the majority of reading disability cases. Through the results of the diagnosis, an adequate remedial program usually can be formulated.

A second consideration was that the amount of testing should be as little as is necessary to give the diagnostician an understanding of each disability case. The plan of procedure is that of first appraising the more general factors, and then gradually taking into consideration as many of the more complex ones as are necessary to understand and prescribe for the difficulty of each.

Among the first appraisals are group measurements; later appraisals can be made only by working individually with the student. In any one factor group measurements, whenever possible, are first utilized; then, if necessary to understand the disability, the factor is analyzed and studied more completely by means of individual appraisals. For example, the initial group appraisal might show that a student was over two years retarded in vocabulary development. In order to find out if the vocabulary deficiency was a general one covering each of the content fields, measurements of knowledge of scientific words, of social scientific words, of mathematical terms, and of literary words would be made. It is very likely that these measurements could be group ones. That is, the vocabulary knowledge of many of the students who were severely retarded in vocabulary probably should be measured more precisely than was possible in the initial all-school appraisal of vocabulary development. This could most expeditiously be done by gathering these students together so that the additional appraisal might be done in a group rather than individually. After each student's degree of retardation in knowledge of the vocabulary of the content fields had been ascertained, the combined appraisals for each student would have to be scrutinized by the diagnostician in order to determine if additional appraisals were needed. Subsequent appraisals very likely would be individual ones. They would in most cases be directed toward locating the cause or causes of the vocabulary deficiency.

In any event, the program of appraisal of vocabulary knowledge for each student would go as far as was necessary to furnish an understanding of the disability and no further. Indiscriminate testing is wasteful of time and energy of both the student and the diagnostician. It is expensive and should always be avoided.

A third consideration in organizing the program of diagnosis was that it should be as easy to operate and as simple as is feasible with good results. It is not felt that elaborate, technical appraisals are needed in order to understand and prescribe for most of the reading disability cases. The diagnostic procedure frequently may be relatively a simple one and one that is comparatively easy for both the student and the examiner. Certain psychological factors such as visual and auditory imagery that might prove important for some few reading disability cases have been purposely omitted from the program of appraisals.

A fourth consideration was that the diagnostic and remedial program entail as little expensive equipment and materials as possible. High schools are not usually able to finance the installation of a fully equipped reading clinic; nor is a fully equipped reading clinic necessary in most high schools. It is often only the rare disability case that requires so complete a diagnosis that the use of expensive equipment and materials is necessary. For those cases a more economical plan is to have them diagnosed by an expert diagnostician in an available reading clinic. The appraisals recommended in this program of diagnosis are ones that are easily accessible and available for use, that entail as little equipment and as inexpensive materials as is possible, and that are, at the same time, productive of results.

Appraisals Needed

The appraisals that should be made are:
1. Mental age
2. Chronological age
3. Grade placement
4. School history
5. Silent reading abilities
   a. Skimming
   b. Locating information
   c. Ability to read graphs, tables, maps, and other pictorial presentations
   d. Sentence, paragraph, and story comprehension
   e. Power of comprehension
   f. Ability to get the general significance

    g. Ability to note details

    h. Ability to organize

    i. Ability to follow directions

    j. Ability to predict outcome

    k. Ability to form sensory impressions of what is read

    l. Ability to read critically

    m. Rate of silent reading

6. Oral reading

    a. Level

    b. Analysis of errors

    c. Rate

7. Ability to work out words in isolation

8. Background of experience

9. Sensory characteristics

10. Physical condition

11. Emotional and other personality disturbances

12. Interest in and attitude toward reading.

The discussions of the above appraisals will include: (1) the nature of the factor being measured; (2) how it may be measured; (3) its general significance in a program of diagnosis. It must be realized that there are interrelationships among many factors. Each factor contributes to an understanding of the reading problem, but the significant consideration in diagnosing the reading case is the total picture rather than any one factor in the picture. One factor or group of factors may be responsible for the disability. However, in making the diagnosis, it would be necessary to see that factor or group of factors in relation to the others.

1. *Mental age.* Generally speaking, the mental age indicates the level of mental growth of the individual. For example, if a given individual is said to have a mental age of 12-6, it means

that his mental growth is roughly equivalent to that of an average child twelve and a half years old. In general, he should be able to read at least as well as a child of twelve and a half. This is true even though his actual chronological age may be fifteen years and two months. As has been indicated in previous chapters, the mental age of reading disability cases should be measured by means of the Stanford-Binet Test of Intelligence, some other individual mental test, or a non-language test.

The measurement of mental ability is among the most significant appraisals that are made in diagnosing reading disability. This measure is used, in the first place, as a basis for selecting the cases which actually constitute remedial problems. In the second place, it is important in the prognosis of each case. Remedial work with the student of high mental ability will usually progress more rapidly than it will with the student of low mental ability. Third, it is essential that the remedial worker know the mental ability of the student in order that materials and instruction can be adjusted to his needs and mental capacity.

2. *Chronological age.* Chronological age is the actual age of the student; that is, the student who has lived for thirteen and a half years would have a chronological age of 13-6. The chronological age is useful in giving some indication of the level of maturity of the individual. This helps in two areas. First, it tells the diagnostician the range of reading interests that the student might be expected to have. Then, by comparing his actual interests with those of the average student of his age, it is possible to estimate the degree of maturity or immaturity of the individual's interests. Secondly, knowledge of chronological age aids in estimating the degree of maturity or immaturity in physical development. Chronological age and mental age considered together form a basis for under-

standing the development of the student in the other areas of appraisal.

3. *Grade placement.* By grade placement is meant the actual grade the student is in. The student or the school records will furnish the examiner with this information. It is important to know the grade placement in order to compute the degree to which the student is retarded or accelerated in school in comparison with his mental and chronological ages. Inasmuch as reading ability is so highly related to school success, the majority of disability cases will be somewhat retarded. This retardation will indicate, in some measure at least, the amount that the reading disability has been a handicap to the student's normal progress through school. When the school placement is compared with the student's actual reading ability, the disparity between the materials he is required to read and those he is able to read is indicated.

4. *School history.* The yearly records of the school will give the diagnostician information about the progress the student has made throughout his school life. They will also indicate the subjects that have been difficult for him. They will tell, too, any periods of prolonged absence or changes of school. In addition, such records help to locate the grade level at which the trouble with reading may have started. The examiner should make a careful study of the school history of the student and should record upon the diagnostic record those circumstances that are related to reading.

5. *Silent reading abilities.* The silent reading abilities listed in the outline (on pages 280-81) have been discussed in Chapter IV. The group measurements (see Appendix) of these abilities should be a part of the yearly testing program. The diagnostician may obtain the results of current measurements and in addition the rating of the student in previous years. He should make more extensive appraisals of those abilities

in which the student has demonstrated a marked or persistent weakness. This may frequently be done by observational methods. For example, if a given case shows a general inferior ability in locating information, the examiner can observe the student in the actual process of locating information in order to detect wherein the difficulties lie.

A comparison between the various silent reading abilities of an individual will prove to be very enlightening to the examiner. If, for example, the student is relatively high in the less exacting sorts of reading, such as skimming or getting the general significance, and is low in the more analytical types, such as reading critically or following directions, there is an indication of rather superficial reading or of a lack of the necessary background. If this is accompanied by a relatively high degree of inaccuracy, the diagnosis should be concerned with a more intensive study of the methods used in attacking words and concepts. This comparison indicates that purposes should be provided that cause the student to gain experience in reading more analytically. If, on the other hand, a student has a relatively high proficiency in the more analytical types and a low proficiency in the less exacting sorts of reading, there is an indication of slow meticulous reading with the possibility of overanalysis of words or other interfering habits. Such a profile indicates that the student may be overcareful when the material does not demand so high a degree of careful reading.

If the student is low, in comparison with his mental and chronological ages, in all these silent reading abilities, or in a large proportion of them, there is a definite indication that a very careful and intensive diagnosis must be made. This implies, too, that the student needs a more intensive and prolonged remedial program than is necessary for the student who is low in but a few of these silent reading abilities. Fundamentally the problem in the latter case is that of enabling the student to adjust his reading to the purpose at hand. In the case of the student who is low in a large proportion of these abilities, it frequently will be found that he has faulty or interfering habits or other conditions which are causing the general retardation.

6. *Oral reading.* In order to obtain a measure of oral reading ability, the student may well be asked to read from each of several books of gradually increasing difficulty.[1] Inasmuch as remedial cases are relatively low in reading ability, the examiner may use selections from a series of elementary school readers. He might assemble a graded series of selections as follows: one from the beginning, middle, and end of a sixth-grade reader, seventh-grade reader, and eighth-grade reader. These selections should be about a half page in length. By having the student read the selections orally at sight, it is possible to estimate his level of oral reading ability. If by his oral interpretation the student seems to the examiner to be understanding most of the words and concepts, he may be credited with a successful performance. When the errors become relatively frequent, it may be assumed that his level of oral reading ability has been passed, and an analysis of the errors should be made. This analysis will show the type of errors the student makes most frequently and will be helpful in formulating remedial work. It may be assumed that the student is making the same sort of errors in his silent reading.

The following classification of oral context errors taken from Gates's *The Improvement of Reading* will prove helpful in isolating the most troublesome errors:

A. Number of seconds required to read each paragraph. (Give the pupil the word if he is unable to get it at the expiration of 5 seconds . . .)

[1] Durrell, Donald. "Individual Differences and Their Implications with Respect to Instruction in Reading," *The Teaching of Reading: A Second Report. The Thirty-Sixth Yearbook of the National Society for the Study of Education*, Part I, Public School Publishing Company, 1937.

B. Total number of errors. This is the sum of errors entered under:

1. Number of whole words omitted. This includes failures to respond in 5 seconds . . .
2. Whole words added.
3. Repetitions of 2 or more words. . . .
4. Mispronunciations of a word in whole or part. Be *sure* to write above the word the mispronunciation made by the pupil. These are later to be analyzed into several types. Unless the mispronunciations are clearly entered, this grouping cannot be made.
5. Also record particular types of errors as follows:

   a. Reversals—*was* for *saw,* etc., due to clear reversal of letters; also *toin* for *into,* or *inot* for *into* (reversal of parts).
   b. Order of parts incorrect—any case not entered under 5a, in which the letters or word-parts are put in a wrong order, viz. *arnely* for *nearly,* or *arenly* for *nearly,* or *linar* for *nearly;* or *aws* for *saw; are* for *ear,* etc.

   In certain cases, it will perhaps be difficult to tell whether the mispronunciation should go under (a) or (b). In these cases, it will not much matter, since the following score is also used:

   c. Total words showing incorrect order. This is merely the total number of words falling under (a) and (b)—that is, total number of words in which the *order* of letters or parts is incorrect.
   d. Wrong beginning. These are cases in which the initial part of the word is wrong but in which the *order* of parts is correct. Thus here would go: *bad* for *had; stove* for *drove; as* for *is,* etc. Cases in which first part is omitted should be included, such as *ad* for *had; rove* for *drove; is* for *his.* Also parts added, such as *into* for *to; almost* for *most.*

e. Wrong middle. Order of elements correct, for example, *hod* for *had; row* for *raw; smelling* for *smiling; alone* for *above.* Or omissions of middle parts, as *door* for *doctor; had* for *head; money* for *monkey.* Also parts added, as *heard* for *head; bearing* for *being.*

f. Wrong ending. Order of elements correct, for example, *it* for *is; dig* for *did; mad* for *made; all* for *alone; also* for *alone; peep* for *peek; cry* for *cried; no* for *now; start* for *stuck,* etc. Ending omitted, such as *some* for *something; brow* for *brown; no* for *not.* Also parts added, such as *smiling* for *smile; rats* for *rat; stopped* for *stop.*

g. Wrong in two or more parts, as *barking* for *donkey; ill* for *silly; biting* for *better; blow* for *brown; balloon* for *all,* etc., when the incorrect word is not a new word made up of parts of the actual word in incorrect order. This classification would include totally different words such as *are* for *his; come* for *sing,* etc.

Care must be exercised to distinguish between errors in which the elements are given in incorrect order, and hence to be classified under (a) or (b) and errors which are not due to rearrangement of word-parts and hence to be included under (d), (e), (f), or (g).

The mispronunciation should be entered in only *one* of the categories. Never should it be entered in more than one of these [except in the case of (c) which is merely the total of (a) and (b)]. The sum of the entries in (a), (b), (d), (e), (f), and (g), in other words, should equal the score under 4—total mispronunciations.[2]

An analysis of the phonetic errors,[3] such as errors in conso-

---

[2] Gates, Arthur I. *The Improvement of Reading,* Revised, The Macmillan Company, 1935, pp. 534-36.

[3] Monroe, Marion. *Children Who Cannot Read,* Chicago University Press, 1932, pp. 34-37.

nants, vowels, diphthongs, will supplement the above classification.

The oral reading of the selections from elementary school readers may be timed to show the number of words per minute the student read the materials of varying difficulty. In order that a comparison may be made between speeds of reading material orally and silently, the student should be timed as he reads similar passages silently. When the speeds of reading orally and silently from the same materials are approximately the same, there is an indication of vocalization in the silent reading.

7. *Ability to work out words in isolation.* Isolated lists of the more difficult words taken from material similar to that used for the oral reading should be compiled. The student should read these lists orally so that the examiner may compare the relative effectiveness with which the student can recognize words in isolation and in content. By comparing his performance in oral reading with his performance on isolated lists, an appraisal can be made of the degree to which he is using contextual clues as contrasted with the more analytical word recognition techniques. If he is relatively high on the oral reading, it is safe to assume that he is making use of contextual clues. If, on the other hand, he is as proficient or more so in reading the isolated words as in reading contextual material, there is an indication of overanalysis.[4]

The examiner should have the student work aloud on those words that were difficult for him in the previous reading of isolated words. The method used in attacking difficult words can thus be determined. One student may work out the word phonetically. Another may use large familiar parts of words. Still another student may resort to a spelling attack, spelling

[4] Gates, Arthur I. *The Improvement of Reading,* Revised, The Macmillan Company, 1935, p. 250.

each letter of the word before recognition of the word takes place. Still another student may have no attack at all and may flounder completely over the words that he does not recognize at sight. Such an appraisal will aid materially in formulating the remedial program for the student who has an inadequate attack upon new words.

8. *Background of experience.* A limited background of meaning may be to some degree either the cause or result of reading disability. In order to estimate the extent of the meaning background of the individual, a semi-controlled interview technique should be used. The examiner should ask some informational questions concerning backgrounds of meanings which would most likely be derived through reading. Then the examiner should ask other informational questions, the answers to which would be derived from experiences outside of reading. For example, questions of the former type might be, "What is a *gaucho?*" or "What method did Widow Douglas use to find out whether Huck Finn was a boy or girl?" After asking such questions, the examiner should find out where the student got the information. Questions of the second type might be, "How can you tell whether the ice is thick enough to skate on?" or "What street car do you take to go to the zoo?" or "How is a street paved?" Again the examiner should ascertain the source of the information. A comparison of the student's background of information derived from books and information derived from experience will give an indication of whether the student's limitation is due to meager experience in general or to deficient reading. The total response will give an indication of the extent of the background.

In order to know more about the background of word meaning of the disability case, the examiner might find it profitable to compare the student's responses on the vocabulary test of the Binet, from which a rough age estimate may be obtained, with the vocabulary age score on the Gates Reading Survey test. The words included in the vocabulary test of the Binet are given orally by the examiner as the student reads them. The student reads the words in the Gates Reading Survey vocabulary test, but does not hear them pronounced. A comparison of the results of the vocabulary test given orally with the results of the one that was read by the student will indicate in some degree whether or not the background of word meanings is a definite handicap to the student's reading ability. If the student ranks considerably higher on the list read to him than on the list he himself read, poor word recognition techniques rather than meager meaning vocabulary are interfering with his reading development. If he ranks equally low or lower on the list read to him than on the one he himself read, it is quite likely that word meaning background is interfering. This comparison will aid in making an estimate of the extent to which remedial instructions should be directed toward the development of word meanings.

9. *Sensory characteristics.* Among the visual characteristics that are frequently considered to be causes of reading disability are nearsightedness, farsightedness, poor acuity for other reasons, muscular imbalance, astigmatism, and lack of ability to fuse or combine the images from the two eyes. The diagnostician should be on the alert for symptoms of visual disability when working individually with reading disability cases. Frequently the examination conducted by the school nurse will give indications of individuals who need visual corrections. Visual perception tests also prove helpful in singling out those students who have defective vision. While there are measures that will aid the diagnostician in locating the visual cases,[5] it is recommended that whenever it is suspected that a student

[5] Betts, Emmett Albert. *The Prevention and Correction of Reading Difficulties,* Row, Peterson and Company, 1936.

has a visual defect, he should be encouraged to have his vision examined by an expert.

Among the auditory characteristics that are considered to be causes of reading disability are poor acuity, poor discrimination, and lack of blending ability. Blending ability is the ability to form words from the sounds which comprise the word. In measuring this ability, the examiner gives the phonetic sounds of a word and has the student pronounce the word as a whole. For example, the examiner might say *di rek shon,* and the student would be expected to say the word *direction.* If the student depends upon phonetic analysis as his method of working out unfamiliar words, lack of blending ability is a great handicap.

Auditory discrimination is the ability to tell the difference between sound patterns. It is this ability that enables an individual to distinguish between words that are very similar in sound and to hear the exact pronunciation of a given word. While poor auditory discrimination is sometimes related to poor auditory acuity, it is not infrequent that reading disability cases are found who have high auditory acuity and faulty discrimination. Auditory discrimination can be measured in two ways. First, by measuring the student's ability to hear and repeat nonsense syllables that contain a variety of auditory patterns, and second, by measuring the student's ability to distinguish between words of similar sounds. Gates[6] has excellent tests of these two types in his diagnostic battery. For high school students it might be advisable to extend these tests. The student who has poor auditory discrimination is handicapped in building a background of words. Since such a student is never sure how a word sounds or is pronounced, he is likely to be insecure in oral reading and conversational situations.

---

[6] Gates, Arthur I. *Record Booklet for Reading Diagnosis,* Bureau of Publications, Teachers College, Columbia University, 1933.

Auditory acuity is the keenness with which one hears sounds. It is this ability which is usually thought of when it is said that someone has a hearing loss. Auditory acuity can be roughly appraised by having the individual walk away from the examiner while the examiner whispers certain directions, such as, "Raise your left hand with three fingers extended; raise your right hand with all fingers extended." If four or five students are given this examination at the same time, the one who first misses the directions or begins to follow the lead of his neighbors in all probability has the greatest hearing loss. If an audiometer (an instrument for measuring hearing loss) is available, it will give a much more accurate measurement. Whatever method is used, the individual suspected of having a hearing loss should be examined by an expert.

10. *Physical condition.* If any interfering physical condition is evident, the student should be referred to an expert. Such conditions as malnutrition, glandular disturbances, infections, lack of energy, or any other condition that lowers the individual's vitality will be reflected, of course, in his schoolwork. The diagnostician and the teachers should be on the alert for physical disabilities.

11. *Emotional and other personality disturbances.* As has been indicated in previous sections of this book, there is a marked relationship between emotional and other personality disturbances and reading disability. Whether or not the personality condition is the cause of reading disability or the result of that disability, the remedial worker should be aware of any such condition. Inventories, such as the Bell Adjustment Inventory [7] or the Bernreuter Personality Inventory, [8] may be used by the diagnostician to advantage in studying the emotional and personality disturbances of the reading case. Such inven-

[7] Bell, H. *The Adjustment Inventory*, Stanford University Press, 1934.
[8] Bernreuter, Robert G. *The Personality Inventory*, Stanford University Press, 1935.

tories should be supplemented by: (1) the personal observations by the teachers in the class situation and in the extra-curricular activities; (2) by the observations of the examiner in the individual test situation and during the interviews; (3) by data derived from interviews with the parents or from other sources.

An understanding of the student as a person is highly essential if adequate remedial work is to be done. Emotional factors that are unrecognized and unadjusted will in some cases make for complete failure of an otherwise well-conceived and well-conducted remedial plan.

12. *Interest in and attitude toward reading.* The reading interests of disability cases are usually meager and immature. In the first place, the severely retarded reader shows little interest in reading; that is, he does not read extensively. This is due to the fact that the task of reading is difficult. Even though the student may be very desirous of improving in reading ability, the difficulty of the task and his constant frustration make him tend to avoid reading. His attitude toward reading is that of dislike. If he is shown that he can become successful and if materials are adjusted to his reading ability and to his natural interests, he will in most cases willingly undertake the task. It is necessary, therefore, to make the experience successful and in line with his natural interests. In the second place, the interests in reading that the student has are likely to be relatively immature. Due to his poor reading ability, his reading has been confined to the reading of juvenile books. There is quite likely to be a discrepancy between the things he is interested in as a person and the things he is interested in reading about. He has found through experience that he is unable to follow up his natural interests through reading. Thus the reading interests that have developed are more or less artificial and are not likely to be of intrinsic worth to the student.

In order to improve the interest of the student in reading and his attitude toward reading, the diagnostician must determine what the interests of the student are. The remedial teacher must find material at the reading level of the student that has intrinsic interest for him. The best methods of finding out the student's interest in and his attitude toward reading are interview and observational techniques.

Outcome of Diagnosis

After the appraisals have been made, the diagnostician should gather the data together. He notes the atypical performances of the student. He studies the interrelationships and forms a hypothesis as to the nature of the difficulty. With the hypothesis in mind he reviews the data to check his appraisal of the problem. Any factors that do not seem to fit the hypothesis are weighed, and the hypothesis is either retained or altered. After making the estimate as to the nature of the case, the diagnostician formulates a remedial plan.

The remedial plan must be considered to be a tentative one. If the student does not respond to the training in a relatively short time—one to three weeks of daily instruction—it is wise to reinspect the data in order that a reformulation of the remedial plan may be made. If the remedial instruction and the diagnosis are done by different people, they should co-operate in making the reappraisal. The remedial teacher will bring to the conference the knowledges he has gained about the student and his disability during the remedial instruction.

Summary

In order to understand the nature of a reading disability, it is necessary to make sufficiently complete appraisals to study the symptoms and to determine, if possible, the causes of the disability. Diagnosis, thus, is undertaken so that the disability may be more thoroughly understood in order that an appropriate program of remedial instruction may be set up. As the poor reader is already insecure, it is especially important for the remedial program of instruction to be one that is appropriate. The program should lessen the hazard of failure, not add to it.

Among the factors that should be considered in setting up a program of diagnosis are the following:

1. The diagnosis should be only as detailed as is necessary to enable the diagnostician to understand the disability.

2. Indiscriminate testing should be avoided.

3. Group measurements, whenever possible, should be utilized. These, however, should be supplemented by individual appraisals when necessary.

4. The program of diagnosis should be as easy to operate and as simple as is feasible with good results.

5. The diagnostic and remedial program should call for as little expensive equipment and materials as possible and yet be productive of results.

In making a diagnosis, it is necessary to see the factor or group of factors causing the disability in relation to the other factors. Appraisals include:

1. *Mental age.* Mental age is one of the measures used in selecting the cases which actually constitute remedial problems. Mental age is important in the prognosis of the case and should be considered in adjusting materials and instruction to the needs of the individual.

2. *Chronological age.* Chronological age tells the diagnostician the general range of reading interests that the individual might be expected to have, and it aids in estimating the degree of maturity in physical development.

3. *Grade placement.* Grade placement tells the degree to which the student is retarded or accelerated in school.

4. *School history.* The school history gives an indication of difficulty in various school subjects, of instructional gaps, etc.

5. *Silent reading abilities.* A comparison of the level of development the student has reached in the various silent reading abilities will prove very helpful to the diagnostician.

6. *Oral reading.* An analysis of the types of errors the student makes in oral reading is helpful in formulating remedial work.

7. *Ability to work out words in isolation.* The method or methods used by the student in attacking difficult words should be determined.

8. *Background of experience.* A limited background of experience may be to some degree either the cause or result of reading disability.

9. *Sensory characteristics.* The handicap under which a student is working because of sensory limitations should be ascertained.

10. *Physical condition.* In the case of an interfering physical condition, the student should be referred to an expert.

11. *Emotional and other personality disturbances.* An understanding of the student as a person is highly essential if adequate remedial work is to be done.

12. *Interest in and attitude toward reading.* The reading interests of disability cases are usually meager and immature. The degree of immaturity should be ascertained. Frequently the remedial case has a strong dislike for reading. It is necessary at the outset to know the student's attitude toward reading and to take it into consideration in formulating the remedial program.

SELECTED BIBLIOGRAPHY

Betts, Emmett A. *The Prevention and Correction of Reading Difficulties,* Row, Peterson and Company, 1936, Chapter 5.

Durrell, Donald. "Individual Differences and Their Implications with Respect to Instruction in Reading," *The Teaching of Reading: A Second Report, The Thirty-Sixth Yearbook of the National Society for the Study of Education,* Part I, Public School Publishing Company, 1937.

Gates, Arthur I. *The Improvement of Reading,* Revised, The Macmillan Company, 1935.

Harris, Albert J. *How to Increase Reading Ability,* Longmans, Green and Company, 1940, Chapters 4 and 6.

McCallister, James M. *Remedial and Corrective Instruction in Reading,* D. Appleton-Century Company, 1936, Chapter 5.

Monroe, Marion. *Children Who Cannot Read,* University of Chicago Press, 1932, pp. 34-37.

Strang, Ruth, and Rose, F. C. *Problems in the Improvement of Reading in High School and College,* Revised, The Science Press Printing Company, 1940, Chapter VII.

Witty, Paul, and Kopel, David. *Reading and the Educative Process,* Ginn and Company, 1939, Chapters 7 and 8.

CHAPTER XIII

REMEDIAL PROGRAM

As materials continue to become more closely adapted to the pupils' power and needs, and as the teachers continue to become more able to adjust these materials to the differences of individual students, the remedial program will envelop fewer and fewer students. Then, from the very first year of school life through the senior year in high school, the developmental program will become the complete reading program for an ever-increasing percentage of the students. However, at the present time many high school students need remedial work. There will always be some students who will need remedial instruction in reading. In other words, there will always be some students for whom the developmental program will need to be augmented by highly individualized instruction based upon a thorough diagnosis.

ORGANIZATION

The organization of a remedial reading program in the high school depends upon local conditions, such as size of school, number of severely retarded readers, financial condition, personnel, equipment, materials. The discussion which follows is based upon the assumption that there is a full-time co-ordinator of reading instruction in the high school. When this is the case, probably about half of his time should be devoted to supervising the developmental program and the other half to reading diagnosis and instruction of the severely retarded cases.

It is recommended that a high school of from 1,000 to 2,000 students have a full-time co-ordinator and that a school under 1,000 have a trained person who devotes a part of his time to the duties of a co-ordinator.

The discussion of the remedial program is based upon the further assumption that the remedial program merely augments the developmental one. Only those students should be included in the remedial program who cannot satisfactorily improve their reading in the developmental reading program alone. It is estimated that on the average such cases will number about 10 to 15 per cent of the school population. If an effective remedial program is organized, many students who otherwise would continue to be remedial cases will be corrected by the remedial instruction. They then will be able to continue their reading growth solely in the developmental program. The per cent of severely retarded reading cases for the entire school population should gradually decrease.

Some schools have found it expedient for the co-ordinator at the start to organize the remedial program around the needs of the freshman class. As time permitted, he was able to extend the coverage. Before the lapse of three years the remedial program was meeting the needs of the reading disability cases of the entire school. While it is better to have a complete coverage of the entire school at the outset, this frequently proves to be too big an undertaking. In other words, it takes time to inaugurate a thoroughgoing reading program. The matter of practicality must be considered. After a three-year period the remedial program is concerned solely with those students of the freshman class who are markedly retarded, those few cases who need more than one year of highly individualized instruction, and the relatively rare case that develops during the high school years.

After the diagnoses have been made, the remedial worker

knows the number of cases that need remedial work, the extent of retardation of each case, and the types of instruction that are needed. With this information the remedial worker is able to organize the instructional program. He knows which students profitably can be taught in groups and what groups they should enter, and which students should be taught individually. Moreover, he knows which students constitute the most immediate problems. If he cannot handle all cases at the beginning, he should place the others on a waiting list. The students on the waiting list should be absorbed by the remedial program as fast as the remedial work of other students is concluded.

The nature of remedial instruction needed by the disability case, the degree of the disability, and the emotional condition are factors which should be considered in determining whether a case should be given group remedial instruction or be dealt with individually. For example, suppose that the diagnoses show ten students are reading too slowly for the purpose of getting the general significance; that the appraisals show seven of them are able to read for the purpose of getting the general significance of materials of about the same level of difficulty and at approximately the same rate; that one must have much simpler material to insure a reasonable degree of accuracy; that another is so concerned with the details that, although he reads the material at about the rate of the first seven, he seems to be unable to obtain any impression of the general significance of it; and that the tenth is so emotional about reading that he cannot profitably be taught with a group of other students. Obviously, group instruction would be arranged for the first seven. Individual therapy, for a time at least, is probably best for the others.

The remedial worker will find, however, that he can successfully guide during the same hour several cases in need of individual instruction. In fact, the remedial instruction for several different types of cases might be going on at the same time. In such a situation the remedial worker should take a few minutes at the start of the period to help each student in the selection of materials for the purpose for which he is reading. While the students are working independently upon their problems, the remedial teacher could work first with one student and then with another.

The remedial teacher should have a room set aside for his use. This enables him to keep in a permanent place the materials, equipment, and records that he uses. The room should be attractive, well-lighted, and centrally located. It probably should be equipped with movable desks. It should have ample shelf space so that each student may keep his materials in a place that is easily accessible both to him and to the remedial teacher. The students should come to this room for their remedial instruction.

A plan that has been found to be administratively practicable is to schedule the remedial instruction of each student during one of his study-hour periods. After the remedial teacher has determined the cases with whom he is going to work, he can secure a schedule of the study-hall periods of the students. He can then organize his remedial classes. Whatever organization of the remedial program is undertaken, it should be possible for students to leave and enter the remedial program at any time during a semester. If a student is no longer in need of remedial work, it must be made possible for him to re-enter the regular school program with little or no readjustment on his part.

It is common practice for remedial reading to be undertaken in some of the sections of English classes. For several reasons this does not seem to be a wise procedure. First, it is not conducive to the necessary flexibility. The student who is no longer in need of remedial work cannot profitably be transferred to another English section without having to make a major adjustment. It is difficult for even the best students to transfer from class to class during a semester; for a convalescent reader, such a transfer is always unwise and is frequently fatal. Second, the poor reader should not be deprived of the regular instruction in English. He is in need of instruction in English just as other students are. It would be as reasonable to use a section of science, mathematics, or any other subject for remedial instruction in reading. Third, the English period constitutes an integral part of the developmental reading program. The remedial reading case, just as any other student, should have the advantages of a well-rounded developmental program in reading.

There should be no stigma attached to receiving remedial instruction in reading. The organization of the remedial program should enable the student to enter and leave that instruction unnoticed. It is frequently the practice for students to use study-hall periods for many types of special instruction. For example, music, art, and gymnasium classes are often scheduled during study periods. The special instruction in reading should very normally be thought of in the same way. Students of high school age are frequently eager to avail themselves of the opportunity to improve their reading and especially so when there is no stigma attached.

Principles of Remedial Teaching

While each type of disability case requires specific procedures, there are principles that apply in general to remedial reading instruction. There are certain considerations in teaching disability cases that are basic. In numerous cases, unless these principles are strictly adhered to, the remedial work will prove to be ineffectual. The principles of remedial teaching will be discussed in the following paragraphs.

1. *Remedial instruction should be based upon a thorough diagnosis.* A large proportion of disability cases results from group instruction that did not take into account the differences between individuals. The remedial cases are, for the most part, those who did not profit from the group instruction. Unless the remedial instruction is adjusted to meet the stages of development and the individual abilities of the reading cases, it is little more than a continuation of the group procedures from which the disability cases have resulted. Remedial programs that attempt by a single procedure to correct faulty reading will result in a high per cent of failures. Even though such programs appear to have been successful, it is likely that, had there been individual diagnosis, greater success would have resulted.

The diagnosis is only profitable to the degree that it aids instruction. In other words, instruction cannot be effective unless the reading disability is understood. The factors that cause a reading disability case are often subtle and interrelated. If the instruction aims to overcome or correct these inhibiting conditions, a thorough understanding of them is necessary. This understanding, for the most part, can be achieved only by studying and appraising the reading abilities of a given remedial case and the factors related to the disability. The diagnosis is basic to adequate remedial instruction.

2. *Remedial instruction should be started through the use of materials at the student's reading level.* At the outset it should be realized that the student has been in difficulty for some time. Reading at best has been a difficult and uninteresting task for him. The student feels thoroughly discouraged with his reading ability and is inclined to avoid reading of any sort. Often the materials that he has been expected to read

have been too difficult for him to read with ease or with any degree of proficiency, if he has been able to read them at all. He is quite likely to feel that he will never become a good reader.

It is highly essential for the student with a reading disability to experience success from the start. One of the most important tasks of the remedial teacher is that of overcoming the feelings of confusion and frustration which so often accompany reading disability. It is essential that the student be comfortable in a reading situation. He cannot be expected to be untroubled so long as the material is too difficult for him to read with ease. The remedial teacher should use at the start material that is carefully adjusted to the student's reading ability. It should have a level of difficulty equal to the student's reading level. Students, for example, who have a seventh-grade reading ability should begin by reading materials that are suitable in difficulty for seventh-grade children. The appeal of the book should be as near as possible to the student's mental and emotional level. The level of difficulty of materials should be advanced as fast and only as fast as the student can read them with facility. The reading case who does not have material that is in keeping with his reading ability cannot be expected to progress rapidly. The reading level of an individual indicates his stage of growth in reading. To have him attempt to read materials that are above that level aggravates the reading disability.

3. *The natural interests of the student should be used in selecting material*. Another consideration in selecting materials for a remedial case is that they must be of high interest value to him. His remedial program should be a pleasurable experience. Indeed it will be when the student is provided with materials that he can read with interest. The remedial teacher who learns the natural interests of the student and who locates

materials pertaining to those interests at the reading level of the student will find that the student will read them. As he meets with success in reading the material, the student will feel encouraged to read other materials of a similiar sort. Soon the student will recognize that reading has something to contribute to him. The use of the natural interests of the student is an effective means of motivating the reading program.

4. *The materials should be interesting in content and in style.* Even though the material is chosen in line with a natural interest of the student, its content might be such that it would not be stimulating. A typical ninth-grade boy who is interested in airplanes, for example, might rebel against a highly romantic story in which the airplanes played a minor role. On the other hand, he might be stimulated by an account of the construction of model planes.

The content of the book or passage should be analyzed from the point of view of the interest value that it has for a student of the chronological and mental ages and sex of the disability case. It is not always possible to find materials that are easy enough for the student to read and are at the same time in keeping with his chronological and mental development. While the material must be at the reading level of the student, the content should at the same time approximate as nearly as possible his chronological and mental development.

The material, in addition to having content that is stimulating to the student, should be written in a pleasing and interesting style. This consideration in choosing materials is subordinate to the others. It will frequently be found that the type of writing that is interesting to the student is not necessarily a literary one. If this proves to be true, literary materials should not be forced upon him. Rather his tastes in style of materials should be developed gradually as his reading ability improves.

In the selection of materials, the first consideration is that of reading difficulty. The second consideration is that of utilizing the student's natural interests. The third consideration is that of choosing materials of appropriate content. A fourth is that the style must be interesting to the student. In other words, the material should be readable. Only through using readable material can the remedial reading case be expected to read.

5. *The purposes for reading must emphasize the techniques and skills to be improved.* The nature of the task determines the techniques and skills that will be employed. The purpose for which a student reads may be helpful in the development of a technique. If a student reads inaccurately, for example, the task set should be such that, in order to achieve his purpose, accurate reading must be done. For example, Jean was a student who had difficulty in locating information and who read inaccurately. She had considerable ability in art. She was planning to make a poster for the forthcoming fashion show.

One day, while talking to the remedial teacher, Jean mentioned the fact that she wished she could think of a topic for the poster. The teacher took this opportunity to utilize a natural interest of Jean's and at the same time set a reading purpose that would entail reading which emphasized both accuracy and the ability to locate information. He suggested that Jean might design an attractive and interesting poster using the topic, "The Cycle of Fashion." Jean was eager to assemble the data for such a poster. She felt that it would be unique among the other posters. It was decided that the next reading period would be devoted to locating descriptions of costumes of the different periods. The teacher told Jean how she could locate materials in the library. Jean was then excused from the remedial class and allowed to go to the library. The books

Jean brought to the next reading class were supplemented by some the teacher had located. Jean read the materials, taking down pertinent details that would help her to draw the styles to illustrate "The Cycle of Fashion." This purpose proved helpful in enabling Jean, under the guidance of the remedial teacher, gain experience in the two reading techniques in which she was deficient.

A purpose for which a student reads may be detrimental to the establishment of the techniques in which he is deficient. If, for example, a student reads slowly because of excessive articulation, it would be harmful for him to have as his reading purpose the preparation of a passage to be read orally. Reading aloud to himself in order to become acquainted with the pronunciation and oral interpretation of the passage would practice the faulty habit that the remedial program was attempting to eliminate. The purposes set must be adjusted to the nature of the limitation. To have such a student read orally is a questionable procedure. However, he should not be eliminated from oral participation in the class, but should participate by giving oral discussions rather than oral readings.

The above illustrations indicate that the task that is carefully adjusted can aid materially in overcoming reading difficulty. The task that is not adjusted may prove to have detrimental effects. Situations such as the first cited above enable a student to gain experience in the techniques of reading in which he is deficient. Situations such as the second force the student to practice faulty habits that he is trying to eliminate. Emphasis can be placed upon the types of reading which need to be developed. The nature of these situations will be determined by the limitations and needs of each student. The task of the teacher is that of setting up purposes for reading that emphasize the technique and skills to be improved.

6. *The purpose for reading should be real to the student.*

The remedial reading teacher, as far as he can, should avoid setting up artificial reading purposes or situations. Sometimes it is only through the setting up of an artificial purpose that a specific technique can be employed. However, such cases are the exception rather than the rule. In general, the material read should have intrinsic worth for the student. It is neither wise nor necessary for the remedial reading program to be something apart from other school experiences of the student. During the remedial class the student may read materials upon the topics that are under discussion in his other classes. This will enable him to make contributions to class discussions. The student will feel that the reading experiences are of twofold use to him: first, they are useful in improving his ability in various reading skills and techniques; and second, they are useful in enabling him to achieve in other school subjects.

7. *The student should be aware of the nature of the disability.* In order that improvement may be as rapid as possible, the student should know the techniques and skills that he is endeavoring to improve. A high school student should be aware of the factors that are contributing to the disability. In fact, the student should have a somewhat complete understanding of the diagnosis, and the steps in the remedial program should be thoroughly explained to him.

As is shown by the following illustration, when difficulty is encountered and remedial measures are necessary in any field, it is desirable for the individual to have full knowledge of both. Two skippers realize that their boats are off their courses. One skipper knows where his boat is, understands wherein the calculations were wrong, and thereby knows why it is that the boat is off its course and how it can reach its destination. The other skipper knows his boat has not reached the destination. He does not know where he is, why it is that he is off the course, or how to go about finding the destination. Certainly the former skipper will stand a better chance of bringing the boat to port.

The student should know where he is, where he is going, and the steps by which he should proceed. After all, it is the student who must take the steps. Such insight will enable him to make a more profitable use of the time spent in remedial reading.

8. *The student should have his progress demonstrated*. In order that the student may see how he is progressing, a record should be kept of his development. It is advantageous to appraise frequently the student's growth in the techniques that he is endeavoring to improve. The student should keep a chart of these appraisals. He will be interested in following his progress, and this will stimulate him to further progress. From time to time the student may find that he is not gaining. When this is true, the remedial teacher and the student together should analyze the situation in order to determine the reasons for the lack of progress and work out a plan of procedure designed to overcome this new difficulty.

9. *Good teaching techniques should be employed*. As can be seen from the above generalizations, remedial teaching is simply good teaching. These general principles are applicable to teaching in any subject, developmental or remedial. The teaching techniques that will be discussed in the pages that follow are for the most part adaptations of these general principles to fit specific needs. In certain instances specialized procedures will be recommended that may violate one or more of these general principles. Such instances are the exception rather than the rule. For example, it may at times be necessary to have the student read materials that have little or no intrinsic worth to him. For a time a fifteen-year-old boy of above average intelligence, who reads at third-grade level, will be obliged to read material that is not stimulating to him. In

such a case the improvement of reading alone would be the student's purpose.

As the result of the diagnosis, the remedial worker can isolate those specific defects that need special attention. It is more frequently true than not that the disability case will demonstrate difficulty in more than one reading technique. It is also true that disability in one technique may be responsible for retardation in several techniques. It is usually advisable to concentrate remedial instruction around that technique or the techniques in which the student is most deficient. Usually the technique in which the student is most deficient is one that is basic to his disability. The fundamental problem is to locate and focus instruction upon the basic difficulty. There are, however, interrelationships among the various areas in which the student is deficient, and all of them should receive attention. For a clear understanding of remedial instruction in techniques which are frequently found to be basic, it is necessary to consider the techniques separately.

Word Recognition

In order to develop the student's ability to recognize words, it is necessary to determine the methods he uses in attacking words. It may be that he is depending solely upon a phonetic attack for the recognition of words. This may prove to be effective with many words. Some words, however, do not lend themselves to phonetic analysis, in which cases the method is inadequate. To depend solely upon this method may be time-consuming. One student who depended upon this attack took several minutes to work out the pronunciation of a word. The remedial work for a student who is depending solely upon a phonetic attack is that of developing other means of word recognition and of suppressing somewhat the tendency to depend upon the sounding of words. What is needed in word recognition is a well-rounded attack, including in addition to phonetics: (1) the use of context clues; (2) the use of the general shape of the word; (3) the use of known parts of words; (4) dependence upon syllabification. The student must be able to apply that degree of analysis that is necessary for the recognition of the word and no more. In most cases the rapid techniques, such as dependence upon the content and the general characteristics of words, will suffice. However, at times it is necessary to employ more analytical visual and sounding techniques.

The technique of using context clues can be developed by reading extensively in relatively easy materials where there are few difficult words. The student, being aware of his problem, will attempt to recognize the words from the meaning. For the development of the ability to use context clues and initial sounds, material may be prepared that includes in the running sentences only the initial sounds of certain key words. The task of the student would be to supply the rest of the word while reading. Such a procedure is somewhat artificial and probably should be used only for the more troublesome cases and for a short time.

Another technique of recognizing words is using the general shape of the word as a clue. This method of recognizing words can be developed by noticing similarities and differences between words. Methods that speed up the reading tend to cause the student to depend for word recognition on the striking characteristics of the word rather than on more obscure characteristics. Frequently various sorts of flash card procedures are used to develop this ability. These procedures are **highly** artificial and should not be used extensively.

The use of large known parts is an effective means **of word** recognition. A person who might not be able to recognize *neighborhood* might know the two large parts—*neighbor* and *hood*—of which it is composed. If such is the case, he would have little difficulty in recognizing the word if he made use of the two known parts. A way of developing this ability is to encourage the student to look for known parts in the words he does not recognize as wholes.

Many students who have difficulty in recognizing words independently find trouble in seeing the word other than in its entirety. If the student is made aware of his problem, his frequent use of the dictionary will help in developing ability to find usable elements within the word.

The oral reading errors of the student who is unable to sound out words will indicate the training that is needed. In some such cases it will be found that there are certain important phonetic elements that the student does not know. For example, one student will consistently make errors on vowels. Another may find certain consonants difficult. A relatively small amount of practice on these sounds will enable the student to make use of phonetic analysis when faster word recognition techniques are not sufficient.

The important consideration is the degree to which the student has developed a well-rounded attack. That is, he should have available several techniques of recognizing words. He should develop the ability to muster up for use in a given situation those techniques that are necessary. An explanation of several ways of recognizing words will help the student who is aware of his problem. Caution should be used against causing the student to be overanalytical or too word conscious.

In the reading situation most words are recognized as sight words. The student may recognize a word just as he may recognize an individual. But just as he may be mistaken in the identity of an individual at whom he has glanced hurriedly, so in reading he may be mistaken in the identity of a word. The student may underemphasize certain parts of words and may therefore be subject to error.[1] One student may habitually underemphasize the beginnings of words; another may not inspect the middle of the word carefully enough; while a third may make his errors in word endings. Whichever of these errors is habitually made, the remedial work should consist of having the student distinguish between words that are similar in the parts other than that which the student habitually neglects.

Another source of difficulty is faulty orientation. The student who tends to reverse whole words or parts of words or tends to read the running words in a sentence in the wrong order is subject to faulty orientation. Reversal cases in high school are less frequent than they are in the elementary school. However, inasmuch as some of the cases in high school actually are readers on the elementary level, a consideration of reversal tendencies is not out of place. Such reversal tendencies can be corrected by methods that force the student to pay attention to the beginnings of words. The continual use of the dictionary is helpful in remedying this type of difficulty. It is frequently necessary to allow the student who is subject to reversal tendencies to resort to the "crutch" of moving the eraser end of the pencil underneath the line of print as the line is being read.

Eye Movements

There are two contradictory points of view regarding the role of eye movements in reading. It is the unquestioned fact that good readers of any given material have effective eye movements. Some research workers in the field of reading believe that faulty eye movements are the *cause* of reading dis-

[1] Gates, Arthur I. *The Improvement of Reading,* Revised, The Macmillan Company, 1935, pp. 534-36.

ability. Others believe that they are the *result* of inability to read the material adequately. The writers hold the latter point of view. The problem does not seem to be one of correcting faulty eye movements; rather it is correcting the poor reading techniques, of which faulty eye movements are simply a result.

Reading Speed

Faulty speed of reading may result from (1) interfering habits, (2) inappropriate differentiation, (3) inadequate sight or meaning vocabulary. Interfering habits are such habits as excessive articulation, word-by-word reading, overanalysis, interfering mechanical habits, and excessive speed. The habit of excessive articulation is the practice of vocalizing the words as they are read. This habit may be accompanied by lip movements or may be subvocal. Forming or saying the words slows up the reading considerably. Excessive articulation is a common cause of slow reading in high school. Whatever the degree of vocalization, the student should be made aware of the difficulty. The material that is used for such readers should be relatively easy. They should be encouraged to read as rapidly as possible, so that they do not have time to form the words. As long as vocalization exists, the amount of oral reading that the student does should be reduced to a minimum. As is true with remedial work for all slow readers, timed tests in easy material are effective. If the excessive articulation is accompanied by lip movements, the student should be encouraged to keep his finger on his lips or compress the lips tightly. When the remedial teacher notices signs of excessive articulation, he should caution the reader that he is again "saying" the words.

Word-by-word reading is the habit of looking intently at each word rather than grouping words into thought units. This faulty habit is frequently found among slow high school readers. It should be demonstrated to the student that it is possible to read by thought units. The students should endeavor to group words into thought units and to read those thought units as hurriedly as possible, while keeping the accuracy at a high level. A day-by-day chart of the student's speed should be kept. He should be allowed to enter a day's speed record on the chart only when the accuracy is high for that day.

Let us consider the case of Henry, who was a word-by-word case. He was fifteen years of age and of very superior intelligence. He was in the ninth grade. His reading ability was in general about fourth grade. He read fourth-grade material at the rate of about 75 words per minute with approximately 65 per cent accuracy. Slowly he read words and not content. Therefore, in spite of his intelligence, his comprehension was poor. Henry was told his difficulty. He was shown how to group words in thought units and to read to get the general significance, was given easy fourth-grade material, and a daily record was kept of his reading speed. The first week of remedial instruction he was allowed to enter his speed on the record irrespective of the accuracy. At the beginning of the second week he was told that he would be allowed to enter the speed only when the accuracy with which he answered questions on the material was 75 per cent. At the beginning of the third week the accuracy standard was raised to 80 per cent. Material of gradually increasing difficulty was used during the five weeks of remedial work. While the remedial period was only an hour in length, Henry was encouraged to read extensively material of high interest value during his spare time.

At the end of the five-week period this boy was reading eighth-grade material at the rate of 250 words per minute with 95 per cent accuracy. When tested on the Gates Silent Reading Test, he was found to have gained slightly over four years in his average reading ability. It must be remembered that in this case the boy was exceptionally intelligent and that there were no complicating factors other than an extreme dislike for reading.

Just as the word-by-word reader looks too intently at the words within a thought unit, the reader who overanalyzes studies too intently the parts of words. His problem is very much like the one just discussed. The procedures that are remedial for the word-by-word reader are also effective for the analytical one. The latter usually is a more stubborn case, and the prognosis is a little less favorable. In addition to other procedures, attention must be given to building up an adequate sight vocabulary and more adequate word recognition techniques.

Interfering mechanical habits, such as finger pointing and head movements, can usually be overcome simply by making the student aware of the faulty procedure and by calling his attention to his faulty habit when he reverts to its use. The teacher can use other deterring devices, such as having the student who points with his finger hold the book in both hands.

It seems paradoxical to say that slow reading can be caused by excessive speed, but nevertheless such is the case. It likewise seems paradoxical that speed of reading may be increased by using procedures that cause the student to read more slowly. The student may be attempting to read so rapidly that he continually loses the content and is obliged to do much rereading. In such cases the task is one of learning to read so that these regressions are unnecessary. At the start the reading should be slowed up considerably. Then it may be gradually increased.

Much of the difficulty with speed of reading is the result of the habit of reading all material at a constant rate. That is, the student is unable to adjust his rate to the purpose at hand. He may read all material as slowly and deliberately as he does where his purpose is that of formulating a critical analysis of a passage. Or he may read for every purpose as rapidly as would be compatible with reading to get the general significance of a passage. Or he may attempt to read difficult material at the same rate that should be used for very simple material. Or he may read simple material with the same degree of care that he does difficult material. The important consideration is not the rate of reading, but whether or not that rate is adjusted to the purpose at hand. The student should be timed when he reads for various purposes and when he reads materials of different difficulties. Then he should be shown that both different purposes and different materials require different rates of reading. He should be given practice under the guidance of the teacher in differentiating his rate of reading.

Comprehension

Getting meaning from the printed page is the major goal of all reading. All other aspects of reading are subservient to reading comprehension. The development of reading techniques is for the purpose of making comprehension more adequate. A rapid rate of reading is of no benefit to the student who does not comprehend what he reads. The development of a large sight vocabulary is necessary only because it makes comprehension possible. The ultimate goal of reading instruction is to develop the ability to comprehend materials of varying sorts for varying purposes. The student who is unable to understand what he reads is indeed in difficulty.

Some of the more frequent disabilities in comprehension are: (1) inexperience in reading, (2) immature or faulty reading habits, (3) excessive speed or speed unadjusted to the purpose, (4) lack of a differentiated attack, (5) inadequate background of meanings, (6) insufficient meaning vocabulary.

A student may have difficulty in comprehending the materials as well as normally could be expected because he has not had adequate experience in reading. If such is the case, the remedial teaching should consist of having the student read material at the level that he has reached and of motivating the reading situation so that the student is encouraged to read more extensively. The student needs the same sort of guidance that is given in ordinary classroom procedures. If other factors responsible for the lack of opportunity to read are still present, whenever possible they should be removed.

Immature or faulty reading habits impede comprehension. Among such habits are faulty word-recognition techniques, word-by-word reading, and overanalysis. The remedial work should be based upon improving the immature reading habits. These have been discussed under word-recognition techniques and speed.

Excessive speed does not permit comprehension. Moreover, unless the speed is adjusted to the purpose and to the materials, comprehension will be hindered. Inasmuch as the ultimate goal is getting meaning from the printed page, speed should be secondary to comprehension. The student who is attempting to read material too rapidly must be made aware of this fact and helped in so adjusting his speed that comprehension results. In the case of a student who reads excessively fast, it might be well to have him read for more exacting purposes, such as reading material to organize and reading to note details. His comprehension should be thoroughly and continuously measured. It is profitable to keep an accuracy chart in order that the student may see whether or not he is progressing.

Lack of a differentiated attack is among the most frequent

causes of poor comprehension. The student who is in this difficulty frequently has a high rating on one or two of the various comprehension techniques. His performance is likely to be an inconsistent one. He may have a high rating, for example, in the ability to draw inferences or read critically and yet have a low rating on all the rest. The remedial work for such a case is similar in nature to that given in the discussion of the differentiated attack in Chapter VII. The remedial case, however, needs more careful guidance and more intensive work than are given in the developmental program. The work should definitely concentrate on those abilities in which the student has demonstrated the lowest performance. Purposes that demand those types of reading should be set up. Adequate and continuous appraisals of comprehension should be made. Above all, the student should understand his problem thoroughly and he should keep an account of his daily progress.

An adequate word and meaning background is basic to understanding a printed passage. Consequently, the individual who does not have an adequate word and meaning background is a poor comprehender. This is so basic to reading that a chapter (Chapter V) has been devoted to the building of word and meaning backgrounds. All the suggestions offered in that chapter are applicable to the remedial case. Putting a student who has a low meaning background in the remedial program makes it possible to concentrate specifically upon the development of backgrounds. The remedial teacher is better able to adjust materials to the student's level than other teachers are. Extensive reading of such materials adds to his background of meanings. In addition, the remedial teacher is the one who is best able to stimulate the desire of the student to use the dictionary and other sources of building word meanings. The remedial teacher can aid also in establishing a large sight vocabulary through the word-recognition procedures. *Reading Aids Through the Grades*[2] by Russell, Karp, and Kelly contains many useful suggestions for enlarging the sight vocabulary.

SUMMARY

Remedial teaching is good teaching. The following principles apply in general to remedial reading instruction:

1. Remedial instruction should be based upon a thorough diagnosis.

2. Remedial instruction should be started through the use of materials at the student's reading level.

3. The natural interests of the student should be used in selecting materials.

4. The materials should be interesting in style and in content.

5. The purpose for reading must emphasize the techniques and skills to be improved.

6. The purpose for reading should be real to the student.

7. The student should be aware of the nature of his disability.

8. The student should have his progresss demonstrated.

9. Good teaching techniques should be employed.

The fundamental problem in remedial instruction is to locate and focus instruction upon the basic difficulty. The chapter includes a discussion of some of the techniques which are frequently found to be basic.

SELECTED BIBLIOGRAPHY

Alexander, Fred M. "Reading in Newport News High School," *Journal of Education,* Vol. CXIII, March 2, 1931, pp. 248-51.

Blake, Mabelle B., and Dearborn, Walter F. "The Improvement of Reading Habits," *Journal of Higher Education,* Vol. VI, February, 1935, pp. 83-88.

[2] Russell, David H., Karp, Etta E., and Kelly, Edward I. *Reading Aids Through the Grades,* Bureau of Publications, Teachers College, Columbia University, 1938.

Deal, A. B., and Seamans, A. "Group Remedial Reading in High School," *English Journal,* College Edition, Vol. XXVI, May, 1937, pp. 355-62.

Deal, Roy W. "The Development of Reading and Study Habits in College Students," *Journal of Educational Psychology,* Vol. XXV, April, 1934, pp. 258-73.

Garrison, Blanche L. "A Contribution of Measurement to Remedial Reading," *Education,* Vol. LVI, November, 1935, pp. 144-48.

Gates, Arthur I. "Diagnosis and Treatment of Extreme Cases of Reading Disability," *The Teaching of Reading: A Second Report, The Thirty-Sixth Yearbook of the National Society for the Study of Education,* Part I, Public School Publishing Company, 1937.

Gates, Arthur I. *The Improvement of Reading,* Revised, The Macmillan Company, 1935.

Harris, Albert J. *How to Increase Reading Ability,* Longmans, Green and Company, 1940.

McCallister, James M. *Remedial and Corrective Instruction in Reading,* D. Appleton-Century Company, 1936, Chapter 6.

Monroe, Marion, and Backus, Bertie. *Remedial Reading,* Houghton Mifflin Company, 1937, Chapters 5 and 6.

Russell, David H., and others. *Reading Aids Through the Grades,* Bureau of Publications, Teachers College, Columbia University, 1938.

Strang, Ruth, and Rose, F. C. *Problems in the Improvement of Reading in High School and College,* Revised, The Science Press Printing Company, 1940, Chapter V.

Traxler, Arthur E. "Group Corrective Reading in the Seventh Grade—an Experiment," *School Review,* Vol. XLI, September, 1933, pp. 519-30.

Witty, Paul, and Kopel, David. *Reading and the Educative Process,* Ginn and Company, 1939, Chapter 5.

SECTION IV

CO-ORDINATION

CHAPTER XIV

CO-ORDINATING THE READING PROGRAM

The discussion so far has been concerned with the improvement of instruction in reading. It has been shown that reading ability must be developed in at least five broad, interrelated areas. It has been shown further that a well-rounded reading program should be an all-school program and that all teachers should participate in aiding the students in developing their reading abilities. Moreover, the reading program should include instruction in both the silent and oral aspects of reading. Then, too, the developmental program must be supplemented by a program of special remedial instruction. It is necessary now to think of the reading program in its entirety.

The developmental reading program must be well organized to be effective and to avoid overlapping and duplication of effort. In any phase of schoolwork that encompasses the entire school personnel, there is a grave danger of wasteful duplication of effort. This is especially true of the reading program because of the complexity of the reading process, the marked degree of interrelationship among those who direct and participate in it, and the need for co-operation among them. Another factor that frequently makes for duplication is that no one teacher can or should give the student his entire reading instruction. Inasmuch as it is necessary for the student to learn to adapt his reading ability to a variety of purposes in each subject, reading instruction for any one individual should be given by several teachers.

The reading program also must be well organized to insure instruction in each of the five areas in both oral and silent reading. Without a rather thorough organization of the individual efforts of the teachers, instructional gaps are likely to occur. Furthermore, some areas are apt to be overemphasized at the expense of others. The resultant lack of balance is harmful to the continued development of reading. For example, when oral reading is overemphasized, the students are likely to become slow, ineffectual silent readers as a result of interfering habits of vocalization. Again, when emphasis is placed upon the sort of reading that is necessary for the effectual reading of the novel, the students may regress in their ability to read the more exacting materials of science and mathematics. Or again, students may become so conscious of establishing a differentiated attack that they fail to realize the relationships that exist between reading in any two fields and for any two purposes.

Organization of the reading program is essential if instruction in reading is to be effective. This organization includes the co-ordination of the factors in the program. These various factors will be discussed in the pages that follow.

Co-ordination between Elementary and Secondary School Reading Programs

The developmental reading program in the secondary school should begin where the developmental reading program in the elementary school leaves off. There should be a close co-ordination between reading instruction in these two divisions of the school system. At the outset those who are responsible for reading instruction in the secondary school should have a complete knowledge of reading instruction in the elementary school. Both the secondary and the elementary schools should have somewhat the same underlying philosophy of reading instruction. Of vital interest to those who teach reading to the students when they reach high school are such factors as the reading materials the students have been using; the number and type of appraisals that have been made; the amount, kind, and extent of diagnostic and remedial instruction; and the kind, completeness, and accuracy of the records of the developmental progress of the pupils.

The gap between the last year of elementary school and the first year of secondary school should be no greater than that between any other two years of school life. Just as the fourth-grade teacher passes on to the fifth-grade teacher the information he has about the reading strengths and weaknesses of his pupils, so at graduation time the elementary school should send on to the high school the information it has about the reading status of the students who will make up the freshman class group the following September.

A close co-ordination between the elementary and the secondary schools will result in a co-operative effort that will enable the instruction in reading to be continuous and developmental from the first grade through the twelfth. It is possible for the high school teachers or authorities to appreciate the level of development in various reading abilities that the students have reached only when there is an understanding of how that development has been achieved. And, on the other hand, it is possible for the elementary school more nearly to prepare the students for the reading activities in which they will engage in the secondary school if those activities are known. A continuous developmental program of instruction in reading will produce more effective readers than will a program not as well organized.

CONSIDERATIONS IN CO-ORDINATING A READING PROGRAM

The way in which the reading program is co-ordinated in

any one school system is dependent upon local conditions. Some of the factors that vary from school to school and which effect the organization of a reading program are: the size of the school, the reading needs and abilities of the pupils, the school facilities, the co-operation and efficiency of the teaching and administrative staffs, and the demands and flexibility of the curriculum.

While the organization of reading instruction is basically the same for all schools, certain modifications of the administration of the reading program will be necessary in order that the co-ordinated program may fit local needs. For example, an overcrowded school will present problems of organization that will not be found in a less crowded one. A school with meager library facilities has a serious problem of adjusting materials to the individual needs of students. In schools where there is a large percentage of teachers who have had little, if any, training in methods of teaching reading, it will be necessary for the in-service training to be more intensive and for the introduction of the reading program to proceed slowly. In schools where the testing budget is limited, more use of teacher-appraisals will be required. In spite of the fact that there are great differences among schools, it is desirable to discuss some of the general considerations in organizing a program for the teaching of reading.

The program schedule of the high school must be so budgeted as to include two or three periods per week for certain phases of reading instruction. In most high schools it is expedient to have this instruction carried on by the home-room teachers. The precise amount of time devoted to this instruction depends, of course, upon the facilities and needs of a specific school system. Two periods of instruction per week in the general aspects of reading should, however, be considered a minimum. Provision should be made for general instruction in reading throughout all four years of high school. Inasmuch as all students should be included in the developmental reading program, other school activities should not be allowed to conflict with instruction in reading.

For the best results, reading possibilities of all parts of the curriculum must be utilized. The development of reading cannot be expected to be accomplished in the two-hour-per-week general reading period. It must be supplemented by special instruction in reading the materials of each content subject. Since the reading of the materials of the various content fields is essential to effective instruction in those fields, the teachers are quite likely to find that instruction in reading and the resultant independence of the students will lessen their teaching load rather than add to it.

In addition to making a full use of the curriculum in teaching reading, it is necessary to adjust the materials of instruction to the abilities of the students. While it may be difficult to make adjustments in the more formal and standardized curricula, nevertheless such adjustments are necessary. As a result of initial appraisals of reading ability, for example, it may be found that the majority of students do not have sufficient word and meaning backgrounds to enable them to read and appreciate the literary materials included in the course of study. If such is the case, curriculum adjustments are needed. When these adjustments are not made, the objectives of neither the reading nor the curriculum can be achieved.

At the outset, an appraisal should be made of the training, experience, and potentialities for the teaching of reading of the members of the teaching staff. Very likely some will have had training and experience that will enable them to help in the organization of reading instruction in various content fields as well as with the initial organization. They may also help with an in-service training course in the teaching of reading for those teachers who have had little or no training and experience in teaching reading.

Making a wise and full use of the services and knowledges of the people within the system who are to carry forward the instruction in reading does not preclude providing for other help and guidance. In order that a reading program may get under way efficiently and smoothly, it may be advisable to make use of outside help. If the introduction of reading instruction into the high school is to be an all-school one, a consultant may be able to help the program proceed with a minimum of overlapping of endeavor. While it is probable that an enthusiastic and co-operative beginning on the part of administrators, teachers, and students will often prove sufficient to inaugurate a program, technical help may be needed in some school situations.

An important consideration in setting up a reading program is that it be simple and easily operated. A cumbersome, complicated program of co-ordination is neither necessary nor desirable. Whatever organization of the program is ultimately undertaken, it should be understandable to the teachers. This implies that the teachers' part should be clearly defined and explained.

The Co-ordinator of the Reading Program

In organizing a reading program, it is advisable to have the administration of the program in the hands of one individual. This is true whether the program is carried on by the existing personnel of the school, or is directed by someone who is added to the staff for that specific purpose. Inasmuch as all teachers are concerned with the development of an adequate reading program, there is likely to be an overlapping of effort. This makes necessary a well-organized program of co-ordination under the direction of some one individual.

In the small high school it is usually advisable to have one who has other teaching duties act as co-ordinator. This person may be a teacher in any of the content fields. The person selected should have an intense interest and a good training in the teaching of reading. If no member of the staff has such training, the person who has a keen interest in reading and other necessary qualifications should be encouraged to become trained. Regardless of the keenness of interest, it is unwise to expect a person with little training in the field of reading to undertake the responsibilities and duties of the co-ordinator. If a vacancy occurs in the teaching staff, it is advisable to fill that vacancy with someone definitely qualified to act as co-ordinator of a reading program. The one who is selected as co-ordinator and given the many responsibilities of organizing a reading program is entitled to supervisory status and the wholehearted backing of the administration. It is only by such backing that desirable outcomes may be realized. The task will be difficult, and so in the beginning progress may be expected to be slow. Consequently, the co-ordinator should not carry a full teaching load and should be freed from other responsibilities.

In the large high schools it is necessary to have a full-time well-trained reading co-ordinator. The problems confronting the co-ordinator in a large high school are fundamentally the same as those confronting the co-ordinator in the small high school. However, they are more numerous, somewhat more complex, and constitute a greater administrative burden. Obviously, the co-ordination of the work of many people will present more problems than will the co-ordination of the work of but few. The problems will be more complex in nature inasmuch as there will be varying degrees of responsibility among the co-workers. This is not so true in the small high school. The task of administrating the reading program

in a school of considerable size is a large one. Direct contacts
with the teachers are less frequent, making it necessary to co-
ordinate the program by administrative devices and group discussions rather than by means of individual conferences.

DUTIES OF THE CO-ORDINATOR

To Appraise and Analyze Available Resources

The initial task of the co-ordinator is to appraise and analyze the resources of the school and community in their relation to the reading program. The appraisals are necessary so
that the co-ordinator may have a fairly complete understanding of the school and community situation before the inauguration of the reading program. In a small school system the
initial survey might take a relatively short time—a week or so.
In a large system it will take a longer time—perhaps a month
or more.

One of the early appraisals should be the extent of training
and interest in reading that the various members of the staff have.
Such an appraisal indicates those staff members who are willing and free to assume responsibilities. It also reveals the extent of in-service training that should be undertaken. In the
ultimate analysis the reading program in no small measure
depends upon the quality of the reading instruction that is
done by the individual members of the staff. Hence, the co-
ordinator must know the quality of instruction that can be
expected and consider means of improving it when the need
for improvement is indicated.

A second appraisal that should be made by the co-ordinator
is the quality and quantity of available materials. The extent,
quality, accessibility, and levels of difficulty of the reading materials should be determined. While this exploration may
need to extend over a period of time, it should be accomplished
as speedily as possible. This is not solely the responsibility of

the co-ordinator. He may direct or delegate it. In any event the services of the librarian as well as those of members of the various departments should be enlisted. The co-ordinator's responsibility is that of initiating and interpreting such an appraisal. The importance, on the part of all staff members, of a working knowledge of available materials cannot be overemphasized. This knowledge is essential if individualization of instruction is to be accomplished. The adjustment of the reading materials to the reading abilities of the students is fundamental to the success of the developmental program.

Inasmuch as there must be a co-ordination between the reading program and other agencies concerned with the adjustment of instruction to the individuals, the co-ordinator must be acquainted with the facilities of the school. There may be a program of guidance in the school. These two divisions—guidance and reading—must be closely allied. There may be a central testing organization available for administering and scoring tests. The co-ordinator will find it profitable to make use of such facilities. Other agencies, such as the health department and the speech department, should also aid the reading co-ordinator materially.

It is necessary also to appraise the community resources that have a relationship to the reading problem. Such resources might include child welfare organizations, clinics, public library systems, museums, and other service agencies.

The reading abilities of the students should also be appraised. The survey of reading abilities should include not only the level and spread of reading in general, but should provide a profile of the levels of ability in various types of reading. Such a profile indicates the areas that have been neglected and thereby aids in providing a well-rounded program of instruction. The results of this survey are useful not only to the co-ordinator, but also to the teachers. The co-ordinator's responsibility in conducting this initial survey is the same as his responsibility in the yearly testing program.

To Keep Records

A second duty of the co-ordinator is that of making available to the teachers all pertinent records and reports related to reading. The exact nature of this responsibility depends upon the type of records already in existence. He may find that the existing records are satisfactory or he may feel that they should be revised. Whatever the situation, it is essential that complete individual records be made easily accessible to the teachers and that the most pertinent data be sent directly to them. A fuller account of the program of appraisals was given in Chapter X.

To Give In-Service Training

A third duty is that of giving in-service training to the members of the teaching staff. The in-service training is designed to help those teachers who have had little or no training in the teaching of reading. In many high schools the great majority of teachers realize vaguely the complexity of the reading process. The teachers frequently know that the reading materials of their courses are too difficult for the students and they undertake to remedy the situation by showing the students how to read for specific reading purposes. But their effort to teach reading is not an organized one. In the main, the reason there is little organized instruction in reading in high school is that the teachers do not know how to provide such instruction, not that they feel there is no need for it. Consequently, whenever a developmental reading program is introduced into a school, it is found that many of the teachers feel that they need more training in the teaching of reading and are interested in receiving it.

The in-service training in the teaching of reading may take any one of several forms. Several faculty meetings, for example, may be devoted to the topic of teaching reading in high school. This is accomplished by having the co-ordinator of the reading program discuss the matter with the faculty. In a small high school several of such group meetings, combined with personal conferences between the co-ordinator and teachers, are sufficient to provide the training needed to undertake the teaching of reading in the home-room periods and in the content course work. Other schools find it feasible to have an institute on the teaching of reading before the school year begins. The co-ordinator may arrange and direct the institute. Or it may be conducted by someone employed for that specific purpose.

Another way of providing in-service training is to conduct a class for faculty members once or twice a week throughout the first semester of the year. Attendance in these classes is optional. When training is handled in this way, the co-ordinator posts before each meeting the topic to be discussed. If "The Teaching of Reading in Science Courses" is the topic, the meeting on this day would interest and benefit the science teachers more than teachers in other departments. However, when the topic is "Providing Experiences in Reading Independence," most of the teachers will feel that it is worth while to attend. By and large, teachers eagerly seize any opportunity that enables them to improve the quality of their instruction and so make the task of teaching easier and more effective.

In-service training is provided sometimes by using the facilities of the Extension Division of a near-by university or college. It is possible to arrange for a member of the staff of a teacher-training institution or of the department of education of a state university to conduct an extension course for teachers if a sufficiently large number of teachers enroll to make such a course feasible. In any event, teachers may be encouraged to include the teaching of reading among the courses that they take for their professional advancement. Whatever form the program of in-service training takes, it is imperative that an opportunity be provided for all teachers to learn how to teach reading.

In conjunction with the in-service training, the co-ordinator should assemble a well-chosen professional library on the teaching of reading. This entails both the collecting of professional books and the making of bibliographies of current articles related to reading. It also entails keeping a file of leaflets and reprints on reading. Inasmuch as this library will prove to be of real value to the teachers, it should be large enough to accommodate their needs and should be made readily accessible to them.

To Supervise Instruction

Supervision of instruction in the reading periods is a fourth duty of the co-ordinator. The general instruction in reading in many schools may be done by the home-room teachers. The co-ordinator can be of invaluable service to the teacher in helping him fit the instruction to the needs of his specific group of pupils. The co-ordinator, in co-operation with the various teachers, may work out units of instruction to use in the home-room period. Such units of instruction can be assembled in mimeographed form. Then a unit becomes the core of instruction in a home-room when such a unit aids in the developmental growth in reading of the pupils in that home-room.

In addition to supervising the instruction in reading in the home-room, the co-ordinator has another responsibility to the teachers. He should be available for consultation with a teacher or with the members of a department whenever reading instruction in their subject troubles them. This responsibility is heavy during the first year or so of a school-wide program of instruction in reading. But as the teachers become more experienced, they handle more and more of the difficulties of instruction themselves. The knotty problem during the first months of instruction in reading consists of questions relating to group methods of teaching procedure; later, when group procedures are well worked out, the teachers turn their attention to more individualized teaching methods.

While the home-room teacher assumes the responsibility of consulting with students and their parents in relation to the students' reading abilities, the co-ordinator occasionally participates in these conferences. This is true especially in those cases in which the students are in the remedial part of the reading program as well as in the developmental.

To Select Reading Materials

A fifth duty of the co-ordinator relates to the selection of reading materials. The co-ordinator may advise the textbook committee of the appropriateness of various books in order that those chosen may be neither too elementary nor too advanced for the readers who are to read them. His advice may be sought by the librarian in making up the list of books and magazines to be purchased by the library. The co-ordinator frequently is of help to the teacher in the daily selection of materials to be used in the classes for various purposes. He, in all probability, has a better knowledge of the reading abilities of the students and of the difficulty of the word and meaning content of the various reading materials than any other person in the high school. His help in the choice of materials should make the instruction better fitted to the needs and abilities of the pupils.

To Organize Diagnostic and Remedial Instruction

The sixth duty of the co-ordinator is to diagnose the reading difficulties of the students who are severely retarded in reading ability and to provide remedial instruction in reading for them. Diagnosis of reading deals, for the most part, with individual children. It should be done by someone trained in diagnostic procedures. After the co-ordinator has made the diagnosis, he outlines the remedial instruction for the individual cases.

While it is true that the remedial instruction must be individualized to a great extent, this does not mean that students needing relatively the same kind of instruction cannot receive it in groups. The co-ordinator determines what students will profit from group remedial instruction and makes provision for the group work. The group instruction may be given either by the co-ordinator or by the teachers designated to aid in the remedial program. When the teachers give the individualized group remedial instruction, they should be carefully supervised by the co-ordinator. Those cases who fail to profit from group instruction or who otherwise constitute troublesome problems should receive individual remedial instruction from the co-ordinator or from a teacher who has been trained to do remedial reading work.

To Report Outcomes of Instruction

A seventh duty of the co-ordinator is to make reports and summaries of the outcomes of instruction. It is through such reports that the effectiveness of the reading program can most accurately be judged. The changes in attitudes, achievements, and personal adjustments may be so gradual that their magnitude escapes notice if some systematic appraisal is not undertaken. Measurements of the outcomes of instruction should be made yearly in order that the extent of growth may be ascertained. It is through such measurements that the effectiveness of various procedures can be determined. These analyses may show weaknesses in the program. When this is so, recommendations should be made for their correction.

The co-ordinator also is aware of the opportunities for research. The reading program on the high school level is in its infancy. Consequently, there are many areas that need to be investigated. The teachers and the co-ordinator can contribute to the knowledge of the teaching of reading on the high school level. If, through their experiences with the reading program, interesting conclusions can be drawn, these findings should be carefully, fully, and accurately reported in a professional journal.

The individual who is placed in charge of the reading program must be well trained in reading. This training includes, among others, (1) an understanding of the reading process; (2) a knowledge and an understanding of how reading ability is developed, including methodology at all levels; (3) a knowledge of books and materials, and skill in critically evaluating them; (4) an understanding of the functions of appraisal and a knowledge of instruments of appraisal, as well as skill in administering and interpreting them; (5) an understanding of diagnostic and remedial procedures and the ability to use them effectively; (6) a sufficient background of understanding the symptoms of disabilities, deficiencies, and related disturbances so as to know when to refer a pupil to a competent otologist, oculist, physician, psychiatrist or other expert. The individual should also have an understanding of the psychology of the adolescent. This includes (1) a knowledge of individual differences; (2) an understanding of the physical, emotional, social, intellectual, and personal development of boys and girls.

In addition to the training indicated above, the reading co-ordinator must have the personal qualifications necessary to present the reading problem to teachers, administrators, and parents and other lay groups. The success of the program depends in no small measure upon the ability of the co-ordinator to enlist the co-operation of the people concerned with the program. Many a program has failed to get under way because the co-ordinator lacked the ability to deal effectively with people. Above all, however, the co-ordinator should like adolescent boys and girls, should enjoy working with them, and should be able to gain their confidence and co-operation.

Summary of Co-ordinator's Duties

Among the more important duties of the co-ordinator are: to make an initial survey of the school and community facilities that are related to reading; to aid in the selecting and giving of reading tests and to make all records and reports related to reading available to the teachers; to give in-service training to the members of the teaching staff; to co-ordinate the general reading instruction and that in the content fields; to aid in the selection and adaptation of reading materials to the needs and abilities of the pupils; to assume full responsibility for the diagnostic and remedial program. The successful performance of the services of the co-ordinator will determine in no small measure the effectiveness of the all-school reading program.

DUTIES OF THE TEACHERS

To Understand the Teaching of Reading

The high school teachers are the ones who do the actual teaching of reading both in the general reading period and in the content subjects. It is important that the quality of instruction be at as high a level as possible. One duty of the teacher is, then, to become familiar with and understand the teaching of reading. Whenever the opportunity affords, he should take courses in the teaching of reading and he should participate wholeheartedly in the in-service training that is conducted in his school.

To Make Appraisals

A second duty of the teacher is to study the reading needs and abilities of the students in his classes and to fit instruction to those needs and abilities. Thus, the teacher makes continuous appraisals of the reading interests and abilities of the students by means of observational and other methods.

To Analyze the Reading Needs of His Subject

In order that the teacher may better adjust instruction to the reading abilities of the students, he analyzes the reading needs of his subject. He acquaints himself with the content of available materials and with its difficulty. Whenever it is necessary for him to do so, he prepares the students for reading those materials. This preparation, for example, may take the form of developing word meaning, so that the student is familiar with the meanings of the words as he reads the passage. On the other hand, a background of facts may be built up for the student so as to enable him to read a passage with understanding. Or, the teacher may make the reading of the student more effective by helping him set up appropriate techniques to be employed. The teacher's duty is, then, to know the materials and the reading needs of his subject so that he may adjust the materials and instruction to the reading abilities of the students. In order to do this, some teachers find it helpful to keep a list of materials indicating their approximate difficulty, as well as to keep records of the reading needs of his subject and of the reading abilities of the students.

To Teach Reading in the General Reading Period

A fourth duty is to participate in the program of general reading instruction in his home-room periods devoted to that instruction. The teacher works with the students of his home-room groups in all five areas of reading instruction. It is during these periods that the well-rounded developmental program of reading instruction begun in the first grade of the elementary school is carried forward. Since he has a somewhat complete picture of the reading development of his students, the teacher is the one who confers with them about their reading progress.

The part of the teacher in the developmental reading program is both continuous and difficult. The instruction, however, contributes to the increased achievement of the students in reading and in other subjects of the curriculum as well.

DUTIES OF THE ADMINISTRATOR

To Secure Adequate Personnel

While the duties of the administrator in the reading program are similar to his duties in respect to other phases of instruction, there are certain items that are important to consider. First among these is to secure an adequately trained personnel. As has been indicated, this may be done by normal replacements or through in-service training of the teachers. Of course, the person who assumes the task of co-ordinator must be specifically trained for the job.

The administrator should realize that the introduction of a reading program is a major task. He should also realize that it takes time to organize and develop such an instructional program. Consequently, he should not be impatient if the results are not immediately apparent. The ultimate results will be satisfactory to everybody concerned with the educational program.

To Allocate Funds

An item should be included in the school budget for the added costs of a reading program. The major expense is the salary of the co-ordinator. In all probability, there will be a slight increase in the testing and material budget. By and large, the introduction of the reading program simply means a wiser and more complete use than was formerly made of the available personnel and materials.

To Schedule Time

A third duty of the administrator is to schedule two periods or more per week for general instruction in reading. It should be so scheduled that every student is enrolled in a section. In addition, rooms and other needed facilities should be provided for the reading program.

To Support Program

When a reading program is being introduced into a high school, it is assumed that the administrator will interest himself in reading and will give the program his enthusiastic support. His enthusiasm will be contagious and will encourage others to become interested in reading. In an undertaking that encompasses the entire school personnel, a high degree of co-operation is needed. There can be a high degree of co-operation only when all participants are interested in and realize the importance of the undertaking.

SUMMARY

Factors that should be considered in organizing an all-school program in reading include:

1. Instruction should be provided in each of the areas in both oral and silent reading.

2. The program should be set up in such a way that a duplication of effort is avoided.

3. Reading instruction in the elementary and the secondary schools should be co-ordinated.

4. Local conditions, such as size of school, the reading needs and abilities of the pupils, the school facilities, the demands and flexibility of the curriculum, must be taken into consideration in setting up the program.

5. Time must be allotted for instruction in reading.

6. Instruction in reading must be an integral part of instruction in each subject of the curriculum.

7. Reading materials must be selected and adjusted in relation to the abilities of the students.

8. The training and the experience in teaching reading of the teaching staff are factors that must be considered in the organization of the reading program.

9. The reading program must be so set up that it is simple and is easily operated.

The reading program should have some one person who co-ordinates it. The co-ordinator should be a person who has an interest in reading and who has had training in the teaching of reading. At the outset, the co-ordinator should acquaint himself with the school. This entails making appraisals of: (1) the potentialities of the teaching staff, (2) reading materials, (3) school facilities, (4) resources of the community, (5) the reading abilities of the students. Other duties of the co-ordinator include: (1) making records and reports related to reading available to the teachers, (2) directing or giving in-service training for the teachers, (3) supervising reading instruction, (4) assisting in the selection of materials, (5) counseling students, (6) providing or directing diagnostic and remedial instruction, (7) appraising the outcomes of the reading program.

The duties, in relation to the reading program, of the teacher of a content subject in high school include: (1) familiarizing himself with the teaching of reading, (2) assisting in the program of appraisals, (3) analyzing and familiarizing himself with the reading needs of his subject, (4) teaching reading in the general reading program and in his subject.

The duties, in connection with the reading program, of the administrators of the school include: (1) securing adequately trained personnel, (2) scheduling instruction in reading, (3) giving encouragement and support to the reading program.

Selected Bibliography

Barry, L., and Pratt, M. "A Remedial-Reading Program in a Public High School," *School Review*, Vol. XLV, January, 1937, pp. 17-27.

Harris, Albert J. *How to Increase Reading Ability*, Longmans, Green and Company, 1940.

McCallister, James M. *Remedial and Corrective Instruction in Reading*, D. Appleton-Century Company, 1936, Chapter 16.

Strang, Ruth, and Rose, F. C. *Problems in the Improvement of Reading in High School and College*, Revised, The Science Press Printing Company, 1940, pp. 126-27.

Witty, Paul, and Kopel, David. *Reading and the Educative Process*, Ginn and Company, 1939.

Yoakum, Gerald A. "The Reorganization and Improvement of Instruction in Reading Through Adequate Supervision," *The Teaching of Reading: A Second Report, The Thirty-Sixth Yearbook of the National Society for the Study of Education*, Part I, Public School Publishing Company, 1937.

APPENDIX

READING TESTS FOR HIGH SCHOOL STUDENTS

Name of Test	Suitable for Grades	Abilities Measured	Approximate Time in Minutes	Publisher
Cooperative English Test—Test CI and II Reading Comprehension	9—12	Vocabulary Speed of Comprehension Level of Comprehension	40	Cooperative Test Service, New York, N. Y. Yearly.
Gates Reading Survey for Grades 3-10	3—10	Vocabulary Power of Comprehension Speed Accuracy	40	Bureau of Publications, Teachers College, Columbia University, New York City, 1939.
Gates Silent Reading	3—8	A—Appreciate General Significance B—Predict Outcomes C—Follow Directions D—Note Details	30	Bureau of Publications, Teachers College, Columbia University, New York City, 1935.

READING TESTS FOR HIGH SCHOOL STUDENTS (*Continued*)

Name of Test	Suitable for Grades	Abilities Measured	Approximate Time in Minutes	Publisher
Haggerty Reading Examination Sigma III	6—12	Vocabulary Sentence Reading Paragraph Reading	30	World Book Company, Yonkers-on-Hudson, New York, 1926.
Iowa Comprehension Test	9—12	Power of Comprehension	36	Bureau of Educational Research and Service, University of Iowa, Iowa City, Iowa, 1924.
Iowa Silent Reading Test, New Edition, Advanced Test	High School and College	Rate—Comprehension (a) Science (b) Social Science Directed Reading Poetry Comprehension Word Meaning (a) Social Science (b) Science	45	World Book Company, Yonkers-on-Hudson, New York, 1939.

		(c) Mathematics (d) English Sentence Meaning Paragraph Comprehension Location of Information (a) Use of Index (b) Selection of Key Words		World Book Company Yonkers-on-Hudson, New York. Yearly.
Iowa Every Pupil Test A— Reading Comprehension	6—8	Paragraph Comprehension Understanding of Details Organization of Ideas Grasp of Total Meaning	50—65	World Book Company Yonkers-on-Hudson, New York. Yearly.
Iowa Every Pupil Test B— Basic Study Skills	6—8	Comprehension of Maps Reading Graphs, Charts, and Tables Use of Basic Reference Use of Index Use of Dictionary	80	

Name of Test	Suitable for Grades	Abilities Measured	Approximate Time in Minutes	Publisher
Michigan Speed of Reading Tests	3—16	Speed	10	Psychological Corporation, New York, N. Y., 1932.
Minnesota Reading Examination for College Students, Revised	College	Vocabulary Paragraph Comprehension	46	University of Minnesota Press, Minneapolis, Minnesota, 1930.
Minnesota Speed of Reading Test for College Students	College	Speed	6	University of Minnesota Press, Minneapolis, Minnesota, 1936.
Nelson-Denny Reading Test for Colleges and Senior High Schools	10—16	Vocabulary Paragraph Comprehension	30	Houghton Mifflin Company, Boston, Massachusetts, 1929.

Progressive Reading Tests, Advanced Battery	High School and College 9—13	Reading Vocabulary (a) Mathematics (b) Science (c) Social Science (d) Literature Reading Comprehension (e) Following Directions (f) Organization (g) Interpretation of Meanings	50-55	California School Book Depository, Hollywood, California, 1934.
Purdue Reading Test	7—16	Speed and Accuracy of Comprehension	40	Lafayette Printing Company, Lafayette, Indiana, 1928.
Reading Scales in History	Junior and Senior High School	Comprehension in the field of History	45	Educational Test Bureau, Minneapolis, Minnesota, 1938.

READING TESTS FOR HIGH SCHOOL STUDENTS (*Continued*)

Name of Test	Suitable for Grades	Abilities Measured	Approximate Time in Minutes	Publisher
Reading Scales in Literature	Junior and Senior High School	Comprehension in the field of Literature	45	Educational Test Bureau, Minneapolis, Minnesota, 1939.
Reading Scales in Science	Junior and Senior High School	Comprehension in the field of Science	45	Educational Test Bureau, Minneapolis, Minnesota, 1938.
Shank Tests of Reading Comprehension	II—7 to 9 III—10 to 12	Comprehension	20	C. A. Gregory, Cincinnati, Ohio.
Strang-Martin Reading Tests	9—16	Speed Comprehension Power of Comprehension		Bureau of Publications, Teachers College, Columbia University, New York City.

READING TESTS FOR HIGH SCHOOL STUDENTS (*Continued*)

Thorndike-McCall Reading Scale	2–12	Power of Comprehension	30	Bureau of Publications, Teachers College, Columbia University, New York City, 1921.
Traxler Silent Reading Test	7–10	Rate of Reading Vocabulary Story Comprehension Power of Comprehension	46	Public School Publishing Company, Bloomington, Illinois, 1934.
Tyler Kimber Study Skills Test	High School and College	Location of Information Use of Index Use of General Reference Books Recognition of Common Abbreviations Use of Card Catalog Interpretation of Maps Interpretation of Graphs Knowledge of Current Periodical Literature		Stanford University Press, Stanford University, California, 1937.
Unit Scales of Attainment—Reading Comprehension	9–12	Comprehension	45	Educational Test Bureau, Minneapolis, Minnesota, 1929.

353

Name of Test	Suitable for Grades	Abilities Measured	Approximate Time in Minutes	Publisher
Van Wagenen and Dvorak Diagnostic Examination of Silent Reading Abilities	Junior and Senior High School	Rate of Comprehension Perception of Relations Vocabulary in Context Vocabulary-Isolated Words General Information Ability to Grasp Central Thought Ability to Note Clearly Stated Details Interpretation Integration of Dispersed Ideas Ability to Draw Inferences	140	Educational Test Bureau, Minneapolis, Minnesota, 1940.
Whipple's High School and College Reading Test	High School and College	Rate and Comprehension	10	Public School Publishing Company, Bloomington, Illinois, 1925.

354

INDEX

abilities, reading, and scholastic achievements, 7-10; varied for each subject, 11; varied in individual, 23-25. *See also* silent reading

ability, to follow directions, 186, 188, 191, 281, 284; to get general significance, 280, 284; to read critically, 281, 284

"Ability to Read Historical Materials as Related to Eighth-Grade Achievement and General Reading Abilities," 8

abstraction, difficulties of, in social studies, 178

Adler, Mortimer J., in *How to Read a Book,* 5

administration, problems of, 22

administrator, duties of the, 342-343, 345

adolescent, psychology of the, 339

Alabama text *vs.* Pennsylvania text, 174

all-school appraisal, 279

all-school developmental program for reading, 325, 330; factors in organizing, 343-344

Americans, reading status of, 4

Anderson, E. M., in "Individual Differences in the Reading Ability of College Students," 31

appraisals, by observation, 236-238; by teachers, 341; factors in, 281; for diagnosis, 278-281; function and instruments of, 339; in content-subjects, 224-229; initial, and adjustment of curriculum, 329; initial, by co-ordinator, 332-334, 344-345; in relation to instruction in reading, 220-225; instruments for, 234-235; number and type of, 327; of good and poor reading abilities, 212; of remedial progress to be open to student, 308-309; of teaching staff, 329; of outcomes in five areas of reading instruction, 232; purposes of, 219; standardized measures in, 218; to aid in selection of materials, 229-230; to aid in student guidance, 230; to contribute to research in education, 231; types of, 235-236; using personal knowledge of, 219

approaches, 13

areas, in which to develop reading ability, 325, 326, 333

artificial reading purposes or situations, to be avoided, 293, 308

As You Like It, material from, 154-155, 158, 159

attack, 284

auditory acuity, defined, 292

"Auditory and Speech Characteristics of Poor Readers," 263

auditory discrimination, defined, 291

author and reader, 207-208

authors and sources, considered for points of view, 173-174

background concepts, development of, 42-43

background of experience, estimated by interview technique, 289; varied meanings of, 258

background of meaning. *See* meaning background; experiences

Bell Adjustment Inventory, 292

Bennett, M. E., in *College and Life,* 209-210

Bernreuter Personality Inventory, 292

Betts, E. A., in *The Prevention and Correction of Reading Difficulties,* 290

Binet. *See* Stanford-Binet

Blackmore, R. D., *Lorna Doone,* 152

Blanchard, Phyllis, in "Reading Disabilities in Relation to Maladjustment," 59

blending ability, defined, 291

Bond, Elden, in "Tenth-Grade Abilities and Achievements," 9, 58, 74; in "Some Verbal Aspects of the 1937 Revision of The Stanford-Binet Intelligence Test, Form L," 258

Bond, Eva, in "Reading and Ninth Grade Achievement," 7, 58

Bond, Guy L., in "Auditory and Speech Characteristics of Poor Readers," 263

book-club days, 182

book reviews, 93, 182

Bowman, Isaiah, in *Geography in Relation to the Social Sciences,* 180

budget, 65; school, 343

Byrns and Henmon, in "Reading Interests of High School Seniors," 134

"Case for Voluminous Reading," 140

Center, S. S., and Persons, G. L., in *Teaching High School Students How to Read,* 6; in *Workbook to "Practices in Reading and Thinking,"* 123, 124; in *Problems in Reading and Thinking,* 206-208

Chicago, study of, by Marshall High School, 125, 127

"Child Development and the Curriculum," 79

Children Who Cannot Read, 59, 265, 287

chronological age, defined, 282; value of, in diagnosis, 282

class management, effective, 202-203

Claude Gueux, 3

College and Life, 209-210

community resources, 333

"Community Studies in Reading," 139

comprehension, and rate of reading, 159-162, 185; discussed, 80-99 (*see under* skills and techniques); of high school students, 21-25

comprehension, disabilities in, 317-318; faulty habits impeding, 318; measurement of, 232; remedial work for, 319

connotations, 105

constructive guidance in reading, 203

consultant, for inauguration of program, 330

consultations, 336-337

content fields, reading the materials of the, 329

content subjects, differentiated attacks for, 169-170; reading in, 340, 341; responsibility of teacher of, 170-172; teaching procedures for all, 172-175. *See also* under subject name

contextual clues, 108, 186; *vs.* word analysis, 288

co-operation, all-school, 330; among students, 228; among teachers, 325, 327; between home and school, 255

co-operative independence in economics, 227-228

co-ordination, between elementary and secondary school programs, 326-327; of factors in developmental reading program, 326-330, 344; under one administrator, 330-332; within one school system, 327-328

co-ordinator, duties of the, 332-340; of reading instruction, 296-297; problems confronting, 332-333; salary of, 343; selection of, for small school, 331; summary, 344; training and qualifications for, 339-340

critical analysis, reading for, 161; training in, 173, 174; difficulties of, 179

critical reading and self-reliance, 204

cue reduction, 70, 104

curriculum, adjustments and initial appraisals, 329; reorganization of, 22

Davis, H. C., in "Improving Reading Ability of High School Seniors," 6

derivation of words, study of pictorial helps for, 124-125. *See also* dictionary

derivatives, 70

developmental program, administrative factors of, 62-65; factors in lack of a, 57-59, 65-66; in content subjects, 55-56, 61-62, 65, 66; individualization of, for less retarded cases, 276; major tasks of, 40; need for, 25-26, 57; reading growth and refinement through, 52-55; scope of, 60-62; teacher training for, 64; to be all-school, 325

Developmental Psychology, 52

developmental reading program, defined, 247

Dewey, John, 207

diagnosing reading ability, summarized, 294-296

diagnosis, and remedial planning by co-ordinator, 338, defined, 277; outcome of, 294; purpose of, 277-278

"Diagnosis and Remedial Treatment of Reading Difficulties in the Secondary School," 30

Dickens, Charles, *A Tale of Two Cities,* 146

dictionary, use of the, 121-124, 199, 200, 319; teaching helps for, 124, 125

differentiated attack, 326; affected by reading for details, 272; appreciation of, 233-234; as revealed by experiments, 159; defined, 44-45, 168; development of a, 44-46, 147; in content fields, 169; purposes of, 82-90; to be taught, 160, 162

differentiation, inappropriate, 314

disability in reading, and personality disturbances, 264-269; causes of, 253, 256, 260-261, 267-268; causes of *vs.* symptoms of, 255, 262-263; diagnosing, 276-296; emotional concomitant of, 266-267; fatalistic attitude in, 269; faulty generalizations concerning, 256, 257; remedial instruction for, 268; result of, 265-266; summary of causes of, 274

discussions, reports, and debates, in motivating voluntary reading, 174-175; periodic panel, 182

Durrell, Donald, in "Individual Differences and Their Implications with Respect to Instruction in Reading," 285

Eaton, H. T., in "What High School Pupils Like to Read," 135

Education and Economic Well-Being in American Democracy, 4-5, 59

Educational Policies Commission, in *Education and Economic Well-Being in American Democracy,* 4-5, 59

Elegy, stanza from Thomas Gray's, 184

elementary school, 326-327

emotional disturbances. *See* personality

"Evaluation of the Free Reading in Grades Ten, Eleven, and Twelve, for the Class of 1935," 6, 141

experiences, in developing meaning backgrounds, 114-130; firsthand, 115-117; wide reading, 117-119; vicarious, 119-121; vocabulary study, 121-125; Marshall High School project, 125-129

experimentation in classroom, 231

Extension Division, 335

eye movements, 29, 31, 72-74; in reading, two theories on, 313-314

eye span, 72

"Failure in Reading and Social Maladjustment," 59, 264

Fendrick, Paul, in "Visual Characteristics of Poor Readers," 262

fixations, 73

follow directions, ability to, 186, 188, 191

France, 1834, "cannot read," 3

Freeman, Frank N. *See* Wood

functional knowledge *vs.* factual memory, 212

Gates, Arthur I., in *The Improvement of Reading, Rev.,* 20, 21, 31, 285-287, 288, 313; in *Gates Reading Survey,* 20, 21, 248, 347; in "Failure in Reading and Social Maladjustment," 59, 264; in "Intelligence and Artistry in Teaching Reading," 181-182, 184-185; in *Record Booklet for Reading Diagnosis,* 291; in Gates Silent Reading Test, 315, 347

Gates Reading Survey, 20, 21; described, 248; scores on, 249-253, 290, 347

Gates Silent Reading Test, 315, 347

generalize, ability to, 193-194

Geography in Relation to the Social Sciences, 180

goal, reading to achieve a, 210

goals in reading, 206-207

"Golden Cup of Kasimir, The," 92

Goodenough, Florence L., in *Developmental Psychology,* 52

grade placement, defined, 283; value of, in diagnosis, 283

graphic material, reading and use of, 78-80, 124-125, 173; difficulties in reading, 180, 189

graphs, developing independence in reading, 212-215; types of, 214

Gray, Thomas, first stanza of *Elegy,* 184

Gray, W. S., in "The Nature and Extent of the Reading Problem in American Education," 19

Greek and Latin derivatives and roots, teaching, 70, 71

group measurements, 278, 279

group methods, problem of, 203, 337

group *vs.* individual remedial instruction, 338
Growth in Reading, 92-93
guidance and reading, 333

Haswell, W. A. *See* Parker
Hathaway, Gladys, in "Purposes for Which People Read," 30
health department, school, 333
Henmon, V. A. C. *See* Byrns
high school, the new *vs.* the old, 6; reading program, need for a, 19; reading program twofold, 46
history, reading, 238
Hollingworth, H. L., in *Psychology,* 104
home background a cause of disability, 260, 272
home-room periods, instruction in all five areas in, 342
home-room teachers, 336
Horn, Ernest, in *Methods of Instruction in the Social Studies,* 73, 79, 131-132, 175-176, 178
Horn and McBroom, in "A Survey of a Course of Study in Reading," 29-30
How to Read a Book, 5
Hugo, Victor, in *Claude Gueux,* 3

Illustrating Hero Stories, exercises, 92-93
Improvement of Reading, The, Revised, 20, 21, 31, 285-287, 288, 313
Improvement of Reading in High School and College, 178-179
"Improving Reading Ability of High School Seniors," 6
inaccuracy, 284
independence in reading, achieving a developmental process, 201; and individual growth, 203-204; appreciation of, 233; co-operative, 202; defined, 44, 215; development of, 44, 56-57; improving habits of, 201, 205; need for, 202; object of instruction, 215; shown by familiarity with library uses, 208
independence in setting reading goals, 206-207
"Individual Differences and Their Implications . . . ," 285
"Individual Differences in the Reading Ability of College Students," 31
Ingles and McCague, in *Teaching the Use of Books and Libraries,* 123

inhibiting conditions, 303
in-service training, 64, 328, 330, 332, 342; Extension Division, 335; methods of conducting, 335-336
institute on teaching of reading, 335
instruction, adjustment of, 22, 30; areas of, 40, 46-47; rate of, in content fields, 226; supervision of, by co-ordinator, 336; units of, for home-room period, 336
instruction, diagnostic and remedial, kind and extent of, 327
instruction in reading, aspects of improved, 325
"Intelligence and Artistry in Teaching Reading," 181-182, 184-185
intelligence and reading efficiency, 256-258; tests for, 258
interest in and attitude toward reading, studied for diagnosis, 293-294
interests and tastes, and reading abilities, 148; and self-reliance, 204; appreciation of, 233; at Negaunee, 140-141; factors affecting, 136-139, 149; in reading, development of, 11-18, 43-44; in the social studies, 120, 121, 131-132 (*see also* Marshall H. S. project); La Brant on, 141-142; of high school students, 132-136; suggestions for guiding, 139-147; summary, 149-150, 181, 182, 194
interfering habits, 261, 271, 272, 284, 285, 314, 326
interviews, 237-238, 289, 293, 294
"Investigation of the Development of the Sentence and the Extent of Vocabulary in Young Children," 51
Iowa Silent Reading Comprehension Battery of tests, Advanced, described, 248; scores on, 249-253, 348; Sub-test 3 in, 86

Jacobson, Paul B., in "Two Experiments with Work-Type Reading Exercises in Ninth Grade," 11
Janney, J. E. *See* Pressey
Jersild, Arthur, in "Radio and Motion Pictures," 119, 121
Jordan, Berglund and Washburne, *Lorna Doone* adaptation, 152

Karp. *See* Russell

Kelly. *See* Russell

Kendall, James, in *A Laboratory Outline of General Chemistry,* 192

key words, 109, 160, 311

Kopel, David. *See* Witty

Kuhlen, R. G. *See* Pressey

Laboratory Outline of General Chemistry, material from, 192

La Brant, L. L., in "An Evaluation of the Free Reading in Grades Ten, Eleven, and Twelve, for the Class of 1935," 6, 141

librarians, 337; co-operation of, 199, 333

library, 133, 197 ff.; Bennett inventory for visits to, 209-210; facilities, encouraging use of, 208; instruction in use of, 208-209; professional, for school, 336; school, 139; trip to the, 195-200

Life: A Psychological Survey, Laboratory Workbook, 215

literature, at reading level, 181; motivating voluntary reading in, 182; purposes of teaching, 181, 183-185; unsuitable school, 181-182, 334

locating information, 198, 284

locating material, 15, 16, 36, 37, 38, 56-57; difficulties in, in content subjects, 179, 190-191

Lorna Doone, passage, adapted by Jordan, Berglund, and Washburne, 152-154, 157, 158, 159, 163

Lowell, Thomas, in *Magic Dials,* 119

Magic Dials, 119

"Making School Excursions Worthwhile," 125

map, use of, 200. *See also* graphic material, graphs

Marshall High School, Minneapolis, project at, 125-129

Mason, E. W., in "Making School Excursions Worthwhile," 125

materials, reading, adjusting reading rate to, 160-162; adjusting to mental capacity, 282; adjusting to student's level, 319, 327, 328, 329, 333; affecting attack in content fields, 169; affecting choice and refinement of techniques, 165-166; appraisal of, 332-333; at student's level, 255, 258, 259, 263, 270;

current, use of, 173; lack of, 255; pictorial and tabular use of, 173; purchase of, 22; recommended, 172; selected or advised by co-ordinator, 337; selection of, 301

mathematical materials, difficulties in, 185-189; reading, 185-189; techniques in, 185

mathematics, appraisal of instruction in, 228

McBroom. *See* Horn

McCague, Anna. *See* Ingles

McCallister, James M., in *Remedial and Corrective Instruction in Reading,* 30, 58

McKee, Paul, in *Reading and Literature in the Elementary School,* 30, 35, 179-180, 181, 183

meaning background, and remedial work, 319; and self-reliance, 204; and sensory impressions, 112-113; and speed, 109, 160; appraisal of, 232; basic to reading, 107; development of, 114-130; difficulties of, in social studies, 178; individualizing reading experience, 113; in following directions, 110; in getting general significance, 110; in locating information, 109; in noting details, 111; in predicting outcomes, 111-112; in word recognition, 108; three phases in development of, 106-107

measurements and appraisals, early, 338

mental age, defined, 281; value of, in diagnosis, 282; *vs.* reading age, 250-253, 256-257, 258, 282

Merriam, G. and C., Company, derivation pictorial slides, 124

methodology, 339

Methods of Instruction in the Social Studies, 73, 79, 131-132, 175-176, 178

Midwestern communities studies, 125-129

mind-set, wrong, in reading mathematics, 188

Minneapolis, study of, by Marshall High School, 125-127

Monroe, Marion, in *Children Who Cannot Read,* 59, 265, 287

Motion Pictures in the Classroom, 120

motivating study, in content subjects, 227

motivating voluntary reading, in content subjects, 172-175; in literature, 182

motivation, inadequate, 272-273
moving pictures, 114, 119-121, 126, 127, 129, 137-138

National Society for the Study of Education, in *The Teaching of Reading*, 58
"Nature and Extent of the Reading Problem in American Education," 19
"Negaunee Reading Experiment, The," 139-141
Northwestern University Educational Clinic, reading analysis at, 30

oculist, 339
oral context errors, classification of (Gates), 285-287
oral reading, 39, 94-99; and speech defects, 263-264; at sight, measuring and analyzing, 288; effect of, upon silent reading, 326; measurement of, 232, 288
organization of ideas, 85-87, 159, 166-168; in social studies, 178-179
organization of reading program, factors affecting, 328; local adjustments of, 328; necessity for, 326; to be simple and easily operated and understood, 330
orientation, faulty, in word recognition, 313
otologist, 339
overanalysis, 284, 288, 314

Parker and Haswell, in *A Textbook of Zoology*, 73, 155-156
Pennsylvania text *vs.* Alabama text, 174
personality, disturbances of, and reading disability, 292-293; compensatory reactions in maladjustment of, 265
phonetic analysis, 312
phonetic attack, 310
phonetic errors, 287-288, 291
phonograph records, 121
physical disabilities that lower vitality, 292
pictorial material. *See* graphic material
pictorial and tabular materials in content fields, 173
Pooley and Walcott, in *Growth in Reading*, 92-93
Popular Mechanics, faulty use of, 200
Pressey, Janney, and Kuhlen, in *Life: A*

Psychological Survey, Laboratory Workbook, 215
Prevention and Correction of Reading Difficulties, 290
Problem-Solution Pattern, 207
Problems in Reading and Thinking, 206-208
problems, requiring reading, 175; reading used for independent solution of, 212
prognosis in remedial work, 282
program diagnosis, character of and steps in, 278
psychiatrist, 339
Psychology, 104
psychology of the adolescent, 339
Psychology of Making Life Interesting, The, 91
purpose, 10, 13, 14, 16-17, 31, 32-39; and types of reading (differentiated attack, *q.v.*), 35-39, 46, 82-90; determining choice and refinement of techniques, 162-168; determining rate, 161-162, 163-164; determining attack in content fields, 169-171; reading for a, 210; teaching, 32-33, 35; to be provided, 284
purposes, 198, 306
"Purposes for Which People Read," 30

questionnaires, 236

radio, 99, 114, 119-121, 126, 127, 129, 137-138; in case of John, 143-144, 149
"Radio and Motion Pictures," 119, 121
Ramseyer, 121
rate of instruction in content fields, 226
rate of reading, adjusting, to suit purpose and material, 160-162, 168, 190; and ability, 75; and comprehension, 159; and differentiated attack, 159; and interest, 147; and interfering habits, 272; and material, 159-160; and reader's content background and vocabulary, 109; defined, 74; experiment in, 152-158; measurement of, 232; readers and, 152
Readers' Guide to Periodical Literature, use of, 209-210
readiness, appraisals of, in reading, 223; in reading ability in content subjects, 228-229

reading, ability, defined, 271; ability in, of a selected group, 247-249; ability in, of high school students, 19-26, 146-147; at student's level, 145, 183, 283; clinic, 280; clubs, 182; experiment at Negaunee, 139-141; experience individualized by meaning backgrounds, 113; extensive and intensive, 117-119, 138, 139-142, 143-144, 146-148, 172-175, 182, 191; factors in complexity of, 31-32; faulty habits in, 218; importance of, 3-7, 18-19; in adult life, 204-205; instruction for each content subject, 11, 25, 30; in the content subjects, 169, 195; in the home, 136-137, 139; motivation and purposes for improving, 11-19; process, 28-32, 46; science and history, 138, 142, 161, 164; units, 206-208. See also rate, speed, and subject names

reading age vs. mental age, 250-253, 256-257, 258, 282. See also mental age

Reading Aids Through the Grades, 320

"Reading Disabilities in Relation to Maladjustment," 59

Reading and the Educative Process, 73

reading instruction by many for one, 325

"Reading Interests of High School Seniors," 134

Reading and Literature in the Elementary School, 30, 35, 179-180, 181, 183

"Reading and Ninth Grade Achievement," 7, 58

reading program in its entirety, 325; organizing the, 326

"Reading and Study Skills as Related to Comprehension of Science and History in the Ninth Grade," 9, 58

recognition of word, first phase of meaning, 104, 106. See also word recognition

Record Booklet for Reading Diagnosis, 291

records, and reports, 327, 334; and research, 339. See also school history

records of reading development, 239-241

reference materials, 119, 126, 127, 128-129; abilities in using, developed in social studies, 175-176; using, 179, 191, 198-199, 200, 213, 223, 233

"Relation of Ability to Read Material of the Type Used in Studying Science to Eighth-Grade Achievement," 8, 193

Remedial and Corrective Instruction in Reading, 30, 58

remedial cases, selecting, 247, 253

remedial instruction, and adjustment of instruction, 221; diagnosis basic to, 303; fundamental problem in, 310; in techniques basic to disabilities, 310-320; materials for, 303-304; students' interests a guide in, 305-307; to supplement developmental, 325

remedial material, at student's level, 304, 305; character of, 294; selected for reader's purpose, 301; with intrinsic interest for reader, 294, 298, 303-305

remedial plan tentative, 294

remedial program, 22, 46; appraisals needed for, 280; co-ordinator responsible for, 276; defined, 298; dependent on adequacy of diagnosis, 277; factors determining therapy in, 300-301; faulty assignments on a, 307; hazard of failure in, 277; intensive and prolonged, 284-285; nature of, 233, no cure-all in, 277-278; organization of, 298-302; outlook for, 298; success the goal of, 277; supplemental, 299-300

remedial teaching, for specific defects, 310; nine principles of, 302-310; no stigma in receiving, 302; place and time for, 301-302

remedial work, expensiveness of, 276; for faulty vision, 262; related to developmental program, 247

reports, students', 238

research, 339

return sweep, 72

Russell, Karp, and Kelly, in Reading Aids Through the Grades, 320

schedule, 343; for developmental program, 328-329

school history of student, sources for and value of in diagnosis, 283

school nurse, 290

Schoonover, Ruth, in "The Negaunee Reading Experiment," 139-140; in "The Case for Voluminous Reading," 140 science, 138, 142, 143, 145; abilities required in, 189; appreciation of instruction in, 229; difficulties in, 190-194; objectives of teaching, 190; reading in, 155, 159, 161, 166-167, 189-194

sensory characteristics and reading disability, auditory, 291-292; visual, 290-291

sensory impressions, learning to form, 183-184

sentences, complexity of, as in social studies, 178

Shakespeare, in *As You Like It,* 154-155, 158, 159

Shores, J. H., in "The Ability to Read Historical Materials as Related to Eighth-Grade Achievement and General Reading Abilities," 8; in "Reading and Study Skills as Related to Comprehension of Science and History in the Ninth Grade," 9, 58

silent reading, 36-38; and oral reading, 325; measuring rate of, 284

silent reading abilities, tests, measurements, and comparisons of, for diagnostic appraisal, 283-285

skills and techniques, ability to predict outcomes, 89-90, 159; appraisal of, 232; comprehending directions, 87-88; comprehension, 80-81; development and refinement of, 41-42, 46; forming sensory impressions, 90-93; getting general significance, 82-83, 146, 159; how determined, 10, 16-17, 42; in content fields, 169-172; interpretive oral reading, 94-99; learning new, 30; locating information, 77-78, 164; noting details, 83-85, 146, 159, 164; organizing ideas read, 85-87, 159, 166-168; power of comprehension, defined, 82; rate and speed, 74-75; reading critically, 93-94; reading graphs, maps, etc., 78-79; refining, 166-168; selecting, 162-166; skimming, 75-77; summary of, 99-102; teacher ignorance of, 68-69; time allotted for, 198; types of word recognition, 70-72. *See also* comprehension, differentiated attack, mathematical materials, purpose, rate, science, social studies, speed

skimming, 13, 36, 37, 38, 280, 284

Smith, M. E., in "An Investigation of the Development of the Sentence and the Extent of Vocabulary in Young Children," 51

social studies, and development of cooperative independence, 227-228; difficulties encountered in the, 177-181; reading abilities developed in the, 175-176

speech department, school, 333

speed of reading, 314-317; an all-school problem, 250; and constant rate, 316-317; a word-by-word case in, 315; causes of faulty, 314; experiments in, 152-160; of high school students, 20-22, 23-25; regressions and excessive, 316-318; use of appraisals of, 226. *See also* rate

standardized measures, in appraisals, use of, 218

Stanford-Binet Test of Intelligence, use of, 20, 21, 258, 268, 282, 289-290

Strang, Ruth, in *Improvement of Reading in High School and College,* 178-179

study-hall periods for remedial instruction, 302

"Survey of a Course of Study in Reading," 29-30

Swenson, Esther J., in "The Relation of Ability to Read Material of the Type Used in Studying Science to Eighth-Grade Achievement," 8, 193

Syracuse high school, reading interests in a, 135

Tale of Two Cities, A, 146

teacher, duties of the, 340-342; efforts, 59-60; of content subjects, 345. *See also* home-room teachers

teacher of content subjects, responsibility of, 170-175. *See also* under subject name

teaching. *See* instruction

Teaching High School Students How to Read, 6

teaching procedures, summary, 194-195

Teaching of Reading, The, 58

Teaching the Use of Books and Libraries, 123

techniques, basic for remedial instruction in, 310-320; comprehension, 317-320;

eye movements, 313-314; reading speed, 314-317; word recognition, 310-313. *See also* skills
"Tenth-Grade Abilities and Achievements," 9, 58, 74
terminology, 109, 186, 190
testing budget and teacher appraisals, 328
testing program, use of, for selecting remedial cases, 278-279
tests, central organization for administering and scoring, 333; questionnaires, 236; reading, for high school, 347-354; standardized group, 235-236; teacher-made, 236
textbook assignments, deterrent to self-reliance, 205-206
textbook committee and co-ordinator, 337
Thorndike, in *Your City*, 173
thought units, 314-315
Traxler Silent Reading Test, described, 248; scores on, 249-253, 353
"Two Experiments with Work-Type Reading Exercises in Ninth Grade," 11

University of Wisconsin, study of reading interests, 134-135
use for what is read, providing the, 211-212

"Visual Characteristics of Poor Readers," 262
vocabulary, and following directions, 110; and rate of reading, 109; appraisal of, 232, 278-279; by student's effort, 118-119; by systematic study, 119, 121-125, 129-130; development of, 42-43, 51-52, 61-62, 70-71, 106-107; enlarging sight, 319-320; for all content fields, 169-170; for comprehension, 317; inadequate meaning, 259; inadequate recognition, 277; inadequate sight, 314; in mathematics, 185-187; in science, 190; in social studies, 177; of high school students, 22; specialized, for locating information, 109; teaching of, 107
vocalization, 288, 326. *See also* interfering habits
Vogel, L. *See* Washburne

Waples, Douglas, in "Community Studies in Reading," 139
Washburne, and Vogel, in *Winnetka Graded Book List*, 138; Jordan, Berglund, and, adaptation of *Lorna Doone*, 152-154
"What High School Pupils Like to Read," 135
White, Wendell, in *The Psychology of Making Life Interesting*, 91
Wilson, H. W., Company, pamphlet: "Cataloguing and Indexing Service," use of, 210
Winnetka Graded Book List, 138
Witty, Paul A., in "Diagnosis and Remedial Treatment of Reading Difficulties in the Secondary School," 30; and Kopel, David, in *Reading and the Educative Process*, 73
Wood and Freeman, in *Motion Pictures in the Classroom*, 120
word and meaning backgrounds insufficient, 329
word-by-word reader, 277
word recognition, 70-72; faulty orientation in, 313; importance of contextual clues to, 108; remedial instruction in, 310-313; techniques of, 311-312; use of dictionary for, 312; well-rounded attack in, 311
words in isolation, analysis of ability to work out, 288-289
Workbook to "Practices in Reading and Thinking," 123, 124
World Almanac, The, material from, 156-157, 158, 159, 163
Wrightstone, in "Child Development and the Curriculum," 79

Your City, Table of Cities in, 173

Zoology, A Textbook of, material from, 73, 155-156, 158, 159; factors in reading, 166-167
zoology, differentiated attack for, 158-159; fixations and regressions in reading, 73; rate of reading in, 155-156